# THE TIMELESS LEADER

# THE TIMELESS LEADER

JOHN K. CLEMENS
and
STEVE ALBRECHT

ADAMS PUBLISHING
Holbrook, Massachusetts

Published by Adams Media Corporation
260 Center Street, Holbrook, MA 02343

ISBN: 1-55850-483-4

Printed in the United States of America.

J   I   H   G   F   E   D   C   B   A


Library of Congress Cataloging-in-Publication Data
Clemens, John, 1939–
    The timeless leader / John K. Clemens, Steve Albrecht.
    p.    cm.
    Includes index.
    ISBN 1-55850-483-4 (hc)
    1. Leadership. I. Albrecht, Steve. II. Title.
HD57.7.C55   1995                                    95-5276
658.4'092—dc20                                       CIP

*This book is available at quantity discounts for bulk purchases.*
*For information, call 1-800-872-5627.*

*For Karyl and Leslie,*
*with gratitude,*
*and for Steve's kids,*
*who we hope will learn from history*
*and then go out and make some*

# TABLE OF CONTENTS

The Father of Western Philosophy • Try a Little Philosophy • The Cave as Comfort Zone • Knowing the Dimensions of Your Own Cave • Comfort Zones and the Frog Factor • Psychic Prisons: Toxic and Nourishing Places • Crucial Cave Paintings • Fellow Cave Dwellers • No Pain, No Gain: Discomfort Zones • The Couch Potato and the Desk Potato • Cave Dweller Mottos: Rationalizations, Excuses, and One Million Reasons Not to Leave • IBM Follies: The Biggest Cave Is Not Always the Best One • Try a Little Risutora • Then There's the Big Three Automakers • Lessons from the Cave

Going on Nantucket Sleigh Rides  •  Leader as Quasi-Maniac  •  The Whale as Quest: Every Organization Needs a Big Goal  •  Mission Statements and Marching Orders  •  Away All Boats: Preparing for Your Quest  •  Becoming Goal-Specific  •  Electrifying the Troops  •  Leading by Asking Questions  •  The Value of an Occasional Failed Quest

# ACKNOWLEDGMENTS

We stand on the shoulders of giants. We are indebted to those characters—both real and fictional—who populate the unforgettable stories on which this book is based. And we are deeply grateful to the authors of their tales, whose pens gave vivid and accessible coherence to lives full of the agonies and the victories of the leadership task.

We would also like to express our deep appreciation to those who have shared our commitment to bringing the leadership lessons latent in mankind's greatest works to those who manage and lead in today's organizations. First to Jerrold C. Brown, professor of Classics at Hartwick College, without whose editorial excellence in the development of the Hartwick Humanities in Management Institute's leadership cases this book could never have been written.

We also want to thank the Institute's case writers, whose extensive research yielded the Hartwick Classic Leadership Cases from which much of our material is adapted: Gerald McCarthy, managing director of OLV Associates, Worcester, Massachusetts; Associate Professor of Management Edward Ottensmeyer of the Graduate School of Business at Clark University; Associate Professor of English Richard Burke of

Lynchburg College; Professor Douglas F. Mayer of Hartwick College; Thomas R. Martin, Jeremiah O'Connor Professor of Classics at the College of the Holy Cross; Richard B. Larson, Organization/Human Behavior consultant and adjunct professor at Assumption College and the College of the Holy Cross; Director of Independent Studies Robert Colley of Syracuse University; Professor of Management Dennis Gillen of Syracuse University; Professor of English William Brown of Philadelphia College of Textiles and Science; Associate Professor of Management Claudia Harris of North Carolina Central University; James A. Bostwick Professor of English Welford Dunaway Taylor of the University of Richmond; Professor of Management Systems James C. Goodwin of the E. Claiborne Robins School of Business Administration at the University of Richmond; Professor of German Wendell Frye of Hartwick College; Associate Professor of Philosophy Michael K. Green of the State University of New York at Oneonta; Associate Professor of Economics and Business Margaret Maguire of the State University of New York at Oneonta; Associate Professor of History and Black Hispanic Studies Ralph Watkins of the State University of New York at Oneonta; Associate Professor of History Peter G. Wallace of Hartwick College; Associate Professor of Philosophy and Religious Studies Julius Jackson of San Bernardino Valley College; Assistant Professor of Sociology Douglas Gutknecht of San Bernardino Valley College; and Professor of History Donald Birn of the State University of New York at Albany.

We want to especially thank our editor, Dick Staron, who has been no less than our creative alter ego in this endeavor. We've had long and rewarding discussions about the nature of leadership with Dick over the past year and a half, and his suggestions have always enriched us and our work. In addition, Merrilee Gomillion's contribution at the final editing stages of the project were invaluable, as were Aron Helser's not-to-be-believed talents with the computer.

Finally, we are extremely grateful to the W. K. Kellogg Foundation, whose generous grant to the Hartwick Humanities in Management Institute has made this entire project possible.

# FOREWORD

by EARL N. SHULMAN
*Vice Chairman, Seafirst Bank*

T he difference between "management" and "leadership" seems to
be more critical than ever. This book underscores the need for
business people to move their thinking as rapidly as possible from
management perspectives to leadership perspectives. Management has
been described as dealing with complexity while leadership is often
thought of as dealing with change and driving change.

John Clemens and Steve Albrecht in *The Timeless Leader* use the
great books of literature in their case studies to drive this theme home in
a unique way. It has been my good fortune to personally experience the
effectiveness of these Hartwick cases in action. In one of my volunteer
labors of love, serving as president of the Pacific Coast Banking School,
an executive education experience for high-ranking potential managers in
the banking industry, I witnessed first-hand the enthusiasm of students
as they considered the leadership lessons found in the messages contained in the great books. The authors of *The Timeless Leader* have based
their book on the ideas gained from actual seminars similar to those they
conduct at the Pacific Coast Banking School.

Because this book is based on "real world" feedback collected by the
authors in executive seminars, those of us in the private sector will find

this work extremely relevant as opposed to academic and idealistic books on management. The wisdom gleaned from Shakespeare and Plato and the many other sources used in *The Timeless Leader* have real meaning for the reader when the cases are carefully considered. The ideas advanced in this book are extremely helpful to the reader and go far beyond the purely academic concepts found in many writings on the subject of management.

In today's business world with its emphasis on rapidly changing conditions, the need to consider technology and the emergence of the information highway, and the clear demand to think strategically versus tactically, it is useful for business people to pause and consider the lessons of humanity's greatest books. While at first look it would not be a natural conclusion to link the two concepts of business leadership and classic literature, after studying *The Timeless Leader* the reader will clearly see the connection and be stimulated to consider the future of business from a new leadership perspective.

Thanks to Clemens and Albrecht, our business minds will be stretched.

# PREFACE

Imagine the following situation: you have just arrived at the site of your company's annual management development meeting. As you unpack your bags and settle into your room overlooking a splendid golf course and tennis courts, you begin to prepare for the first session of the seminar scheduled for 8:00 A.M. next morning. When you open the thick binder containing your seminar materials, you are amazed to discover that your reading assignment for tomorrow's course is a 25-page excerpt from Herman Melville's story *Billy Budd.*

Incredulous (you assumed you'd seen the last of Melville in high school), you search for the more familiar—and easier to read—literature you thought would be required for this course: things like Harvard Business School cases, *Wall Street Journal* articles, selections from *Fortune* magazine, chapters from the latest management best sellers, or perhaps a book on leadership theory. Yet all you find are more excerpts from literature, from history and biography, from philosophy and drama. This seminar, you realize, is going to force you to read everything you've successfully been avoiding for years.

What's going on here? After calling to cancel your 6:00 P.M. tennis match, you begin to understand. At least the seminar's introductory materials contain quotations from two authors with whom you are vaguely familiar. "Management," writes management guru Peter Drucker, "deals with people, their values, their growth and development—and this makes it a humanity. Management is thus what tradition used to call a liberal art—'liberal' because it deals with the fundamentals of knowledge, self-knowledge, wisdom, and leadership; 'art' because it is practice and application." The second quotation comes from Luigi Salvaneschi, the retired Blockbuster Entertainment Corporation president, who says, "The essence of commerce does not reside in spreadsheets or flow charts. Rather, it springs from culture, communication, education, and philosophy."

Culture? Philosophy?

Welcome to the exciting—and sometimes intimidating—world of leadership as liberal art. Our goal is simple: to add some intellectual heft to all the bland superficial management and leadership advice that's out there. Our method is also simple: the ideas in this book come directly from managers like yourself who've attended our leadership seminars. Over the past eight years, we and our colleagues at the Hartwick Humanities in Management Institute—with the help of a major grant from the W. K. Kellogg Foundation—have conducted hundreds of these seminars at places like IBM, Aetna Life & Casualty, Heller Financial, American Cyanamid, Campbell Soup, Prudential, Pacific Coast Banking School, Colorado Banking School, and The Southwestern Graduate School of Banking.

We kept notes. And when something that a fast-track manager read in Plato's *Republic*, or Sophocles' *Antigone*, or—you guessed it— Melville's *Billy Budd* struck a familiar chord or revealed a truth about leadership that he or she had not considered before, we filed it away.

What we later discovered as we researched these notes was that, in terms of leadership, the 20th-century looks astonishingly like most other centuries. A recent *Wall Street Journal* article, for example, described the ideal leader. He, or she, it suggested, should be a conglomerate, made up of equal parts of the following: Barry Sanders, the Detroit Lions running back who's fleet of foot and capable of changing directions in a flash; Walter Cronkite—after all, a leader needs credibility; Franklin Delano Roosevelt—his fireside chats would be guaranteed to calm a recalcitrant workforce; Leonardo da Vinci—what leader doesn't need to be a renaissance man or woman? Philip Marlowe, the fictional private eye—business leadership, full of paradox and ambiguity, resembles nothing more than detective work; and former New York mayor Ed Koch, who frequently asked his colleagues the empowering question, "How'm I doing?"

We agree with this assessment of the ideal leader as far as it goes, but we'd add others to the leadership gene pool: Plato, whose dialogues and allegories constitute nothing less than a handbook of leadership; Shakespeare, who perhaps more than any other writer seemed to know what makes people "tick"; Sophocles, the Greek tragedian who understood how leadership and the heroic go hand in hand. We'd include characters as diverse as Cleopatra, Herman Melville's fictitious sea captains, and Martin Luther King. There'd be a certified military genius like von Clausewitz (business is, at least sometimes, like war, is it not?) and a pol the likes of William Penn Warren's Willie Stark (just to prove that real leadership is sometimes stranger than fiction). And as you'll soon discover, we turn the lives of two larger-than-life leaders, Winston Churchill and Gandhi, into a primer on leadership.

What you are about to read is the result of our study of these, and other, unforgettable characters. You'll read marvelous leadership success stories, and you'll learn about leadership failures. Whether you see our writing as role model or cautionary tale, we hope you'll compare the people, places, and events described in this book with your own career, your own management style, your own leadership goals and skills, and your own organization.

You'll notice that throughout the book we make a distinction between "manager" and "leader." Some have argued that making such a distinction is a useless exercise. We disagree. Although it's fine to be a manager, today's organizations demand much more—they demand leadership.

It's a role that can be refreshing, challenging, and sometimes dangerous. Change—the elemental "stuff" of leadership—can, after all, be painful. As one of our favorite writers, Niccolo Machiavelli, put it: "... nothing is more difficult to handle, more doubtful of success, nor more dangerous to manage, than to put oneself at the head of introducing new orders." For this reason, we argue that leaders must be flexible, comfortable in ambiguous situations, and long-term players. Quite obviously, leaders inhabit a vastly different world than their managerial counterparts.

It's a world we hope you'll want to explore with us—a world where you'll discover that leaders are careful risk-takers, diligent and tireless workers, occasional rule-breakers, empowerers and guiding forces for the people around them, goal-setting questors, and skilled and charismatic communicators. Most importantly, they are persons who are never satisfied with the way things are. Leaders, unlike ordinary mortals, abhor comfort zones. They seek new experiences, new challenges, new opportunities.

In this book, you'll discover that the past can teach us much about leadership. We want to encourage you to leave your own "comfort zone" and begin the difficult transition from manager to leader.

Successful, powerful, and balanced leadership is a learned skill. We hope *The Timeless Leader* will help in this life-changing learning process. And as you embark upon this journey, keep in mind that Oscar Wilde once said: "The one duty we owe to history is to rewrite it."

—JOHN CLEMENS
—STEVE ALBRECHT

## CHAPTER 1

# LEAVING THE COMFORT ZONE: PLATO'S "ALLEGORY OF THE CAVE"

*Man—a being in search of meaning.*
— PLATO

## KEY POINTS

- LEAVING YOUR COMFORT ZONE AND HELPING OTHERS TO LEAVE THEIRS
- HANDLING AND MANAGING CONFLICT
- DEALING WITH CHANGE AND TURMOIL FROM ALL SIDES

Imagine that you're trapped deep inside a cave with a crowd of strangers. They slowly mill around you, transfixed by a bizarre sort of slide show projected onto the far wall. To your amazement, they seem to have no interest in leaving this gloomy dungeon. You walk among them, urging them to escape the darkness of their self-enforced imprisonment, but their apathy is impenetrable. Reality for them consists only of the images of light and shadow that play eerily across the wall in front of them. It's hard to believe, but they seem quite satisfied with their lives in this make-believe world.

You alone escape this place. Fighting your way up the near-vertical rock face, you slip and fall repeatedly. Battered, bleeding, and bruised, you finally make it out of the cave and into the light of the real world. The good news is that you are finally free; the bad news is that your challenge has just begun. You must re-enter the cave and force its lethargic captives to leave the familiarity of the world they know and emerge from the cave with you.

This "Allegory of the Cave" is a story almost as old as humanity itself. Not surprisingly, it is documented in a book that provides the cornerstone for all of western philosophy: *The Republic*. It is here that Plato describes a place that we all sometimes inhabit—the cave.

The famous "Allegory of the Cave" teaches us something fundamental, something that is universally true in life and in leadership: that it is sometimes tough to leave the safety of our comfort zones. Of course, good leaders understand that change—leaving your comfort zone—can be most unpleasant, just as it was for our cave dwellers, but in terms of survival, it's frequently necessary. And Plato, it turns out, can help.

## The Father of Western Philosophy

Plato's greatest written work, *The Republic*, was shaped by two main influences in his life: one was his student-mentor relationship with another great philosopher, Socrates; the other was the fact that much of his life was spent watching the many bloody battles of the Peloponnesian War, which raged over the Greek countryside for twenty-seven long years. His position as a student of Socrates, although fruitful from an intellectual standpoint, was short-lived. Due to the political turmoil of the time, Socrates became caught up in the vicious rivalries, infighting, coups, and counterrevolutions among the Athenian aristocracy. Tried for "atheism and corruption of the youth of Athens," Socrates was executed, an act for which Plato never forgave his government. What's more, living in a world at war for nearly three decades affected him, as might be expected: Plato became cynical and distrustful of Athens' military and political leaders, all of whom he felt were ruining his nation.

These two influences, wisdom and war, forged in Plato some deep-seated beliefs about how organizations might best be structured and governed. (Granted, he was thinking about nation-states whereas our interest is modern corporations.) Perhaps that is why *The Republic* is replete with sound leadership principles for any age. For our purposes, we'll focus on one small part of the book, Plato's "Allegory of the Cave". It is one of *The Republic's* strongest messages, a kind of primer on the challenges and rewards of change.

In this brief but powerful story—it takes up only two pages—Plato urges enlightened leaders to leave the dark corners of the human cave. He implores them to experience new life outside it and then return to share their wisdom with the cave dwellers who remain.

So with that in mind, put your miner's helmet on, switch on the lamp, and prepare to explore the "leadership cave." Here's the setting:

> *Imagine men living in a cave with a long passageway stretching between them and the cave's mouth, where it opens wide to the light. Imagine further that since childhood the cave dwellers have had their legs and necks shackled so as to be confined to the same spot. They are further constrained by blinders that prevent them from turning their heads; they can only see directly in front of them. Next, imagine a light from a fire some distance behind them and burning at a higher elevation. Between the prisoners and the fire is a raised path along whose edge there is a low wall like the partition at the front of a puppet stage. The wall conceals the puppeteers while they manipulate their puppets above it. Imagine, further, men behind the wall carrying all sorts of objects along its length and holding them above it. The objects include human and animal images made of stone and wood and all other materials. Presumably, those who carry them sometimes speak and are sometimes silent.*[1]

What Plato has described is a group of people who are captives of their environment. They are their own worst enemies. Rooted to the spot where they stand, they see unreality as reality and—like mindless automata—they don't seem to care. They are in their comfort zone.

But one among their group is unlike all the others; one is a person who is about to break out of the chains and escape from this place:

> *Imagine now how their liberation from bondage and error would come about if something like the following happened. One prisoner is freed from his shackles. He is suddenly compelled to stand up, turn around, walk, and look toward the light. He suffers pain and distress from the glare of the light. So dazzled is he that he*

*cannot even discern the very objects whose shadows he used to be able to see.*

Once the person actually sees light, he is blinded by it. In effect, the truth, or some form of it, is staring him in the face and, at least for now, he can't comprehend it. Yet our cave dweller does not let this stop him. He leaves the cave to see what kind of light exists above:

> *Then let him be dragged away by force up the rough and steep incline of the cave's passageway, held fast until he is hauled out into the light of the sun. Would not such a rough passage be painful? Would he not resent the experience? And when he came out into the sunlight, would he not be dazzled once again and unable to see what he calls realities?*

Clearly, leaving the cave has been a transforming experience. But Plato's more important point is that our former cave dweller must now re-enter the cave. It's a trip that won't be easy:

> *Consider further, if he should go back down again into the cave and return to the place he was before, would not his eyes go dark after so abruptly leaving the sunlight behind? They would. Suppose he should then have to compete once more in shadow watching with those who never left the cave. And this before his eyes had become accustomed to the dark and his dimmed vision still required a period of habituation. Would he not be laughed at? Would it not be said that he had made the journey above only to come back with his eyes ruined and that it is futile even to attempt the ascent?*

The brave soul who left the cave, who risked all to seek truth and then returned to reveal it, is now being ridiculed for even attempting the journey. If this sounds all-too-familiar, consider how many times you have experienced similar criticism or scorn from a legion of "I-told-you-so"-ers in your organization who attacked you for taking what you thought was a bold, and perhaps even a noble, step.

> *By the same token, would you think it strange if someone returning from divine contemplation to the miseries of men should*

*appear ridiculous? What if he were still blinking his eyes and not yet readjusted to the surrounding darkness before being compelled to testify in court about the shadows of justice or about the images casting the shadows? What if he had to enter into debate about the notions of such matters held fast by people who had never seen justice itself?*

What struggling entre-(or intra-)preneur has not been faced with this modern situation? What leader fighting to change the status quo has not faced armies of critics who offer one thousand and one reasons why something cannot or should not be done?

But if you want to create effective leaders, suggests Plato, go back to the allegorical cave, where it's dark, uncomfortable, and inhospitable, to convert as many followers as you can:

> *So down you must go, each in turn, to where the others live and habituate yourselves to see in the dark. Once you have adjusted, you will see ten thousand times better than those who regularly dwell there. Because you have seen the reality of beauty, justice, and goodness, you will be able to know idols and shadows for what they are.*

There's more than improved vision here. Your difficult journey up and back has made you a better person and an effective leader. You are no longer one of the sheep; you are now the shepherd. Leaving the cave has shown you another world. And, forearmed with the knowledge of the world outside the cave you can speak and act with wisdom.

## Try a Little Philosophy

If philosophy was not your favorite subject in school, fear not. We've intentionally left out any mind-numbing references to Aristotelianism, Cartesianism, Kantianism, and the like. Our point is, rather, a modest one: to provide you with some philosophical guidance—with a tip of our hats to Socrates and Plato as well as to the many practicing managers and leaders who have participated in our seminars—that you will be able to apply to your life and your work.

As you've no doubt already discerned, Plato's marvelous allegory strongly suggests that you and your organization must leave your comfort zones. Why? Because they can too easily become caves, keeping you in a suspended state of ease where you don't experience anything uncomfortable, unpleasant, conflicting, difficult, or physically or mentally challenging.

Escaping Platonic caves is an apt metaphor for trying to change organizations. Both activities are fraught with difficulty. It's hard to stir up the organizational soup without getting some spilled on your lap. No wonder it often feels better to stay in one place, to maintain the status quo. But while this may sound safe and inviting, it's often the first indication that you and your company will quickly be left behind as the rest of the world moves forward.

Leadership success starts with a sense that you must pick up and move ahead from time to time, just to stay competitive—inside, with your own work group, team, division, or company, and outside, with your competitors, customers, and markets. And from a personal development side, leaving the safety of the comfort zone is the first step toward becoming a better leader.

### The Cave as Comfort Zone

Plato's cave is a powerful symbol of the need for change. As we've said, it is nothing less than a metaphor for change in our own personal and business lives by stepping outside our comfort zone. But what is a "comfort zone?" A good working definition might be: "a place, real or imagined, that offers you a feeling of stability, safety, and protection from outside influences." To put it into even simpler terms, a comfort zone is a psychological place where you have a sense of well-being; a place where you are relatively stress-free and secure. Our world is full of comfort zones.

In most cases, your home serves as a comfort zone; there is a familiarity in the routine there that makes it a place where you want to stay. Leaving your warm bed to sleep on the ground outside would be more than just uncomfortable for you physically; it's mentally uncomfortable as well.

The desk in your office is another comfort zone. You feel comfortable and familiar there, surrounded by your personal things—photos, notes, coffee mug, and favorite pens. It offers you a safe haven and a place to work in relative peace and quiet.

Amazing as it may seem, even your job can be a comfort zone of sorts. It's safe to say that in these uncertain economic times, one awful day of employment is better than any moment of unemployment. What's more, your job offers you certain routines, familiar events and episodes that make you feel relatively safe, confident, and knowledgeable; it's a script you know well. There's little ambiguity, only a bit of uncertainty as to what will happen or what to do next, and little hard-core "fear of the unknown."

But a comfort zone can be much larger than your own personal world. Your organization and, in fact, your whole industry, can become one big comfort zone. And this leads to a profoundly strategic question: is your company so "comfortable" in the way it operates, moves, responds, and does business in this changing world that it is too much of a comfort zone? If you work in an organization which, like many, is reactive rather than proactive, are you too comfortable to change? And if the culture of your company does not embrace the concept known as "churn management," or change just for the sake of it, do you go to the other extreme which says, "Not wanting to upset the order of things, we'll do nothing?"

The now-famous case of IBM's demise is really a story about comfort zones and their profound effect on organizations. Listen to what one writer, chronicling the downfall of IBM, had to say in his post-mortem:

> ... IBM was once such a great company—great to its customers, great to the towns, cities, states, and countries where it operated. In many people's eyes, IBM wasn't so much a company as an institution. Yet the things that made the company so widely admired are what now make it vilified. People once referred to IBM's passion for being right, its rigorous processes, its thorough training of employees, its focus on customers' desires, its guarantee of lifetime employment. But the computer industry has moved out of the horse-and-buggy days that produced IBM's values and into a relativistic universe where everything is moving at the speed of light. So, referring to the same vaues IBM has always had, people talk about IBM's fear of risk, its civil-service mentality, its brainwashing of employees, its failure to make innovative products that anticipate customers' desires, its inability to adapt its work force quickly enough to react to shifts in the industry.[2]

Are you (or is your organization), like IBM, living and working in a dark cave of your own? Are you unable to react and move when the situation calls for it? Have you created such a professional comfort zone for yourself that you're either unwilling, unable, or too afraid to move out of it? And if you are willing to step outside the realm of your own comfort zone and take on projects and problems that demand a period of discomfort, does your organization support your efforts or does it hinder them? Do the people above and below you encourage movement out of the corporate comfort zone or do they try and pull you back into their own caves?

If so, you may be suffering from the same malaise that did so much damage to IBM. Hopefully, however, your organization more closely resembles a lesser-known but clearly heathier outfit like the Denman Tire Corporation of Leavittsburg, Ohio. Although the tire and rubber industry has changed dramatically since the company was founded in 1919, Denman Tire survives, proving convincingly that even rust-belt relics can compete and even prosper. And it is no wonder. Denman has stayed about as far away from its comfort zone—its metaphorical cave— as an organization can. According to Denman President and Chief Operating Officer Charles R. Wright, the company's formula for success would have made Plato proud. "If you get comfortable in the way you do things," said Wright, "you might get left behind. Yesterday's results will never be good enough for tomorrow."

### Knowing the Dimensions of Your Own Cave

Let's face it—we all need the safety and security of our personal comfort zones from time to time. And no wonder. They serve as positive places where we can ground ourselves in familiar or routine things. The challenge, of course, is knowing how—and when—to leave them. To do this, it helps to know the territory. Perhaps a little self-analysis would help us understand this process of change. The danger of remaining in comfort zones comes when we allow them to control us; they become much like spider webs, holding us stickily in one position because we are too fearful, too apathetic, or too comfortable to make any significant changes that would alter the status quo or make us feel uncomfortable.

Comfort zones that exist in your personal life can include some surprisingly familiar components: your spouse and family relationships, boyfriend or girlfriend relationships if you're not married, your relationships with close friends, relatives, neighbors, and acquaintances. In your business life, these comfort zone relationships are with bosses, peers and colleagues, and subordinates who work for you or in your department.

If you're like most people, you also have your own comfort zone relationships that come from within. Some people would never go skydiving or bungee jumping, others could never contemplate giving a speech to a group of one hundred people, and still others would never think of quitting their jobs and moving to another part of the country to open their own business.

Why? As you can guess—especially if you're one of those people who would not want to do any of these things—such activities have the potential to be difficult, stressful, potentially painful, and filled with great risk.

**Comfort Zones and the Frog Factor**
There is a story often told by people who want to make a point about change and levels of comfort that is about a frog in a pan of water. As a metaphor for change, it's certainly apt. The story goes like this: If you put a frog into a pan of boiling water, it will jump out as soon as it touches the water. The water is too hot and too uncomfortable for the frog to linger in the pan. But, if you place the frog in a pan of water that's at room temperature and then slowly turn up the heat until the water boils, the frog will die in the pan.

Why? As the metaphor points out, the frog gets used to the gradual rise in temperature of the water and will not have the will to leave the pan until too late. The frog lives—and dies—in its comfort zone.

As you consider this story, think about your own reality, personally and professionally, and about those things that might be keeping you in your comfort zone. What kind of "frog factor" events are you involved in now? With your personal relationships? In your work relationships? From an organizational perspective, are you so tied to a project, a product, a service, or a mission that you can't let it go even as the water boils around you? The business newspapers and magazines are filled with stories of seemingly bright people working inside seemingly well-run companies who have failed to heed this lesson and, in effect, have ended up in very hot water.

**Psychic Prisons: Toxic and Nourishing Places**
Another way to look at comfort zones is to consider the toxic or nourishing effects these places have upon your personal or professional life. The descriptive word "toxic" refers to unpleasant or difficult people, places,

events, or decisions that make life either inside or outside your comfort zone unbearable.

A difficult employee who constantly breaks the rules, argues with everyone, including you—his boss—and generally makes everyone feel drained after even the shortest encounter, is a prime example of a "toxic" entity inside your corporate comfort zone. This person negatively effects the world around him, including yours. Your equilibrium, along with everyone he contacts, is disturbed by this person, who could be called a kind of comfort zone "terrorist" employee due to the psychological or physical havoc he creates. In short, this person takes you and others out of your comfort zones by his very presence. The threat of the unknown, the specter of downsizing, the possibility of "re-engineering"; all can serve to move you out of your comfort zone.

On the other hand, "nourishing" events are those episodes or feelings that are healthy, positive, and pleasant. And just as there are toxic companies to work for, there are nourishing ones as well. Indeed, a "nourishing" atmosphere is what we strive for when we build our comfort zones in the first place. We want things to be pleasant, we want a sense of balance and equilibrium. Given a choice, we would all choose nourishing events and feelings in our lives—at home and at work.

Those who seek to avoid discomfort (read "any form of change") might say, "Develop a new product or service? Not me. Sorry, not interested. I just don't have the time. I'm too busy handling what I have on my plate right now."

Conversely, the leader thinks, "Will this make our organization stronger? Will my efforts on this tough project make me better for the company and make the company better for me and my career plans? If so, let's do it. I can make the necessary changes in my workload. In fact, I know just who I can recruit to help me meet this challenge. With the right team in place, we can beat any deadline and come up with something superior."

It happened at a little-known company headquartered in Augusta, Georgia, called Greenfield Industries.[3] In the 1970s, this manufacturer of rotary cutting tools went the way of the automobile industry when the oil crisis hit, according to one of its senior executives. Things had hit rock bottom. But when Greenfield was hauled out of its comfort zone by a buy-out in 1986, things began to turn around. The new buyer invested in plants, purchased badly needed new equipment, and acquired smaller companies.

The result was nothing less than a complete departure from the comfort zone: near-monomaniacal focus on one thing—high-volume taps. To date, the company has made more than 900 million Sears Craftsman drill bits. And 1994 revenues were a hefty $229 million!

Was this transformation easy? Certainly not. The workforce was trimmed from 375 to 130. But Greenfield has seen the light. As one executive put it, "Once you get rolling on change, it just keeps going. Everyone has to sign on, however, because if you don't make a commitment to change, you're just going to get lost."

Plato would be delighted. You've just seen a brief example of people and organizations who willingly leave the cave—their comfort zone—see the light, go back to bring out others, and step out into the new sunlight of a different comfort zone.

### Crucial Cave Paintings

Sometimes it's necessary to step back and read the writing on the cave walls around you. Just as Plato demonstrated in his allegory, knowing what's *really* on the walls in front of you can help you understand that there is another world outside the cave. This leads to the realization that you can leave the cave and meet the outside world, that there is indeed learning and new opportunity outside the cave. You can experience life outside, re-enter the cave to tell the others what you have discovered, and then bring them out into the light.

This is the crux of leadership, your method for success, and a point we will continually drive home as this book progresses. You can't be afraid to step outside your comfort zone—your cave—to see what's out there. Throughout history, as you'll see in these pages, you will discover how and why various real and imaginary leaders learned that no matter the price, they had to force themselves to tackle their difficulties, fight painful battles, and take the necessary risks that placed them squarely outside of their comfort zones. This was, and still is, an elemental prescription for leadership success.

### Fellow Cave Dwellers

The "cave" in business is frequently filled with three different groups of dwellers: mere managers, manager-has-beens, and that rare bird, the leader (or the budding leader).

Mere managers do the work that is given to them, follow the rules, and hope for the best. They tend to be quite comfort zone-oriented and are committed to maintaining the status quo, both personally and professionally. They seek to avoid the pain of leaving their cave, so much so that they may miss opportunities. "Go and tell my boss I think we're having production problems? That's not my job. Quality control or personnel difficulties? Better to leave that to someone else better suited to bring it up. Handle a situation between my department and another? I'm not a negotiator, I'm a manager." And so it goes.

Other examples of not always pleasant changes that strike fear into the hearts of mere managers everywhere might include the following:

- Going back to graduate school
- Taking on a project nobody wants
- Traveling to places that make business life stressful
- Taking on additional duties, assignments, responsibilities, or personnel
- Hiring, disciplining, or terminating people
- Assuming temporary or permanent command of a new work group, team, or division
- Being asked to develop new strategies, new systems, or new policies and procedures
- Developing a new product or service
- Working with difficult or challenging customers
- Moving to a new office in another part of the country

Manager-has-beens, by definition, are those bosses who have either been burnt out from overwork or burned themselves out because they were not challenged—by the organization, by the work, or because they lacked that specific talent that some people seem to have that says, "Challenge me. If you don't give me interesting projects, I'll make my own." The manager-has-been may have also missed several opportunities to rise in the organization. He or she may have missed out on promotions that went to other seemingly less-qualified people; been passed over when the time came to find someone to head a new project; overlooked on a choice reassignment; or otherwise been left standing still in their careers.

Sometimes these events come along by accident or happenstance— they were not in the right place at the right time. In other cases, the company is just not a good place to work: it does not nurture its people, provide new opportunities, or offer any ways or means for advancement. Or, more accurately, the manager-has-been has physically, emotionally, and mentally thrown in the towel before the fight has ended.

Then there are the true leaders or the budding leaders, people who are willing to move out of their cave when given the opportunity. Armed with new information, new challenges, or even new problems with no apparent solutions in sight, these folks can see past narrowly defined job descriptions, outside the standard boundaries created by The Rule Book, and into the seemingly dark unknown or impending change.

## No Pain, No Gain: Discomfort Zones

We all know how easy it is to sit on the couch with the TV remote control in one hand and unhealthy snacks in the other. The treadmill, stairclimber, or exercise bike gathering dust in your bedroom might call out to you, but if you turn up the volume on the TV loud enough, you can successfully block it out. It's easier, safer, and more fun to sit in one place than get up and move about. The brain says, "Vigorous exercise might mean some discomfort. We don't care for that. Let's go back to the couch."

Plato's cave is not much different. After all, it's more fun to stay inside where it's safe, quiet, warm, and non-threatening. It's hard to go out into the blinding light and deal with all the problems that suddenly overwhelm you. Leadership is all about your willingness to be uncomfortable more times than not. It is, truth be told, all about your tolerance—not for comfort, but for discomfort. This readiness to move into a "discomfort zone" has proven to be one of the hallmarks of leadership.

Lee Iaccoca took over the reins of Chrysler in the early 1980s when the automaker was at its nadir. Thanks to a dismal financial picture and no apparent hope for recovery, the future of Chrysler seemed hopeless. The phrase "Abandon All Hope, Ye Who Enter Here," could have been carved over the door to Iaccoca's office, and yet, he was the first to admit that he relished, even welcomed the challenge. Tough times? Bring 'em on! No comfort zone in sight? That's fine, just give me the reins and let me start leading the horse in the direction I think is right. No supporters in the vicinity? Even better, I'll go into the company and personally recruit a team of go-getters who aren't afraid to leave the comfort zones surrounding their desks and come ride to the sound of the guns with me.

This company will come back from the near dead to be one of the best carmakers in the world.

Hype? You bet. Overtly patriotic? Surely. And yet, it happened. Iaccoca took generous loans from the federal government and turned the company around. Gone was the gas hog, in came the minivan, and a transportation revolution took place as nearly every other car maker on the planet followed suit. But what ended as an afterthought for Ford and Chevy, Nissan and Mazda, and any other newcomer to the minivan race was a rock-solid beginning for the new Chrysler.

For his part, Lee Iaccoca talked the "let's get out of the cave" talk. Love him or hate him, Iaccoca went out into the marketplace and "took the point," on TV, on the radio, and in print. His face and his demeanor became so associated with Chrysler that the buying public couldn't help but jump onto his bandwagon.

It's a dead certainty that working at Chrysler during the Iaccoca turn-around years was filled with long periods of "discomfort"; you don't go hat in hand to banks and the feds without feeling your collar tighten. But no amount of this kind of psychological pain seemed to stop Iaccoca; he developed his plan, moved out smartly, and gathered a cadre of enthusiastic supporters along the way, some from surprising places such as the automaking trade unions. Almost single-handedly, this scrappy leader dragged his organization—kicking and screaming—out of its psychic cave.

How about you? When a new challenge, difficulty, or problem arises, are you ready, willing, and able to leave the relative safety of your cave, your comfort zone, for however long it takes, until you get the job done?"

Leaders lead, managers manage. Leaders leave their caves. Mere managers tidy up. Manager has-beens stay.

### The Couch Potato and the Desk Potato

Whoever said, "All change is good," was probably not thinking too clearly. All change is of course not good, but change is a fact of business life; and it frequently gives you the opportunity to improve your situation. And since change is taking place faster than ever, you have to be able to respond and react accordingly.

Yet "couch potatoes," and their business counterparts, "desk potatoes" need not apply. Our American lexicon has given us the term couch potato to describe a person who is glued to his or her couch and whose most vigorous activity is channel surfing.

In the best case, the couch potato is a do-nothing, someone who just sits there and watches life go by. In the worst case, the couch potato actually causes himself or herself harm with lazy or even self-destructive behavior. This is not to say that being a couch potato is all bad. We've all felt like plopping ourselves in front of the TV after a hard day at work. Sometimes it's fun to let someone or something else make our decisions for us.

But couch potatoes become real problems when remaining inert is all they do. If and when they ever come out of their stupor in six months or even one year later, they find themselves no better than they were, and probably even worse. For the couch potato, those extra pounds didn't get there by accident. Thanks to a complete lack of motivation, momentum, or any desire to make a change, these people can deteriorate quickly.

And so it goes in business, since we define the desk potato as a mere manager who mirrors some of the same habits belonging to his or her home-based counterpart. They are inveterate cave dwellers. Desk potatoes abhor pressure, conflict, and anything that requires more than the usual effort to accomplish. They become masters in the use of avoidance, buck-passing, and delaying tactics, knowing that if enough time passes, the unpleasant tasks, job, or duty falls onto someone else's lap. They are history's great bureaucrats.

While you may work in an organization that does nothing to change desk potato behavior for the better, consider yourself lucky. It could be worse: you could work for an organization filled with desk potatoes or, in a nightmare of nationwide proportions, you could work in an industry full of desk potatoes.

It happened at San Diego's Teledyne Ryan, long a maker of helicopter fuselages and unmanned drone target aircraft. With the end of the so-called Cold War, many of our oldest defense manufacturers and contractors have found themselves literally dead in the water (and in the air). Teledyne failed to see the light. As a result, the firm has had to initiate massive layoffs, and even furloughs (better known as unpaid vacations) for its employees. This is the company that built the plane that flew Charles Lindbergh across the Atlantic. Cave dwellers take note: It's also the company that failed to see the end of the defense boom that lasted from World War II until the early 1980s.

Widely reported interviews with Teledyne Ryan company managers and executives showed a group of people who were not sure what to do next—desk potatoes seemed to typify the company's management team. The usual "next big contract from Uncle Sam" was suddenly not in the pipeline. When your company makes something that only one customer—the Pentagon—wants to buy, and it suddenly changes gears on you, what do you do with your helicopter bodies and your planes?

This is not to go out of our way to pick on the aerospace/defense industries, where such desk potato behavior often seems to have reached epidemic proportions. People who thought their engineering or manufacturing skills would give them a job for life in the gun, bomb, and rocket business have had a rude awakening. The time to ask, "Gee, what do we do next?" should come long before the final RFP (Request For Proposal) comes from your one and only customer in Washington, D.C.

As we have said, there are those who hate change, fight it, and avoid it, and there are those who deal with it, welcome it, and even embrace it. As Plato's journey from darkness to light and back again demonstrates, your success as a leader begins by doing something fundamental and seemingly paradoxical: changing your response to change.

Effective leaders, as Plato knew so well, look upon their tasks, daunting as they may appear, and say, "There is some tough sledding now, but it will end and I—and my organization—will be better for it." If that means you need to retool your factory, change the location of your plant, develop completely new products or services to match the new economy, or start from scratch, you had better be ready to move.

## Cave Dweller Mottos: Rationalizations, Excuses, and One Million Reasons Not to Leave

We think the following advertisement, run several years ago by TRW, Inc., says a lot about how cave dwellers can kill good ideas. It goes like this:

*I have an idea ...*
*A word of caution ...*
*A little too radical ...*
*I like it myself, but ...*
*We tried something just like that once ...*
*Let me play devil's advocate ...*
*It's just not us ...*
*I wish it were that easy ...*
*Oh, it was just an idea ...*

"It won't work." Those three simple words have probably caused more good ideas to come to a grinding halt than any others in our English language. Yet, as destructive as these words can be for a new and fragile idea, some people still insist on trotting them out every time a new idea threatens their—you guessed it—comfort zone. An idea is a fragile thing. Don't turn it off.

As Plato has pointed out in his allegory, the person leaving the cave suffered the slings and arrows of his fellow cavemates, who heaped scorn upon him or her for (a) wanting to leave, (b) leaving, and (c) returning to explain what he or she had seen on the outside. In that respect, the world has not changed much since 300 BC; we still hear from the critics, naysayers, and other "can't-do"-ers who offer many so-called valid reasons why something won't work and not much in the way of positive help.

Thanks to the Wright Brothers and their successful flight (accomplished only after many failures), the phrase "Back to the bike shop, Wilbur" is a favorite among people who like to question the reasons behind any good idea. It's always easy to point to the distinct possibility of failure. That way, some people reason, if an attempt does flop, they can say, "I told you so" as often as they like.

As we've suggested, Plato would be the first to agree that cave-leaving is never easy. It's a hard, tough, bloody climb. No wonder many companies have failed to leave the cave of their industry, marketplace, product, or service. The reasons are legion. Here are just a few:

*The Sunk Cost Theory*
"We've already spent X dollars on this project and so, even though it's been an abysmal failure, let's throw some more money at it in the miraculous hope that something might change for the better."

*The Crippled Race Horse Theory*
"We've come this far (on a broken-down nag, no less) with the people we have in place already on this project. Let's give them even more rope to hang themselves instead of putting newer, smarter, fresher horses on to the track."

*The Leaky Boat Theory*
"We've already patched this boat and bailed lots of water from it.

Let's stick with this faulty design, this outdated technology, this worn-out equipment for one more trip across the ocean."

*The Let's Wait 'Til ... Theory*
"Let's wait until the marketplace improves, our survey data comes in, the recession goes away, unemployment goes up or down, the prime rate changes, the stock market settles down, our competitors raise their prices, or the cow jumps over the moon before we take any risks. Conditions have to be just exactly right before we can move."

And what may be even more disturbing is the notion that self-satisfied companies, unwilling to change even when all of the signs are trying to bring them out of the cave, are too prideful even to see the signs. As we will note in this next section, big is not always best.

**The IBM Follies: The Biggest Cave Is Not Always the Best One**
A favorite quote of financial analysts and management consultants everywhere comes from guru Peter Drucker, who wrote the prescient lines, "Whom the gods must punish, they first grant forty years of business success." As we suggested at the beginning of this chapter, nowhere is this more applicable than with Big Blue, IBM. Few huge companies have demonstrated the concept of comfort zone life more fully than this computer giant. Even though IBM seems to be resuscitating itself as this book goes to press, IBM's long and distressing downward profit spiral has alarmed shareholders, financial analysts, and IBM leadership for several years now, with only a few quarterly upturns to provide much optimism. For a company long known for its cradle-to-grave employment policies, there is a sea change in the air at many IBM offices. Many longtime employees are being asked to take early retirements, reassignments, and other career-threatening events.

Big Blue is still learning a lesson that serves to contrast the good old comfortable cave with the realities of the marketplace. Mainframes—those behemoth databank computers attached to satellite PCs—are no longer popular with customers who used to rely on them in days of old. With the desktop PC now as a common as a coffeemaker in organizations, many people realize they can do more with less.

Instead of filling this need, IBM has continued to stress mainframe sales as the bulk of its business. The market shifted to "IBM-compatibles," a generic phrase used in parlance nowadays like "Xerox copies," "Kleenex tissues," and "Band-Aids." (This ironic use of their corporate name must cause much pain around IBM corporate headquarters when you consider how often it's used to describe their competitors' machines.) What will it take, everybody still wonders, to get IBM to leave its cave and abolish its current comfort zone?

## Try a Little Risutora

Behemoths like IBM might do well to try a sure-fire cave-exiting technique the Japanese are using to transform Matsushita, the world's largest consumer electronics company. And the sooner the better. At Matsushita (a company known for its slow, bureaucratic management structure), sales have topped out at about $70 billion dollars over the past four years and pre-tax income has plummeted.

It's called "risutora" and means (what else?) "restructuring." It can be Draconian. Matsushita executives have decided to kill the bureaucracy. Six thousand corporate paper pushers are being told to transform themselves from cost centers to revenue producers. Translation? They're being transmogrified into marketing and production personnel. Not only that, but life-time employment, so long a standard at Japanese firms, is *out* at Matsushita. Increasing white collar productivity means that scientists who work on special projects have become "temps," with short-term five-year contracts.

Perhaps the most dramatic change at Matsushita, though, is the appointment, in 1993, of Yoichi Morishita as president. Only a junior executive vice-president before his appointment, he was young and—perhaps more damning—had only served in sales. (Matsushita had always been headed by engineers.) Yet, nothing communicates more clearly to the established comfort zones in an organization than the personnel moves you make. Morishita's selection said it all: Matsushita was making a clean break with the past. It would leave its comfort zone.

## Then There's the Big Three Automakers

Like Matsushita, the U.S. auto industry had for too many years been a victim of its own success and its own comfort zone mentality. Why did it take them so long to move their designs from gas-guzzling four-doors to more economical and fuel-friendly models? Upstart car models like the Saturn have tried to shake each of the Big Three into a new mindset, with middling success. Although at this writing the Saturn model is still not a profit-making entity for GM, it has helped every U.S. (and foreign) car maker to say, "Hmm, maybe we should build cars we know our customers will want to buy rather than cars we want them to buy."

For their part, the Big Three are starting to respond to the mandate for change at the buyer's behest. Behind both the Japanese and the European car makers in sales just several years ago, U.S. car makers were, as one wag put it, the "ultimate not invented here" companies. For too long, the thinking in Detroit went, "If we didn't dream it up, it must not be any good." And this apparent lack of strategy hit their bottom lines hard. U.S.-based auto sales fell from over 77 percent in 1984 to just under 70 percent in 1991.

Yet by leaving their comfort zones, American automakers have, in just three years, pulled off one of the greatest turnarounds in their history. It wasn't easy—leaving your comfort zone never is—but they managed to reorganize their top management structures, introduce a myriad of new products, improve on existing models dramatically, slash costs, beef up productivity, and forge new alliances with their suppliers, their unions, and their customers.

The result has been nothing short of a corporate Renaissance. Chrysler, GM, and Ford recently posted their best quarters in their histories (at one point, the three firms combined were earning galloping profits of $51 million every day!) And market share of U.S. auto sales has rebounded to over 75 percent. Kicking and screaming, no doubt, the leaders of the U.S. auto industry have started pulling their organizations out of their caves.

At Ford, for example, leaders have been ushering the company through a complete redesign. Widely touted as the most sweeping change in Ford's ninety-one-year history, "Ford 2000" required nothing less than a massive corporate exodus from the auto maker's comfort zone. There were costs, certainly. Eighty thousand jobs redefined, three hundred senior and middle managers let go, and four thousand high-level managers taking on different, broader responsibilities. But the process itself seems to have great value, according to a *Wall Street Journal* article describing Ford's makeover. Some of the changes include the following:[4]

- *Down-up as well as top-down involvement.* Ford tried recasting itself in 1967 and failed miserably. Why? Because employees didn't understand the goals. This time out, Ford has been getting the people who will be affected by the changes involved in the planning process.

- *An opened-up process.* Enough of secret meetings—internal memos and newletters inform everyone about what's going on. There's a weekly faxed newspaper, an electronic bulletin board, and even an in-house TV show.

- A *super-fast schedule.* How? By putting all the key decision makers in one building, mountains of memos and reports were eliminated, while the really big decisions were more than likely to be made around the water cooler. Reported one member of the "reorg team," as it's called, "a long-term assignment around here is five days."

- *Managed confusion.* It's chaos: careers are being profoundly affected, lives changed. People are, understandably, afraid. (Some European employees, it is said, joke sadly that FAO, which stands for Ford Automotive Operations, which will include the long-autonomous Ford of Europe, stands for For Americans Only.) Yet through it all, the "reorg team" presses on, changing the Ford Motor Company forever.

Yet, unhappily, most companies are not following Ford's example; the list of continuing corporate cave dwellers is still nearly endless: Texas and California real estate companies, convinced the apartment and office building boom would last forever, got comfy. Oil in Alaska and Texas would flow forever, went the common thinking of the oil and gas pumping and distribution outfits. No need to import foreign oil from politically unstable countries—there's plenty right here, until the marketplace demonstrated to them that it was cheaper to get it over there. And manufacturing and service industries have learned or are learning the same things: we need to be new, better, different, customer-centered— and we need to be that way now.

A printing company we know demonstrates the comfort zone/cave principle yet again. You would be impressed to see their warehouse with the large offset printers whirring at top speed. And yet, their business is in the doldrums. Why? Like IBM and so many others, new computer technology is passing them by. Smaller, sleeker, more service-oriented printing firms have found that by making a substantial investment in computers rather than in huge and expense-laden printing presses, they can offer their customers one-stop shopping.

From an idea on a piece of paper to computer-generated artwork, to the negative plates to the final print run, these smaller litho firms can do it all. Add another product photo to your brochure? No problem, we'll just make some space on your computer floppy disk. Change the type size or style in the entire document? Easy. We'll just press a few keys and print out a new master. Our friends at the big print shop didn't buy into this computer-based design "fad" when it first came along. Now they find themselves using antiquated equipment, charging higher prices than the smaller full-service firms, and not being able to offer the same design flexibility or product quality.

Leaving the comfort zone of the cave is tough, no question. But faced with technology that will pass you by and changes in the way your customers want to use your products and services, you must be willing to do it.

### Lessons from the Cave

Plato's *Republic* was such an important book in philosophy that it was said "everything since is merely a footnote." The same could be said for the wisdom this text contains about leadership. And surely the "Allegory of the Cave" is one of its most profound leadership lessons. Lest you find yourself becoming a corporate spelunker, some final thoughts on caves and comfort zones:

1.  *When things get too comfortable around here, it's best to take cover.* It's called complacency, and it is a terminal organizational disease. And it doesn't just happen to the giants like IBM. But wherever it occurs, the trajectory of stagnation that results is classic. You've no doubt witnessed it. A friend founds a small company that becomes a leader in its industry, commanding respect, high prices, and even higher margins. This seems to be a career made in heaven. Increasingly, however, something all too human happens. Your friend becomes overconfident, even arrogant. He or she is in the comfort zone. Feeling invincible, a disdain for customers develops. Then sales begin to stagnate; profits plummet; a key customer chooses another supplier; a product is recalled. Smaller, more agile—and, we might add—

less comfortable companies begin to capture share of market. Employees are laid off; a plant closes. It's a near-mythic journey you must avoid.

2. *Kill the bureaucracy every day.* Nothing gets you into the cave, and keeps you there more effectively, than the grinding official-ism we call bureaucracy, with its specialization of functions (i.e., "it's not my job, buster!"), adherence to fixed rules (i.e., "do it my way or don't do it at all!"), and hierarchy of authority (i.e., "so what if it's wrong, it came down from corporate headquarters!"). Such beadledom fairly breeds in the dark corners of the cave, spawning the cave dweller's god, conventional wisdom. Light, happily, eradicates such nonsense.

3. *Try telling the truth.* The whole point of Plato's "Allegory of the Cave" is that truth is power and responsibility together. Nothing, it seems, does more to move people out of their comfort zones than the kind of reality check that comes with conveying the truth, well-told. So important, in fact, is *credibility* to the health of both the individual and the organization, that it is the subject of a book by the same name. In *Credibility,* management gurus Barry Posner and Jim Kouzes assert that simple honesty has another payoff: it is the single most identified characteristic of effective leadership. Simply put, tell it like it is.

   Not too many years ago, the Dana Corporation ran an ad in leading business publications that dramatized the practical value of honesty. "Talk back to the boss," read the headline. "It's one of Dana's principles of productivity," continued the ad. "Bosses don't have all the answers. The worker who does the job always knows more about it than his boss. But all that he knows can't be used unless he's free to talk about it. Especially to his boss."

   Such sanctioned sassiness seems to have paid off. Dana's ability to increase productivity in quantum leaps is legendary.

4. *Practice healthy paranoia.* If this sounds sick, think again. Such a strategy is precisely what accounts for Hewlett-Packard's ability to cut operating expenses from more than 40 percent of rev-enues in 1988 to 28 percent in the first quarter of 1994. The result, a "leadership cost structure" built on a corporate culture that rewards managers for always looking over their shoulders at the competition. And what a memory-jogger. "HP" no longer

means just "Hewlett-Packard." It also stands for—you guessed it—Healthy Paranoia.

In *Managing as a Performing Art*, author Peter Vaill writes:

> For Plato, leadership is an art, and some contemporary theorists draw a distinction between the functions of management and those of leadership and argue that, whereas management requires certain organizational skills and is perhaps captured by the preceding theories, leadership is an art form, specializing in the articulation of a vision of an organization's goals and creation of the conditions necessary for the achievement of those goals.[5]

We would agree. The remainder of this book will further paint the distinction between being a mere manager and becoming a leader in the broadest of brush strokes. It won't be easy to make this journey to leader, nor will it be comfortable. But why not leave the cave and see the light?

## CHAPTER 2

## CLIMBING THE CAREER LADDER: SHAKESPEAREAN SECRETS FROM THE HENRIAD

*Be not afraid of greatness: some are born great, some achieve greatness and some have greatness thrust upon them.*
— WILLIAM SHAKESPEARE

### KEY POINTS
- LEARNING TO LEAD
- MATURITY, GROWTH, AND DEVELOPMENT

If you've ever marveled at the meteoric career of someone you've always considered disreputable or a general ne'er-do-well, you have unwittingly proven that life really does imitate art. It was none other than history's greatest playwright, William Shakespeare, who described this surprising, but archetypal, up-the-career-ladder phenomenon. It's all in his series of three plays known to afficionados as the Henriad. (Stay with us here; there's *Henry IV, Parts I and II*, and *Henry V*.) Reading these works, you'll join in Shakespeare's great exploration of the nature of kingship—the personal traits and political skills that will enable you to become an astute and capable leader.

The journey begins with young Prince Hal, who appears to be wasting his time in the company of thieves, drunkards, and fools. It ends with an older and wiser Hal, known as King Henry V, a valorous leader who not only unifies his contentious countrymen, but also soundly beats the French at the Battle of Agincourt in 1415.

What's especially fascinating about this story of achievement is that none of it could have happened without Hal's misspent youth, which was actually a calculated plan to prepare him for leadership. How else could he have developed an understanding for the common people who made up the majority of his subjects?

### Shakespeare: The Consummate Management Consultant

In a word, poet and playwright William Shakespeare was an Elizabethan; that is, a man who lived during the age of Queen Elizabeth I and Britain's world dominance that ran from 1558 to 1603. This period of history was filled with noble deeds and forward thinking in terms of literature, art, music, politics, and exploration. It was a time of heroic voyages across the sea, as noted sailors Sir Francis Drake and Sir Walter Raleigh plied the oceans in search of new lands and new discoveries. During this dynamic period, Shakespeare quickly established himself as one of his nation's premier men of letters and the arts. Although little is known about his life, his written work is well-known and it has certainly outlasted that written by all his dramatic competitors.

Shakespeare was born in 1564 in Stratford-upon-Avon, England, married at eighteen, and with his wife had three children. And while knowledge of his personal life may not fill the shelves, his literary life certainly has done the job. To say that Shakespeare (also known as the Bard of Avon or, more simply, the Bard) was prolific would be a vast understatement. He could and did write about all aspects of the human condition, creating comedies and tragedies, histories and romances, sonnets and poems that resonate with the times, then and now. So prolific was the Bard that quotations from his works outnumber all others chronicled in *Bartlett's Famous Quotations*.

Above all else, Shakespeare had the unique ability, as a playwright, to communicate with audiences of every social class, education, and background. His stories and their built-in messages about love and life, war and death, duty and honor, crossed all social barriers and made him a writer for the people. The more well-known of his thirty-seven plays include *Romeo and Juliet*, *Macbeth*, *Othello*, *Julius Caesar*, *The Merchant of Venice*, *As You Like It*, and *A Midsummer Night's Dream*.

Most of your early exposure to Shakespeare probably came at the hands of well-meaning junior high and high school teachers who made you and your classmates read his plays aloud. (It's still a good way to really understand what is being said and done by the characters.) Since the language is more than a bit archaic and the metaphors, similes, and other more abstract images don't always translate easily, it's no surprise many people found their school-age encounters with Shakespeare less than pleasant.

However, thanks to motion pictures and television, scores of people have had the chance to see many of Shakespeare's works in a new and more appealing light. (Suggestion: If you haven't yet, rush right out and rent the video versions of Kenneth Branagh's *Henry V* and Mel Gibson's *Hamlet*. You'll be transformed!) Indeed, much of Shakespeare's work has now fallen into our vernacular. Even if you know nothing of the play, you're sure to be familiar with the phrase "To be or not to be?" from *Hamlet*. No wonder the late Orson Welles said, "Now we sit through Shakespeare in order to recognize the quotations."

## The Henriad: Lessons In Leadership

The essential lesson of The Henriad is this: it's not enough to have the title of "Leader." In order to lead and lead well, you have to know your role, your people, and your organization. You also need the strength and wisdom that comes, more often than not, from time (if available) and hands-on experience.

The Henriad, like many of Shakepeare's plays, is full of lively main and supporting characters. It opens with the rise of Henry IV after he has wrested the kingship from the unpopular King Richard and caused his death. When we meet him, Henry IV is having problems with his personal, political, and family life. Among other things, his son and heir, Prince Hal, is keeping company with a disreputable bunch of thieves, drunkards, and fools, and is apparently uninterested in preparing to become king. From a political standpoint, King Henry IV has little support from his countrymen, including a character named Hotspur Percy. Percy is hugely affronted, believing that he and his family have not been adequately rewarded for their support of Henry. He plots an overthrow.

In the first act of *Henry IV*, we find the new king about to be beset by two problems: Hotspur urging his family and other cohorts to try and overthrow what he feels is a clearly traitorous leader; and Prince Hal and his slovenly and vulgarly hedonistic friend Falstaff, planning to rob the king's couriers of their gold. Granted, Hal's acquiescence to Falstaff's plan makes him as culpable as any common thief. Yet Hal has a plan of his own, which he reveals in the famous soliloquy early in the first act of the play. If you read between the archaic lines, you'll discover a future leader engaging in what seem like juvenile pranks and shenanigans so that when he does, in fact, become a leader, he will look all the better. Quite a strategy.

But there's more here. Hal's apparent dissipation is really a part of his strategy to "get to know the employees" as no strait-laced MBA type could ever do. To lead, Hal knows he must first be "of the people." As he puts it:

> ... *herein will I imitate the sun,*
> *who doth permit the base contagious clouds*
> *to smother up his beauty from the world,*
> *that, when he please again to be himself,*
> *being wanted, he may be more wond'red at,*
> *by breaking through the foul and ugly mist*
> *of vapors that did seem to strangle him.*[1]

Hal concludes his soliloquy with the words: "So when this loose behavior I throw off ...", telling us that he knows he will, at the right time, assume the mantle of leadership.

After the robbery, King Henry orders his son to meet with him and explain himself. He finds Hal neither repentant nor ashamed of his deed. Unaware that Prince Hal's behavior is part of a strategy to get to know his people, the king describes in no uncertain terms how his son is destined for failure. (Be thankful, as we are, that your father never gave this speech to you):

> *I know not whether God will have it so*
> *For some displeasing service I have done,*
> *That in his secret doom, out of my blood*
> *He'll breed revengement and a scourge for me,*

*But thou dost in thy passages of life*
*Make me believe that thou art only mark'd*
*For the hot vengeance, and the rod of heaven,*
*To punish my mistreadings. Tell me else,*
*Could such inordinate and low desires,*
*Such poor, such bare, such lewd, such mean attempts,*
*Such barren pleasures, rude society,*
*As thou art match'd withal and grafted to,*
*Accompany the greatness of thy blood ...*

Talk about a low performance rating! It's fortunate that Hal can't be fired. After all, he's the boss's son.

In the meantime, Hotspur and his rebel group have been making plans to go to war with the King's soldiers. Because he is so volatile and hotheaded, Hotspur has a hard time making alliances with the people who should be his allies. As such, he foolishly wants to begin the fight with less support than is safe. Once the battle begins, Prince Hal fights bravely, rescues his father, and kills Hotspur.

When the next play, *Henry IV Part II*, begins, Hotspur's father decides to avenge his son's death and continue his plans to overthrow the king. King Henry IV, although aging and weary, is encouraged to see that while Prince Hal still associates with Falstaff and his misfit friends, he is on his way to becoming a leader. As Henry lays dying, Hal enters and, thinking that his father is already dead, removes his crown and places it on his own head. The king awakens and is angered, wrongly believing that Hal has stolen his title from him. In the ensuing discussion, the dying King realizes his son meant no ill and is, in fact, bound for greatness.

When Hal's drinking companion Falstaff learns that his friend is king, he greets him with a backslapping informality that angers the new leader. Hal rebukes Falstaff for his lack of deference. Not only has Hal made the transition to leader, he takes his new role quite seriously.

*Reply not to me with a fool-born jest,*
*Presume not that I am the thing I was,*
*For God doth know, so shall the world perceive,*
*That I have turn'd away my former self ...*

Anyone estranged from a newly appointed leader who feels it is no longer appropriate to continue a personal relationship can empathize with Falstaff's reaction to this kingly rebuke.

Friendly or not, the new king had quite an agenda. Before he died, Henry IV had urged him to try and unite England's quarreling factions by the simple expedient of going to war against the French. (Showing near-genius for ensuring domestic tranquility, Hal's father had admonished him: "... be it thy course to busy giddy minds with foreign quarrels ...")

From the beginning of the third play (*Henry V*), it's clear that war with the French is almost unavoidable. So offended and cocksure are the French that they make war inevitable when the French prince publicly insults the new king. History records that this indignity was the result of a gift, elaborately presented but hugely inappropriate: three tennis balls. This royal putdown backfired marvelously, for it gave Hal (now Henry V) the opportunity to finally reveal himself as a great leader. In front of his entire court, young Hal seizes the moment, giving a rousing speech that both puts the French on notice and motivates his people to follow him into battle.

> *We are glad the [prince] is so pleasant with us,*
> *His present and your pains we thank you for.*
> *When we have match'd our rackets to these balls,*
> *We will in France, by God's grace, play a set*
> *Shall strike his father's crown into the hazard.*
> *Tell him he hath made a match with such a wrangler*
> *That all the courts of France will be disturb'd*
> *With [missed returns].*

The threat worked. The French king, not wanting a war, offers Henry V some land and his daughter, Katherine, in marriage. Henry refuses and the war against the French begins in earnest.

Outside the walls of the French city of Harflew (Honfleur), Henry's call to battle appeals to his men's honor and manhood. It's a rouser:

> *Once more into the breach, dear friends, once more;*
> *... On, on, you [noblest] English,*
> *Whose blood is [proved in battle]!*

*Fathers that, like so many Alexanders,*
*Have in these parts from morn till even fought,*
*And sheath'd their swords for lack of argument.*
*Dishonor not your mothers; now attest*
*That those who you call'd fathers did beget you.*
*Be [an example] now to [men] of [less noble blood],*
*And teach them how to war. And you, good yeomen,*
*Whose limbs were made in England, show us here*
*The mettle of your pasture; let us swear*
*That you are worth your breeding, which I doubt not;*
*For there is none of you so mean and base*
*That hath not noble lustre in your eyes.*
*I see you stand like greyhounds in the slips,*
*[Straining] upon the start. The game's afoot!*
*Follow your spirit; and upon this charge*
*Cry, "God for Harry, England, and St. George!"*

Not surprisingly, the British troops dispense with their French enemy quickly. Following the surrender of the city, Henry V decides to move his victorious army further into France. But by now, his troops—hugely outnumbered by the French—are bloodied, battered and weary. The French army, sensing this, prepares to attack. As both sides wait for daybreak, dissension and fear grow among the English ranks. Henry, aware of his men's disquiet, demonstrates his increasing leadership skill by disguising himself and visiting and talking with his men, learning their hopes and dreams; their grievances, complaints, and fears. Think of it as a kind of medieval "managing by wandering around."

Gathering his troops the next morning, he uses much of what he learned the night before. The result is one of history's most effective calls to arms, a truly motivational message—the famous speech before the battle of Agincourt. More about this later. Thus enabled, the English troops, under the command of a hard-charging Henry, storm the French side and rout them. As the play ends, Henry and the King of France make peace. Henry takes the French king's daughter, Katherine, as his bride and the two countries enter into a new era of accord.

## What the Henriad Means to You as a Leader

In our leadership development seminars, business managers as well as, we might add, business leaders have discovered that Shakespeare's story of Prince Hal says a great deal about the challenges of leading. In "The Henriad," as in many of his plays, Shakespeare places his characters in periods of great stress, introduces further conflict into their lives, and then forces them to make their own way out—not unlike organizational life today. In the process, he teaches us much about the differences between leaders and managers and the process of becoming a leader.

As "The Henriad" shows so well, in leadership, what you do early on has a lot to do with how you finish up. Although he despairs of his son's behavior, King Henry IV tries to serve as a mentor to Hal. He attempts to teach his son the things he needs to know in order to assume the responsibilities about to land squarely upon his shoulders. While it's not obvious until his father's death that the young prince is listening and learning from his father, indeed he is—but he's learning from others as well.

From the start of the first of the three plays, it's clear that Hal's father sees his son's drinking and carousing as a hindrance to assuming the mantle of leadership. But as Hal's opening soliloquy demonstrates, the prince does in fact have a plan for his life and his early behavior is part of that plan. By associating with the common man instead of keeping company only with other royals, Hal demonstrates a surprising ability to be "of the people" and understand what they think and feel. And as unlikely as it may seem, Falstaff and his cohorts play a kind of mentor role for Hal. His association with these miscreants is a unique, but highly effective way to learn about the people he will one day lead. Hal is sowing the seeds for greatness, learning not only from the role models we might expect but also from rather unusual experiences and associations. Although his father does not recognize it at the time, Hal will be ready for kingship, in his own time and at his own pace. But while the prince watches, waits, and learns, tumultuous events around him force him to seize the initiative much sooner than he would have liked.

The mentor relationships that benefitted Hal are not unlike ones occurring in today's organizations. In similar circumstances, a member of the Old Guard takes a young manager with recognizable potential under his wing for the express purpose of imparting the knowledge the manager needs in order to survive and lead. And, just as it happened for Hal, this education can be cut short when this Old Guard mentor loses power or authority due to downsizing, semi-forced retirement, a transfer, or even a termination. Increasingly in today's chaotic environment, this education process can be expected to move at breakneck speed, just as it did for Prince Hal.

The lesson for you as an aspiring leader is to take advantage of mentors where you find them—from the top of the organization to the bottom; from established leaders to the rank and file as well.

## Management Missile Silos: Every Organization Has Its Fiefdoms

But there's more to "The Henriad" than lessons on mentors and protégés. The story also teaches much about organizations in which departments care more about competing with each other than with the *real* competition, the other companies participating in their market. In Henry's case, there is deep divisiveness. The allies have not embraced him or his causes and Hotspur and his family continually try to sabotage his plans. If this sounds to you like many contemporary organizations, you're right.

In their book *Customer-Focused Re-Engineering*, authors Crego and Schiffrin refer to an odd, but all-too-common, phenomenon known as "missile silo management."[2] In this scenario, perfectly good companies deconstruct themselves into various departments that fit neatly into little cubicles, attached to each other only by thread-like lines and dashes that imply (and we do mean *imply*) that some kind of communication among them is possible. This strange organizational geometry reminds us of a pod of missile silos viewed from the air, wholly separate and hugely destructive—sub-organizations linked together only by a fragile communications system.

Management gurus call this "departmental suboptimization." We call it "missile silo management." And it's everywhere. Problems arise when each leader sees his or her specific department as an entity unto itself, separate from the rest of the company. They begin to engage in "silo wars" with other teams, departments, divisions, or groups, all in an effort to advance their private agendas and protect their turf. (You've probably already recognized that some departments in your own company, or even companies in your own industry, are prone to factionalism, dislike, and "missile launchings.")

The marvelously-named Hotspur, to no one's surprise, is a consummate missile silo commander. He's bent on running his own "silo war," even if it means the end of the kingdom as he knows it. By plotting to end Henry IV's reign, Hotspur puts his own selfish interests in front of his nation's. He's not unlike managers who allow their personal, political, or other hidden agendas to sabotage the organization.

What does all this mean to you? In order to have any influence on your company's hierarchy (trust us, even in today's "flattened" and "empowered" organizations, vestiges of the hierarchy still survive!), you need to know the power structure—to put it bluntly, who the missile commanders are. What this knowledge tells you is:

- Who rules where
- How you fit into each of these realms
- Who the behind-the-scenes powers are

Leaders know—as did Henry—that there is always more to the organization than meets the eye. As one wag put it, it's more important to be able to read the white spaces on the organization chart than all the dotted lines and little boxes. If, as you look at yours, you see missiles pointed at you, best to take cover.

### Dispelling the "Us" Versus "Them" Mindset

One of the things that made Prince Hal such a compelling figure was his innate ability to be genuinely "one of the guys." (We will avoid the temptation to compare today's "royals" with their talented forbear.) But how often do you hear of a contemporary CEO lunching in the company cafeteria or (even less likely) quaffing a beer with the boys down at the local pub?

For Prince Hal, that was standard operating procedure; he kept company with people like the larger-than-life Falstaff, a man given to great excesses of food, drink, and other more earthly pleasures. And Hal's friendship with these common people was not based on guilt, pity, or superiority but rather on the fact that he enjoyed their company and, importantly, he wanted to get to know them better. How else, he must have wondered to himself, could he ever lead them?

There's a compelling "work hard, play hard" message here for leaders, too. Even though Hal could mix with people who did not share his station, he possessed the ability, whenever necessary, to shed his frivolous side and get down to the business of being king and leader. This ability to switch roles is paramount to your own success as a leader. Being able to interact with and understand how your peers, subordinates, and superiors think is a capacity that all true leaders share.

One colleague we know puts it this way:

> *I have a fairly high executive position in my company. Yet for all my power lunches with the bigwigs and my high-powered meetings with various CEO's, clients, and ranking executives, I still feel like one of my strongest assets is that I can talk to everyone equally, and on their level, whatever or wherever it is. That means I can talk banking with the Chief Financial Officer one minute and still exchange pleasantries about some subject of mutual interest with the cleaning lady who empties the trash in our building the next. My father taught me to treat everyone as I would expect to be treated, whether it's your boss or the man who pumps your gas at the service station.*

This capacity, unfortunately, is all too rare. Many managers who do an adequate job in exhorting their employees to get the products or services out the door, are abysmally inept at dealing with the more human side of the organization.

Prince Hal knew that there must be a careful balance between being a hard taskmaster and an "all play and no work" leader. Too much emphasis on job performance, at the expense of taking the time to create a nourishing work environment, can be the downfall of any leader who fails to consider the human element. Put simply, Hal's strength as a leader stemmed from his willingness to understand—better than most—what makes humans tick. It's an important lesson. Leaders who fail to appreciate the harm an "us" versus "them" culture can do should not be surprised by the growing indignation and resentment that is now spreading throughout the nation's work force. An example of this, told to us by a participant in one of our seminars, is illustrative:

The union representing a number of professional government employees decided to sponsor a barbecue tailgate party at their city's major league baseball stadium. The members paid one price for hamburgers, hot dogs, sodas, and beer, along with a ticket to the ballgame that night. The union sponsors roped off an area of the stadium's parking lot, brought in picnic tables and chairs, and set up a buffet-style line for the food. During the party, the employees ate burgers and hot dogs, socialized with their friends, co-workers, and families, and generally had a great time. An additional roped-off area remained vacant, even after the start of the cookout. There were several tables and chairs set up for a group that had not arrived as yet.

Suddenly, and with a noticeable flourish, a group of senior executives and the head of the department himself appeared and were led into their "private dining area" to eat their meals, adjacent to the other party-goers. As the union members sat or stood, eating their hamburgers, the cooks manning the barbecues brought steaks and baked potatoes over to the senior executives. This did not go unnoticed, of course, and many people in the crowd asked the obvious question, "Why do we get burgers and they get steaks?"

As the meals continued, one rank-and-file, non-management employee leaned across the roped-off executive area to take a few plastic chairs so that his family could sit near him. He was politely told by the department head's chief assistant, "Don't touch those chairs. They're not for you. They're for the chiefs' use only." Going inside the stadium only made this us versus them gap worse. While the employees sat together, all in one section, cheering and laughing, the ranking executives sat in another section entirely, away from their people.

This one event, originally slated as a way for everyone to gather together, eat, drink, and blow off steam, turned into a management disaster of morale-busting proportions. Talk of the "suits and their steaks and separate seats" went on for weeks after.

At no time during this event did the head of the department or any of his subordinates take the initiative to cross the literal and figurative boundaries that separated the two groups to engage in what Prince Hal might have called "creative mingling." This event did nothing to break down the strong sense of union-management disharmony that had already permeated the organization. Indeed, even when people from the rank and file tried to mix with the "suits," they were in effect told to stay in their place.

The moral of this sad tale is simple: Be willing—as Hal was—to get your hands dirty from time to time. Work the trenches. Fly tourist. Make the transition from management to labor when the chance arises. Imagine how it would have looked if the head of the department, the ranking executive in this government organization, had rolled up his shirt sleeves, loosened his tie, slipped on a chef's apron, and started cooking hamburgers and hot dogs for his employees. What good feelings it would have generated if everyone—management and labor alike—had sat together for a few innings of the baseball game. It is only out of such creative mingling that the "us" versus "them" mindset can be destroyed.

## Assuming a Role: The Art of Disguise

A pivotal point in young Henry's leadership career comes when he disguises himself as a common soldier and, before the biggest battle of his career, spends an evening talking with his men. He knows it's important to "really listen" to his "employees."

Contrast Henry V's genuine interest in learning what his men think to the typical "inspection" of a company's factories, offices, or headquarters by corporate bigwigs. Typically, everyone knows about these "surprise" visits well in advance and can prepare for them. The result is usually high fiction: a make-believe world of workers heigh-ho-ing their way off to work in spic-and-span factories where not a thing is out of place. Such fairy tales serve no purpose. Instead, leaders need to doggedly seek the truth, uncomfortable as it may be at times. Perhaps one of the important lessons *Henry V* teaches is that every organization needs its own brand of "mystery shoppers," those observers who can interact with the people and systems on a number of levels. Consider the possibilities:

Your company promises the best customer service in the industry. Yet when you, with a properly disguised voice, call the toll-free number to request help, you are placed on hold for twelve minutes before being told that the department you want is located in West Fargo and—get this— "No, you cannot be transferred." What's more, "we don't have the number handy."

Or consider what one of us recently discovered when we made a surprise visit to a campus office whose mission was to serve students' counseling needs. It was a hand-written sign stating, "No Students Allowed! You Must Receive Written Authorization from the Department Chair to Enter!"

Quite obviously, as a leader, it's up to you to initiate, as Hal did, your own "inspection of the troops." What you learn from the people who serve the customers and work in the trenches can tell you much about the health and happiness of your firm. You might look rather silly wearing a disguise, as did Henry, but why not pay a visit with little or no advance notice to one of your branch locations? Why not stop by the division office on your way back to headquarters? Why not shop in your company's retail store, eat lunch with the head of your production or assembly units, or call your own in-bound customer service lines and see if they can solve a hypothetical problem for you?

As one executive who is skilled at "breakfast with the foot soldiers" puts it, "It's not about what's important to you that matters. It's what's important to the people doing the work that should count to you. Learn to ask what they want, what they need to do a better job, and be prepared to give it to them, or explain why you can't." And if antediluvian policies exist in your firm, e.g., "Management shall not eat lunch with labor," "Labor shall come through the side employee gate and not the lobby entrance," etc., rewrite them! Stories of employees who are not allowed to use certain bathrooms, break rooms, or soda machines abound in too many organizations. No wonder there is a great deal of tension among the workers in such restrictive gulags.

If part of your job includes the nasty task of writing policy manuals, think about changing your focus from "Here's what you *can't* do ..." to "Here's what you *can* do ..." or "Here's what *we can do together* ..." The truly courageous leaders among us might even ask "What would *you* like to do?"

Leadership, according to Henry, is more than just power, titles, and perks. It's about people. Henry knew he couldn't fight the biggest battles of his career (at Agincourt and at Harfleur) alone. He needed the support and commitment of his men. He earned it by walking, talking, and working among them in a variety of innovative ways.

**Suggestion Box Blues: Getting Feedback and Taking Action on It**
By appearing in front of his men in disguise, Henry took a personal risk—that he might overhear some things about himself and his reign that he would not like. This is difficult to hear under any circumstances, especially when the attacks get personal or seem to come from all sides. Nobody likes criticism, but as the many leaders we review in this book will prove, having real leadership skills means you'll at times need a thick skin, a tough coat of armor, and the ability to take the bad with the good.

When was the last time your organization conducted a survey of your employees? If your answer is "never," you're not alone. Gathering feedback from employees (and, just as importantly, from customers) is not easy or pleasant work. Creating survey materials, handing them out, and then collecting, entering, and processing the data can be time-consuming and one of those "we'll get to it later" kinds of projects.

But for all its built-in difficulty, survey information can serve as the lifeblood of your organization. How else will you know what your employees and customers want, unless you ask them? This is no time for educated guesses. If you're planning to make significant changes in your method of operation, either on the employee side (for example, with work schedules, job positions, or service systems) or on the customer side (such as new products or services, colors, shapes, sizes, prices) you had better know what both parties really want. Don't guess, ask.

Here are a few suggestions to help you get feedback from employees and customers.

1. Create cost-effective, reliable, and easy ways for your employees or customers to give you feedback, using mail-in survey cards, questionnaires, follow-up telephone calls, etc.

2. After you've reviewed the responses (and tossed out the obvious pranks and other strange responses), be adult about what is in front of you. This hard data should be telling you something: "Here's what works and here's what does not. Here are some employees, departments, products, or services that need adjustment."

3. Try to read everything with an open mind. Don't harbor grudges if you know who made the suggestions.

4. Share the bona fide ideas up and down the chain of command. Give reports to the executives, managers, department heads, and supervisors concerned.

5. Reward the best suggestion-givers with real rewards. To an employee, for example, you could give half a day off, a good parking space, or donuts and coffee for the department, and to your customers, perhaps gift certificates, coupons, free products or services, etc.

6. Be prepared to report on the feasibility of all valid suggestions to the employees or customers. Since they gave you honest answers to your survey, they want feedback from you as well.

7. Follow up at intervals on the progress of the suggestions you plan to implement.

## Henry as David, France as Goliath

In the final scenes of the Henriad, King Henry V faced the greatest challenge of his career. He and his rag-tag troops were about to fight the battle of Agincourt.

The French side was stronger and much larger. In a word, Henry would play David to France's Goliath. He knew that looks can be deceiving and that size is not always the only factor in victory. Agincourt, in other words, was the ancient archetype of something very modern: the on-going competitive battle between small companies and large ones.

These battles frequently prove that big is not necessarily better. Smaller companies can be faster, smarter, flexible, more responsive to change, and better suited to meet the needs and expectations of their customers. They can make decisions in six days that might take a giant conglomerate six months.

A competitor's apparent market domination should not, at least at first, mean that it's time to throw in the towel. The United States Postal Service is the largest civilian employer in America. While they may have a lock on delivering first-class letter mail, they had a weak spot: they had no monopoly on package delivery. Penetrating that weak spot has allowed the likes of United Parcel Service, Federal Express, DHL, Airborne, and other large and small package deliverers to capture much of what might have been the Postal Service's natural business domain.

IBM is not the only player in the personal computer market, Nabisco is not the only cookie maker, and as Snapple has recently so successfully demonstrated, Pepsi and Coke are not the only products that can quench your thirst on a hot day.

And so it goes. High-tech dollars frequently get badly beaten by low-tech smarts. As Henry and Shakespeare knew so well, what separates winning organizations from also-rans is often anything but rocket science. It is, in fact, far more likely to be committed creative colleagues rather than computer chips. As an example, look at Silicon Graphics, a highly-successful Mountain View, California, company that transforms computer graphics into three-dimensional images.

This firm is known for things like packing huge amounts of arithmetic functions onto microscopic chips, creating intuitive interfaces, integrating and manipulating 3-D images with powerful enhancements like stereo audio, and generally being at or near the summit of the fast-moving digital media industry. But Silicon Graphics' most important core competency is its people. As its CEO, Ed McCracken, recently told the *Harvard Business Review*, the company's people-oriented philosophy boils down to one thing: hire highly talented people and trust them. The result? Productivity akin to what Henry got from his troops at the battle of Agincourt.

Indeed, when competitor Hewlett-Packard was the same size as Silicon, it employed six times as many workers! McCracken put this into perspective when he said,

> *It's much easier to manage fewer people. We can be faster on our feet, we can concentrate, and we can rely on our intuition, which is extremely important in an industry where the pace of technological change is so rapid.*[3]

Seeming more like a modern-day Henry than a 20th-century manager, McCracken holds frequent "All Hands" meetings with his employees which focus on what's working and what's not. And remember how Henry visited his troops the night before their big battle? Proving that not much in effective leadership changes, McCracken says,

> *I try to be approachable and visible. This means wandering through the R&D labs talking to people. It means going out with our people on sales calls. I do these things a lot and the top managers who work for me do too.*[4]

All this attention to people must be working. Silicon Graphics is the firm that helped bring the Jurassic Park dinosaurs to the screen as well as the liquid metal cyborg in Terminator 2. The company earned more than $95 million on revenues of $1.09 billion in 1993.

### The Language of Leadership: Positive Persuasion

Henry V's speech to his troops on the eve of the Battle of Agincourt is one of history's greatest motivational moments. And it was badly needed. His troops were outmanned, outgunned, and surely doomed to defeat. Listen to the lament of one of his officers the morning of the battle:

> *O that we now had here*
> *But one ten thousand of those men in England*
> *That do no work to-day!*

Henry's response to this naysayer? Unforgettable. Listen to his words:

> This day is call'd the feast of Crispin;
> He that outlives this day, and comes safe home,
> Will stand a'tiptoe when this day is named,
> And rouse him at the name of Crispin.
> He that shall see this day, and live old age,
> Will yearly on the vigil feast his neighbors,
> And say, 'Tomorrow is Saint Crispin.'
> Then he will strip his sleeve and show his scars.
> And say, 'These wounds I had on Crispin's day.'
> Old men forget; yet all shall be forgot,
> But he'll remember with advantages
> What feats he did that day. Then shall our names,
> Familiar in his mouth as household words,
> ... Be in their flowing cups rememb'red...
> From this day to the ending of the world,
> But we in it shall be remembered—
> We few, we happy few, we band of brothers;
> For he to-day that sheds his blood with me
> Shall be my brother; be he ne'er so vile,
> This day shall gentle his condition;
> And gentlemen in England, now a-bed,
> Shall think themselves accurs'd they were not here;
> And hold their manhoods cheap whiles any speaks
> That fought with us upon St. Crispin's day.

Thus does young Henry motivate his men to think, not about their fears, but about their destiny, their place in history, and how the world will remember them. Who wouldn't want to be part of this organization?

What worked for Henry can work for you. Think of the well-known leaders of American business and industry. Aren't many of them masters of persuasive speech and communication? Don't many of them have that rare ability to motivate the seemingly unmotivatable? Is that not the reason the CEO makes a command appearance at a national sales meeting or other large gathering of the organization's people?

While Microsoft's Bill Gates may not strike you as a fire-and-brimstone type of speaker, his mere presence at the unveiling of a new Microsoft software program says something to the people who work for him: this is our leader. As he goes, so do we. His success is our success and ours is his. What he says here can touch something in all of us.

Car makers are also not shy about their products. When Ford, GM, or Chrysler unveils a new line or a new car, it's time to unleash the balloons and strike up the band. The respective CEOs stride to the lectern, full of confidence and words of motivation and encouragement for their troops. They tell their manufacturing employees, their vendors, and their dealers, "We believe in these cars. We want you to believe in them as well. We will give you all of the advice, support, and information you need so you can go forth and sell them."

And is not the annual stockholders meeting a chance for the dynamic leader to step up to the dais and say, "We had a tremendous year. Sales and profits are up, expenses and costs are down. Here's what you can expect from me and this company in the months to come."

And conversely, it is also incumbent upon the leader to deal with the bad news in much the same fashion, with honesty, humility, integrity, determination, and that rare quality, the ability to give people hope. "We had a truly regrettable year. Sales and profits are down, expenses and costs are up. Here's what you can expect from me and this company in the months to come."

You may not ever need to face the public eye like this, but learning to be a leader means standing up and telling it like it is. And even if you don't now speak in huge meeting halls, you will certainly have to address groups, meetings, and gatherings of people in your company at some point in your future as a leader.

No one expects you to speak like Hal, General Patton, or Winston Churchill. But a few pointers might be helpful:

- *Get a good book on public speaking.*
  The goal is not to become Mr. or Ms. Toastmaster, but to improve the way you communicate in groups and to groups. We all know business people who have great ideas on paper, or when they're one on one, yet cannot articulate those same good ideas when they are in front of a group of people. Even a simple staff meeting can send these folks into a tongue-tied spin. Try these

informative, information-packed books on successful speaking: *Fearless and Flawless Public Speaking with Power, Polish, and Pizazz*, by Mary-Ellen Drummond (Pfeiffer & Co.; San Diego, 1993) and *I Can See You Naked*, by Ron Hoff (Andrews & McMeel; Kansas City, 1992).

- *Choose your words with care.*
  Different situations call for different speeches. Sometimes you'll simply need to impart some relatively ordinary information; other times you'll need to announce good news or break some bad news. Whether it's good news or bad, a presentation to your employees, a formal client meeting, or a presentation to an important customer, you'll need to know what to say in advance. When it's important, don't hope for inspiration and shoot something off the cuff; plan it, write it, and review it beforehand.

- *Know your audience.*
  Different groups have different levels of understanding, knowledge, and subject expertise. Gear your message to match the general vocabulary and education of your audience. It's always best to err on the side of simplicity rather than rocket science.

- *Practice, practice, practice.*
  There is a technique therapists, psychologists, and self-hypnosis experts use called future pacing. To use it yourself, sit quietly at home or at your desk, close your eyes, and spend a few minutes actually visualizing what you are going to say and how you are going to say it. When this technique is working well, you can actually hear yourself speaking and see yourself in front of the group. By rehearsing in your mind first, you can relieve much of the built-in anxiety that comes with giving a speech. Future pacing allows your mind to say, "Hey! We've done this once before already!"

- *Lastly, follow the three best rules for speaking to any size group:*
  1. Tell 'em what you're going to tell them.
  2. Tell 'em.
  3. Tell 'em what you told them.

Or, as one wry professional speaker puts it, "Stand up, talk, sit down."

## Lessons from the Bard

It has been said that Henry's speech at Agincourt is the model for all half-time talks given by football coaches every autumn in America. (Try reading it out loud to your kids and you'll see why.) But the fact is that Shakespeare's entire play is a model for leadership. Some ideas:

- *Talk the talk.*

  As Hal proved so well, there *is* a language of leadership. Leaders do, it turns out, talk differently. Just listen. A real leader uses little of the rational, logical kind of verbiage that's become so much a part of our MBA culture. You know: mechanical, without much energy or emotion. Instead, leaders appeal to the heart and to the gut. What they know, that mere mortals do not, is that people aren't motivated solely by rational discourse. (Lest you think they are, consider the last time you discussed the monthly budget with your spouse.) Leaders know that people need to be inspired, not merely informed.

- *Gain commitment to your mission.*

  Sounds easy, but it's not. Happily, researchers have identified some techniques you can use. Pick out a few clear values that you know people care about. (If it's a health care organization, dramatize the saving of a baby's life. Produce something as mundane as automobile tires? Turn drab into dynamite by playing up their safety on a busy, wet road. You get the picture.) Then connect these basic values to the overall mission you're trying to establish.

- *Remember that leadership is about transforming.*

  Hal consistently focused on England's well-being and on unifying his realm. You need to do the same thing, perhaps a little less grandly. Hal exhorted his men to perform beyond what they thought they were capable of. All this is called "transformational leadership"—the ability to get people to focus on team goals rather than individual ones, to increase the need to achieve at a higher level. The result is that everyone finds new satisfaction by doing more than they ever thought possible.

- *Learn to manage ambiguity.*

  Hal was saddled with confusion about his position as king, huge troubles with France and Spain, traitorous conduct by his men, and a lousy reputation. Lesser mortals might have thrown in the towel. Yet Hal seemed buoyed up by all this chaos and disorder. He knew life was not orderly, rational, or predictable. Hal was right. Security, a very wise person once said, is a myth. In life, as in business, there is no security, only risk. We wish for clarity, but we can't see through the fog. We want answers, but in reality there are only questions. We live, in other words, in a world full of ambiguity and paradox. Some have called this condition "permanent white water." Navigating successfully in this environment requires that, first, we recognize it is no illusion.

- *Realize that leadership development is nurture and nature.*
  Leaders aren't just born, they're made. Like Hal, you can develop leadership ability, even if you do not possess it now. How do we know this? A major study of personality conducted at the University of Minnesota. The researchers studied 350 pairs of twins, some of whom were raised together, some apart. The bad news is that the study concluded that about 60 percent of leadership ability is inherited. The good news is that fully 40 percent of leadership ability is entirely up to you!

- *Go out with the boys (and the girls).*
  This used to be known as "managing by wandering around." Before that, it was known as "being overly familiar with employees." Whatever you call it, it's the only way a leader can find out what's really going on. Compare, for example, the depth of understanding one gains in the formality of the conference room versus the insight that magically comes over a a slice of pizza and a beer after the place has shut down. As Hal's experience proves, best to do this after hours. And another thought. Don't institutionalize all this by scheduling yourself to appear in the plant every Monday at 3:00 PM. Such clock-like regularity belies the integrity of your interest. Just let it happen! Surprise 'em.

- *When it comes to your career, always have a strategy.*
  Hal's was brilliant. He decided, early on, not to raise expectations but to *lower* them. He knew that his later performance would seem all the better. Translation: when setting goals, always think in terms of "optimistic," "most probable," and "pessimistic" outcomes. Then when the boss asks you to commit to a plan, use Hal's strategy: promise to deliver somewhere between "pes-

simistic" and "most probable." The result will be your growing reputation as a leader who regularly leaps tall buildings in a single bound. You become known as the person who always delivers more than you promise, not less. (It's called "coming in ahead of plan!") Remember, no one expected Hal to win at Harfleur or at Agincourt. This, alone, made victory all the more sweet.

## CHAPTER 3

# THE ANTIGONE SYNDROME: HOW NOT TO FIGHT CITY HALL

*The gods plant reason in mankind, of all good gifts, the highest.*
—SOPHOCLES

**KEY POINTS**

- LEARNING TO LEAD
- BREAKING THE RULES
- MATURITY, GROWTH, AND DEVELOPMENT

Have you ever tried to fight the powers that be? If so, welcome to the arduous and complex world of the naysayer, rabble-rouser, and social activist. The uninitiated may think that such troublesome types are light years away from what effective leadership is all about. But the fact is that leaders frequently find themselves in the sometimes uncomfortable position of opposing the status quo, rousing followers to act against the establishment, and reforming their organizations. What it boils down to is this: part of the leader's job is to disagree.

It goes without saying that the role of resident revolutionary is never easy. The English poet John Milton put it succinctly. "Long is the way and hard," he wrote, "that out of hell leads up to the light." He was right, of course. Changing the way things are done around here frequently transforms a loyal follower into a high-stakes gambler. Translation? You bet your job. Taking on the establishment and standing up for what you believe in, it turns out, can be one of the toughest tasks you face. This is particularly true, of course, when the boss interprets your intransigence as—what else?—a challenge to his or her authority.

It's a theme made famous by the Greek tragedian, Sophocles. In his tour-de-force, *Antigone*, he scrutinizes what can happen when you try to take on the establishment. Most readers of this play breezily blame its tragic ending on the dismal leadership of the Theban king, Creon. Yet it's Antigone's unwillingness to negotiate that "kills" her as well as "the deal."

## Athens' Polymath

Sophocles, like Plato, was a larger-than-life figure in early Athens. Handsome, muscular, aristocratic, gifted in both the art of music and the combat art of wrestling, he was much admired in his city. His name means "wise and honored one" and for as much as we know about the man, this was true. He lived to ninety-one, a robust age for any man of his era. He served as the treasurer for the city of Athens, one of its military generals, and was a trusted colleague of Pericles, the father of Athens' Golden Age.

In the midst of all this activity, Sophocles found time to write plays. For that, he is also known as one of humanity's greatest "tragedians," a playwright of the formulaic Greek tragedy where good and bad collide, usually resulting in a horrible end. While we have already described William Shakespeare as prolific, the Bard's efforts pale in comparison to Sophocles', who managed to pen 123 plays in his long life, a number that overtakes Shakespeare by more than double.

As a storyteller, Sophocles was skilled at showing his audiences the effects of individual human behavior on the organization. His characters are cast into seemingly impossible situations, and it is from their anguish that we learn many of life's and leadership's lessons.

As might be expected, *Antigone*—the name means "born to oppose"—is no story of laughter and good times. Indeed, it speaks of a very modern problem: one woman's struggle as she tries to take on the establishment. In the play, Sophocles writes both of the dangers of being overly persistent and overly inflexible. The title of the play and name of the main character suggest that a power struggle is in the offing and that much of the story will center on one person's challenge of the organization's rules.

It was Sophocles' belief that an organization could survive only if the needs of the individual and the needs of the organization came together as one. His plays—and *Antigone* is a prime example—show us vividly what happens when these two—the person and the organization—oppose each other.

## Antigone: Lessons in Rule Breaking

As the play opens, we learn that two young soldiers have been killed in combat outside the walls of the ancient Greek city of Thebes. Creon, the Theban ruler, decrees that one of the soldiers, Eteocles, be buried with honors, while the other, Polyneices, known by Creon to be a traitor, is to be left unburied, a move that to the Greeks would condemn his soul for all eternity. Since Creon's word is law, any violation of his order is a capital crime and leads to a death sentence.

Enter Antigone, Polyneices' sister, who, as we have suggested, went against the direct orders of Creon and buried her brother in the custom and manner of the time. She was fully aware that her act consisted of treason against Creon and his organization, but she pressed on anyway. It was her firm belief that she should obey the "laws of gods" and not the "laws of man." Besides, as she tells her sister, Ismene, "Creon is not strong enough to stand in my way."[1]

We see early on that Antigone is prideful, headstrong, and not afraid of death. She tells her sister, who is too afraid to join her,

> *Leave me my foolish plan:*
> *I am not afraid of the danger;*
> *If it means death,*
> *It will not be the*
> *Worst of deaths—death without honor.*

Creon soon discovers that someone has gone against his law and buried Polyneices. Incensed, he orders the culprit arrested immediately. His sentries arrest Antigone and she is brought before him. She admits her part in the burial and tells Creon his laws are not hers:

*It was not God's proclamation. That final Justice*
*That rules the world below makes no such laws.*
*Your edict, King, was strong,*
*But all your strength is weakness itself against*
*The immortal unrecorded laws of God.*
*They are not merely now: they were, and shall be,*
*Operative forever, beyond man utterly.*
*I knew I must die, even without your decree:*
*I am only mortal. And if I must die*
*Now, before it is my time to die,*
*Surely this is no hardship: can anyone*
*Living, as I live, with evil all about me,*
*Think Death less than a friend? This death of mine*
*Is of no importance; but if I had left my brother*
*Lying in death unburied, I should have suffered.*
*Now I do not.*
*You may smile at me. Ah Creon,*
*Think me a fool, if you like; but it may well be*
*That a fool convicts me of folly.*

Antigone continues to show her true colors and her contempt for laws and rules she feels do not apply to her. In his fury, Creon orders her sent to a stone vault, a cave where she will soon die.

Creon's son, Haimon, is in love with Antigone, and protests her imprisonment to his father. He tells the ruler that public sentiment favors reducing her punishment.

*Whoever thinks that he alone is wise,*
*His eloquence, his mind, above the rest,*
*Come the unfolding, shows his emptiness.*
*A man, though wise, should never be ashamed*
*Of learning more, and must unbend his mind.*
*No, yield your wrath, allow a change of stand.*
*Young as I am, if I may give advice,*
*I'd say it would be best if men were born*
*Perfect in wisdom, but that failing this*
*(Which often fails) it can be no dishonor*
*To learn from others when they speak good sense.*

This appeal fails miserably. Creon scolds his son for his misplaced devotion to such a willful woman as Antigone and tells him what's done is done.

Following the confrontation with his son, Creon hears from Tiresias, the city's blind prophet. He tells Creon that he must right his wrongs and release Antigone immediately or risk the wrath of the gods. Creon orders Antigone released, but when he rushes to her cave prison, he finds she has killed herself. Creon discovers his son in the cave with her and, in his rage, Haimon draws his own sword, lunges at his father, misses him and stabs himself to death.

As the grief-stricken Creon returns home to his palace, he learns that his wife, angry with him and aware of the deaths of Antigone and Haimon, has also killed herself with a knife. In the closing scene of the play, Creon can take no more:

> Lead me away. I have been rash and foolish.
> I have killed my son and my wife.
> I look for comfort; my comfort lies here dead.
> Whatever my hands have touched has come to nothing.
> Fate has brought all my pride to a thought of dust.

In this unforgettable closing scene, we see Creon, devastated and desolate, a broken man.

## The Role of the Female in a Male-Dominated Organization

It's easy to look at the themes revealed in Antigone and start pointing fingers at who is to blame. But the story goes much deeper than that; there are agendas at work—hidden and otherwise—on a number of different levels. Both sides—Creon, as the rule of law, and Antigone, as the rule of gods or the natural order—made fatal mistakes. The question is, what can be learned about the way rules and order and power and leadership take shape in your organization? What did Creon do right or wrong? And what about Antigone?

Creon was certainly no stranger to the gender dilemmas in his organization. The play centers around the greatest conflict of his life, and it's with a woman. Creon, revealing a thoroughly chauvinistic attitude, thought his adversary was a man. He asks, "And the *man* who dared do this?" and "I swear by God and by the throne of God, / The *man* who has done this thing shall pay for it!" (Italics added.) But how wrong he was! His leadership was being challenged by a woman. Creon, it seems, never stopped to consider that a woman could even think about disobeying his order. And yet, Antigone rose to challenge his leadership and take on the role of his opponent, as well as his tormentor.

Some see Antigone as an example of one woman's failed attempt to change the rules of her organization by successfully confronting her boss. Unfortunately, there's not much that's new about all this. Two recent studies confirm that, like Antigone, females too frequently still face tough sledding in the executive suite.

One of these studies, conducted by the law firm of Strock, Strook & Lavan, reported that upward female mobility in organizations was severely hampered by the way in which women managers were evaluated by senior management. After surveying more than four thousand executives, the study found that job smarts and job performance counted less than subjective factors like personality, networking ability, and loyalty—the kinds of things that have forever held the "old boy" network firmly together.

And the Center for Creative Leadership in Greensboro, North Carolina, also pondered the plight of female executives. Its study found that most female executives don't even get a shot at bigger jobs because they're not given high-visibility assignments. Asserting that women, even those who had done well at crucial turnarounds and entrepreneurial start-ups, were frequently passed over for truly fast track assignments, the study's directors concluded that females still simply don't get the kind of career-building challenges that their male counterparts get. Some people may call this the glass ceiling; we call it the "Antigone Factor."

Would Creon have treated Antigone differently if she had been a man? Perhaps. And it would have surprised few. For, as we have already pointed out, many women today have complained that they have bumped their heads against the well-known glass ceiling in their attempts to make the bold move from manager to leader. While success stories of skilled and competent female leaders abound, many women still wonder if they are getting the same opportunities for advancement as their male counterparts.

And many women have stated flatly that, in the corporate world, they must work doubly hard to prove themselves. The sad fact is that, just as in Antigone's ancient world, in our male-dominated business culture, women have a harder climb to make it up the career ladder.

If this is the case in your own organization, perhaps it's time to take a hard look at the ways qualified and skilled women are treated.

### The Leadership Dilemma: What's Right versus Who's Right

In the play *Antigone*, Creon is faced with some tough decisions: Antigone did break his law and freely admitted it. She felt no compulsion to apologize and, in fact, explained her actions as the right thing to do under the circumstances. Creon felt he had no choice but to discipline her for violating his rule.

He made his decision, just as Antigone made hers, and followed through with it, just as she did. And just as Antigone did not take her sister's advice to stop and consider the consequences of her actions, neither did Creon take the advice of his son or any of his surrounding advisers. Both sides stood their ground.

How many times have you been faced with a similar dilemma in your organization? Have you ever been placed in an uncomfortable situation when you had to make a choice between doing what you knew was right and what was required by the policies, procedures, rules, or mores of your company? How did you feel before this decision? Uncomfortable? Determined but nervous? And how did you feel after you took action? Relieved? Worried about your future? Or confident and willing to stand your ground, no matter what?

And did the nature of your decision and your subsequent actions take place only after you tried to negotiate an alternative solution with the other party? Or were you unable to reach an agreement or find common ground?

Creon's leadership is flawed for a number of reasons, but mainly because he was far too autocratic. His firm belief that his word was absolute did not allow him to consider other options or even hear other alternatives, suggestions, or ideas from those around him. His "my way or the highway" approach led him into a trap that many fall into: "I've made my decision, it turned out to be a wrong one, and now I'm caught between reversing myself and looking weak, foolish, or indecisive and continuing down this same wrong road in the vain hope that everything will turn out okay in the end." And as this classic play so sadly demonstrates, things did not end well at all.

## The Leader-Manager Grid: A Model for Understanding Leadership Traits

We've already touched on the concept of managers versus leaders, suggesting there are substantial differences between the two. There is, we have said, the "mere manager," who tends to thrive on the status quo; after all, it's safe, relatively calm, and unambiguous there. In short, as Plato's trip out of the cave demonstrated in chapter 1, mere managers tend to stay in their comfort zones.

Contrast this to the leader. Leaders want more from themselves and more from the people who work for them. They set high goals, place difficult demands upon themselves, and are constantly striving in one direction—upward. The leader embraces—even welcomes—ambiguity in business situations and doesn't fear the lack of a perfect or obvious answer. He or she is comfortable with the unknown and sees it as an opportunity to grow, improve, or succeed.

The sad fact, of course, is that most organizations are populated by a great many managers and very few leaders. Whether you are a manager or a leader, you'll spend the vast amount of your time working with other managers. The working relationship possibilities of all this are fascinating, and can be summarized in the following grid.

*Your Boss*

|  | Leader | Manager |
|---|---|---|
| **Leader** | **BEST CASE** | **THREAT** |
| **Manager** | **OPPORTUNITIES** | **WORST CASE** |

*You*

The point? To get you to think about the current working relationship you have with your boss. What role do you think he or she plays in the organization? Is he or she merely a manager or a leader? What role do you play—in harmony or disharmony with your boss? How do you think he or she perceives your management (or leadership) style? Potential for leadership? Ability to make the right choices and decisions?

Is there room for improvement in the working relationship between you and your boss? Does he or she allow and encourage you to grow and develop and even move on to another position? Are you allowed to take credit for your successes instead of just the responsibility for your failures? Do you feel empowered by your boss or held back? In short, is your boss a leader or a mere manager? And are you a mere manager or a budding leader?

The grid may help you organize the way you look at your relationship with your boss. It will point to the various combinations that can occur when managers and leaders work in the same office, team, unit, division, or company. As you review each indicator, consider the leader/manager relationship between Creon and Antigone. What kind of leader or manager was he? How about Antigone's leadership style? What traits does she reveal?

As the grid demonstrates, there are four possibilities: you and your boss both have many leader-like qualities; neither of you has leadership qualities; and two combinations where one person does and the other does not. Let's look at each of them in a bit more detail to discover where you fit.

*Best case.* Both you and your boss are leaders.

Your boss has the traits of a leader and you do too. For the most part, this is an ideal situation. Your boss serves as a leader and a mentor for you and others around you. You're given time to learn, chances to show your initiative and creativity and, on occasion, the chance to lead yourself. Your boss does not feel threatened by your leadership skills. There is little in-fighting, few disagreements that lead to long-simmering hard feelings, grudges, secret agendas, back-stabbing, glory-seeking, or other signs of a toxic relationship.

He or she encourages your growth as a leader and even helps you "leave the nest" and go out on your own if and when the time comes. In many ways, this boss sees himself or herself as a sort of "station master" for you and tries to help you as much as possible so that you may repeat the leadership education process with someone who will work for you.

*Worst case.* Both you and your boss are mere managers.

This is not good because of the element of stagnation built into the relationship. You're not being stretched, and neither is your boss. There is no additional activity other than what it takes to get the work done. Each person tries his or her level best to stick to the status quo, always toe the mark, and not make waves. The anthem? "Rules were meant to be followed and it's our job to see that the work gets done with a minimum of controversy, eruptions, or other comfort zone-busting irregularities."

In this case, each person moves at a take-no-risks, in-at-9-and-out-at-5 pace. There is little room for growth or leadership development because neither party wants to move in those directions. Both of you may feel mired in jobs you can't or don't want to leave and this can be even worse if the company does not provide much hope for advancement or even job performance improvement.

*Next best.* Your boss is a leader and you're a manager who may strive toward a leader position.

Here, you have the benefit of working for someone from whom you may be able to learn a bit about leadership. This position on the grid is similar to the best case scenario, where you and your boss share the same goals and desires to move ahead. The difference may be found in your movement along the leadership evolutionary continuum; that is, you may need more training and job and organizational experience before you can begin to grasp some of the more abstract concepts of leadership.

*Next worst.* Your boss is a mere manager and you're striving to be a leader.

This position may lead to plenty of conflict as your working style conflicts with your boss'. Here, your boss does everything he or she can to keep you down. The possibilities for advancement, promotion, or a job change within the organization seem slight. Worse yet, the atmosphere may be highly charged with negativism between the two of you. Any efforts on your part to move ahead in the company may come off as acts that seem threatening, manipulative, or not in the best interests of the team, division, unit, or organization.

In these instances, your boss may perceive you to be a wave-maker, naysayer, whistle-blower, or other form of corporate subversive.

Remember that these kinds of bosses are comfort zone dwellers and will see any attempt by you to change the status quo as uncomfortable or threatening to their well-protected environment. If you find yourself in this, the most difficult of the leader/manager, boss/subordinate relationships, you'll need to choose your allies and your battles carefully.

**Managing Your Boss: Needs and Expectations**
In the scores of service management books you'll find in bookstores today, there is much talk about the customer's "report card." Here, the customer has certain needs and expectations that are either met by the service experience or not.

When you eat at a fast-food restaurant, you may have a certain need, that is, to feed your family quickly and with a minimum of expense. Your needs are relatively simple and your expectations are fairly low. Once in a great while the fast-food restaurant or its employees do something out of the ordinary for you and then you have your expectations exceeded by the service experience.

If you were to eat at a five-star restaurant, your needs might be much higher than at the fast-food place. Here, you'll be looking for outstanding food, superior customer service, and a fine dining experience not matched by any lesser restaurant. Your needs are more complicated and your expectations are very high. While your expectations are much higher for the five-star restaurant than the fast-food place, you can still be surprised by some gesture made by the restaurant or kitchen staff that makes your dining experience even better.

Of course, the converse of all this is true as well. The fast-food restaurant can fail miserably to meet your needs and not even come close to exceeding your expectations. And it's the same with the five-star restaurant, where one service gaffe after another can ruin your experience, not meet your needs, and certainly not exceed your expectations.

Whether these events in the respective restaurants are positive or negative, they all go on your mental report card. Each service establishment you patronize, whether it's a mail-order firm or a steel foundry, gets a grade—literally or subconsciously—from you, before, during, and after each encounter.

This customer service parallel holds true in your relationship with your boss. He or she has certain needs that must be met, either by you, the organization itself, or by other members of the organization around you. Your boss also has certain expectations and, like the example using the restaurants, they either get met or, on rarer occasions, happily exceeded. And your boss also has his or her own report card to evaluate whether those all-important needs and expectations get met by you.

Leadership is also about anticipation; so much the better if you can anticipate what your boss's needs are, what kind of expectations he or she has—reasonable or otherwise—and how you can go about meeting or actually exceeding both.

Creon had certain needs; namely, to be a powerful leader, to rule with unbending authority, and to know that his word was law throughout his domain. Antigone had her needs as well: to do the honorable thing for her brother, to show that the concept of what is right can be defined in different ways, and to stick to her guns, no matter the cost.

And both sides had their own expectations as well. Creon expected to be obeyed and Antigone expected to be allowed to bury her brother without interference. Neither party understood the others' needs or expectations and both sides failed to understand the significance of this failure.

### Negotiating Strategies: The Added Value Method

On its face, the *Antigone* play illustrates another important and neglected part of leadership, which is the ability to negotiate and do it well. In all events where there are two sides, there are always going to be ways to win and ways to lose. The trick is to create a deal where both sides go away from the encounter thinking that they both got a pretty good deal.

While this sounds simple enough, too many of the negotiating books and training courses on the market today still teach methods that were probably better suited for Creon's times, i.e., the old "grind 'em down, butting heads" approach, which relies on tricks and tactics, secrecy and subterfuge, and one-upsmanship and leverage. Indeed, the vocabulary of negotiation is still filled with the same war-like words and phrases that appeared in Creon's day. It's not uncommon to hear the words "opponent," "battle plan," "strategic approach," "ploy," "opposition," or "hardball," attached to the subject of how people negotiate. With these power-based phrases in place, it's easy to see why negotiation in general is usually seen as a distasteful process by most business people who don't consider themselves to be "professional" negotiators.

These days, with humanity, ethics, and values making a comeback in business, the old phrase "win/lose" is out. What works today is a real form of win/win negotiating called added value negotiating (AVN), which helps two parties search for their mutual interests and then create a number of deal packages to replace the "take it or leave it, this is my final offer" approach that always, always leads to counteroffers and counterattacks.

Antigone negotiated "around" people and not around problems and situations. She serves as a model of a failed negotiator. Her desire to stick to one approach with Creon—"I am right and you're wrong"—did not allow her to see any form of compromise or concession.

And for his part, Creon was not much of a negotiator either. His stubbornness, name-calling, and general obstinacy matched equally with Antigone's hard-boiled style. As is typical in situations where one so-called "tough" negotiator deals with another so-called "tough" negotiator, not much was accomplished by either party.

As one of us has pointed out in our book (co-authored with Karl Albrecht) *Added Value Negotiating*:

> *In the arena of international politics, it is usually a high form of flattery to refer to someone as "a tough negotiator." Henry Kissinger is often described as a tough negotiator. At the height of the arms race talks, the Soviets were described frequently as tough negotiators. Israelis and most Arabs are usually thought to be tough negotiators.*
>
> *But what does being a tough negotiator mean? Basically, it seems to mean that people can't get much out of you. You are a person who stands his ground, makes very few concessions, and eventually gets what he wants. Being tough means that you rarely bend, offer little without getting more back, and generally exhibit all of the mobility, flexibility, generosity, and openness of a park statue. Being a tough negotiator means you don't surrender, you don't concede, and you don't give up anything without getting something of equal or greater value in return. It seems to be more a definition of what you don't do than what you do.*
>
> *What happens when two tough negotiators deal with each other? The answer: not much. Study the history of business and political negotiations handled by tough negotiators and you'll see that they make progress very slowly, if at all.*[2]

The added value approach is a five-step method that starts by clarifying interests and then moves on to identifying options, which are ways to satisfy those interests. If you said, "I want to be rich," then that would be an interest. You could choose from several options to satisfy that particular interest, i.e., win the lottery, marry a wealthy spouse, rob a bank, strike oil in your backyard, etc. All of these alternatives are options for serving your interests. Once the interests and options are out on the table, the next step in the added value negotiating process is to create a group of deal packages that cover the interests and options you want to achieve. The difference between the added-value approach and most conventional negotiating methods lies in this multiple-deal opportunity, which makes AVN unique.

By creating two, three, four, or even five different deals, you give the other party a chance to pick the one he or she likes best. Since you created them—with a sense of fairness, balance, and wanting to keep the interests of both parties in mind—you can live with any one of them. And since the other party can pick from a variety of deals, he or she may feel more empowered. Choice, especially in the often stressful situations that surround many important negotiations, can make both sides feel more comfortable.

With several deals on the table, it's easier for the other party to choose one and move the AVN process into its final two steps: select a deal and perfect it. Once the best deal has been agreed upon, all that remains is to finalize it with contracts, handshakes, letters of agreement, etc. If, during this final wrap-up time, the negotiation starts to deteriorate, you can always stop, back up, and start again at the interests or options development step.

Contrast this approach with the typical negotiating method which usually starts with an immediate offer followed by an immediate counteroffer. This cycle continues until one or both sides finally throw in their respective towels and, in the closing moments, come to some hard-fought agreement that is almost always smaller than the first deal that was put on the table. This reductive process takes away from the deal rather than adding to it; hence the difference between added-value negotiating and the standard win/lose approach still being taught and written about today.

Looking at the on-going struggle between Antigone and Creon, several negotiation flaws come to light. First, and certainly most significant to the end of the play, is each side's total unwillingness to change viewpoints once they began talking to each other. The highly charged atmosphere and the outright resentment both sides felt toward the other seemed to ruin any chance at positive communication. And since neither side could talk calmly to the other, there was little chance for them to find some kind of common ground. With no place to meet in the middle, both sides dug in, refused to budge, and waited for the other one to blink.

Unfortunately for Antigone, Creon was in the stronger position because he had more figurative and literal power than did she. He had soldiers, sentries, and other servants to carry out his rulings. Antigone had only her family and, even then, she could muster no support from her sister, who refused to expose herself to the risks she knew were ahead. To quote an old negotiating phrase, Antigone "didn't have too many friends in the room." Her fiancé, Creon's son, could do little to change his father's mind and was himself caught between defying his father and not supporting the woman he loved.

As you consider the past three or four truly significant negotiations you have been involved in, what parallels to Antigone's plight do you recall? Did you ever find yourself in a weak and vulnerable negotiating position where you could dictate neither the terms nor the price? Did the other party play games with you, act uninterested in your offers, or otherwise use tricks, traps, and tactics designed to confuse or victimize your side?

And did you ever find yourself involved in a negotiation where it seemed as if the other party had all the answers, all the resources, and all the people neatly stacked on its side? In these difficult situations, it's easy to find your stress level at stratospheric levels, which can really hinder your ability to think creatively, logically, or fast on your feet.

Antigone's crisis points out the need to look for compromise points when you're faced with difficult situations that look as if they have no apparent solution. More often than not, there are a number of answers to the negotiating problems you and the other person are trying to solve, but you have to look hard and be prepared to think outside the boundaries of the norm to find them.

The trick to any successful (and added value) negotiation is to be able to bob and weave, so to speak. Don't commit to any one position too early or too often. Look hard at the mutual interests that are either readily apparent or beneath the surface. Know what you want going in and, if the other party won't tell you what his or her interests are, make educated guesses and tell the other party you will make deals based on your best guess. This fact alone may prod the person into telling you more than he or she had originally planned.

Finally, consider the many advantages of the multiple-deal idea. Don't just make one offer and stand by it as if it were the Rock of Gibraltar. Create a number of deals that are equally balanced, but different. Even the toughest negotiator can't argue with you if you give him or her more than one choice.

## Doing the Right Things Versus Doing Things Right

Following the policies and procedures manual is not always the only way to do things in any organization. Recognizing, of course, the need for control, careful thought, and a sense of ethics, it's perfectly acceptable to bend the rules when the situation dictates it.

This is also a habit you should encourage in moderation in your employees, especially at the front line with the customer. True service quality advocates know when, where, and how to bend the rules to meet their customers' needs and try to exceed their expectations whenever possible. By acting as the customer's agent and taking on a problem-solving role rather than a "that's not the way we do things around here" attitude, good service providers know when to ditch the rule book and get the job done for the customer. As *Antigone* points out, there is a time to go up against established thought, the rule book, peer pressure, or even (truth be told) the culture of the organization. Obviously, how you go about it makes all the difference. A service case will tell the tale. This story illustrates a problem both with service systems and the dreaded rule book.

A woman goes into a large grocery store and brings a dozen or so items up to the checkout stand. After the clerk rings up her food, he tells her the total, and she writes a check for ten dollars over the amount. Taking her check-cashing card and verifying her check, he then closes the cash register drawer and hands her the receipt.

"But you forgot my ten dollars cash back," the woman says, putting her hand out.

"Oh! You're right," says the clerk, slapping his forehead in remembrance. "I'll get it for you in just a second."

That said, he begins to ring up the purchases of the next customer, who happens to have an entire shopping cart full of food.

"What about my change?" asks the puzzled woman again. "Oh, I'm sorry," says the clerk, "but we're not allowed to open the cash drawer unless we're ringing up a purchase."

With that, the clerk returned to his chores, rang up all of the items in the next customer's shopping cart, collected his money, and then and only then did he reopen the drawer and give the woman her ten dollars. Talk about a service nightmare, and all because the clerk did not have the good sense to say, "I'll get a manager to come right here and open my drawer," or "Here's your ten dollars, ma'am," or "Sorry for the delay, I'll open the drawer right this second, without making you wait for a manager to come by."

Lots of mere managers know how to do things right. They may have plenty of job knowledge, product expertise, and can read and quote the rule book, chapter and verse. But as Antigone and the other leaders in this book demonstrate, there's more to leadership than just knowing the policy and procedures manual backwards and forwards.

Leadership is also about taking risks, calculated, extreme, or otherwise. History books and the business pages are full of stories of people who defied the odds, didn't listen to other experts who told them something couldn't be done, and went ahead with their ideas anyway.

## How to Be a Safe and Successful Naysayer

Just as there's nothing wrong with bending the rules when events dictate (as we will see in chapter 9 which reviews the story of Melville's *Billy Budd*), it's also just as important to know what's wrong and how to tell someone about it. After all, everyone has a bit of Antigone in them. Best not to always sublimate that primal urge to take on the establishment.

Don't be shy about voicing your opinion—if, that is, you have the ammunition to back it up. Chief executives like facts more than bluster, data more than hunches, and solutions rather than idea-killing. Lots of people can tell the president of the company why something won't work. What he or she wants to hear is what things will work and when and how to do them.

As we have suggested, leadership involves taking risks, acting on hunches, going with your gut feelings and, to quote a Civil War aphorism, "riding to the sound of the guns." And in the course of these events—which often take place outside your comfort zone and those of others—you may have to tell someone in power and authority, "I'm sorry, but from the way I see it, your idea will not work and here's why ..."

One of Antigone's greatest flaws was her inability to convince Creon that he was wrong in a way that could have helped her position. Her actions flew in the face of Creon's edict and she did nothing to garner his support before she took the steps she did. Part of being the person who says, "This won't work," means you also should be ready to say, "Here are five or ten or fifteen things that will work and here's how we might put them to use."

Too bad this happens so infrequently, particularly during that biggest time-waster of all, staff meetings. It's been our observation that in some companies where the managers who support the senior executives are too shy or unwilling to voice their opinions for fear of going against the corporate grain, these confabs turn into one big yes-fest, an endless exercise in group-think.

At the other extreme, some companies are overpopulated with negativists who waste everyone's time criticizing every single idea, person, place, or thing in the organization. To them, brainstorming sessions are a waste of time; better to bash ideas that might move them out of their comfort zones. How to turn such corrosiveness into productive behavior? The key, of course, is to offer additional alternatives, better suggestions, or new ways to do old things, instead of just folding your arms and shaking your head. You'll earn a reputation for being a problem solver instead of a mere idea-killer.

## When You're Right, You're Probably Wrong and Other Business Paradoxes

Antigone and Creon shared two traits that made them flawed leaders: righteous indignation and the fault of being "too right." Creon refused to believe he could be wrong and Antigone decided early in the play that she was ready to die to defend her beliefs. The lesson to be learned from this all-too-modern Greek tragedy is that true leadership is more about compromise than you might at first think. Because Creon and Antigone were unwilling to negotiate with each other and unable to reach a compromise, they both failed.

True leadership is not about proving to everyone that your knuckles are tough or that your skull is thick. Just as the willow outlasts the oak in a windstorm, there is power in flexibility and strength in knowing when to bend. Creon and Antigone, unhappily, did not know this.

## Lessons from Ancient Thebes

Oliver Wendell Holmes wrote that "the best of books is not the thought which it contains, but the thought which it suggests." That is certainly true of Sophocles' great tragedy, *Antigone*. Its lessons on leadership, uncomfortable as some of them might be, are compelling and timeless. Next time you find yourself trying to "fight city hall," best to keep them in mind.

- *Remember that it's part of the leader's job to disagree.*
  Unless you spend most of your time on another planet, you'll find that—like Antigone—the *right* thing to do frequently is to oppose the status quo, to rouse followers to act against the established way of doing things, to reform your organization. The key, of course, is to be sure that (1) what you're trying to accomplish is good for the organization, not just you, and (2) that you keep your eye on the long-term goal so as to not find yourself mired down in righteous indignation along the way. Also, don't make the incorrect assumption that going to battle with the boss is necessarily bad. Sure, you may feel you're avoiding conflict in the short term. But, over the long haul, it's best to get what's nagging you off your chest. It'll help your self-image as well as provide you with the information you need to do your job better.
- *When it comes to negotiating, perception is reality.*
  Creon believed he was doing what was right for his organization. He was concerned, above all else, with preserving Thebes. He was decisive, strong, and uncompromising; he stuck to his principles. But the same could be said of Antigone. *Her* reality, her perception, was that she was right; that her principles, based as they were on higher, divine law were uncontestable. The point is that frequently your perception of the situation is vastly different from the perceptions of those you are trying to lead. Best to understand where they're coming from before you try to get them to go where you're trying to take them.
- *In a negotiating situation, concentrate on interests, not positions.*
  Such savvy at Thebes would have saved a great deal of trouble.

Here's how it works: your position is something you have decided upon on; your interests are what caused you to do it. In *Antigone*, the two antagonists staked out tragically unshakable positions. Two immovable objects come to mind. Instead, negotiate not on position, but on interests. Creon's interest was to make Thebes great. Antigone's was veneration of her brother, Polyneices. Doggedly holding to position, instead of interest, almost always makes for bad negotiating. If Sophocles' characters had been better negotiators, his great play might well have been a mere history, rather than one of literature's great tragedies.

- *Individual and organizational interests are frequently in conflict.*
In *Antigone*, the behavior of an individual conflicts with what could be called "corporate culture." What else is new? This situation is so common that Sophocles saw it as archetypal; the stuff, in fact, of great drama. With lines written in subtly different ways, the same kind of theatre plays itself out in all organizations, for this tension (between individual and society or "organization") is as old as humanity. The best leaders find ways to bring the interests of the individual into alignment with those of the organization. It's an ideal to shoot for, but don't be surprised when you discover there's wide divergence between the two. Creon's mistake was that he did nothing to try to narrow this divergence.

- *Leadership cannot be separated from ethics.*
Ethics, in fact, drive much of leadership behavior. Consider the marriage of the two in *Antigone*. On the one hand Antigone insists, as classicist Thomas Martin and organizational behavior consultant Richard Larson argue in their analysis of the case, that her only responsibility is to her family. That is her ethical position. On the other hand, Creon bases his ban on the burial of Polyneices on the ethical obligation of the citizen to be loyal to the community. Questions of values and ethics may have seemed important in Sophocles' time; they are even more critical now. What's worrisome is that few people are prepared for the kind of ethical challenges they face. They lack what one wag has called "ethical fitness." And this is happening at the very time

when the context in which ethics operates has changed hugely. Increasingly, seemingly small decisions have greater and greater impact. From Chernobyl (unpardonable carelessness on the part of the power station's operators) to Orange County, California (one man leading a county to financial ruin), one person's ethics can be another's disaster.

- *Watch out for that "zone of indifference."*
The good news is that leaders get to boss people around. The bad news, of course, is that rarely do underlings behave precisely as planned. After all, they may not see those orders as acceptable or in line with their own system of values. In such a case, your lofty edict falls *outside* their "zone of indifference." Everyone, it turns out, has this "zone of indifference." Think of it this way: When you have no strong negative opinions about an order coming down from on high, you comply. How can a leader manipulate this zone? It helps, as Creon learned to his deep regret, to base one's power on more than authority. The point to remember is that leaders are powerless until followers grant them the power to lead.

- *Try switching roles.*
Consider what might have happened had Creon and Antigone switched roles and argued it out. Robert Kelley, author of two books on employer/employee relations relates the following story of a software programmer and his boss at a $300 million California computer company at odds over a piece of software. "I suggested that they switch roles and argue it out," said Kelley. "They actually switched chairs and the subordinate sat behind the boss' desk. At first it was difficult for them. But after about five minutes, when they realized how silly they each appeared to the other, they started to laugh, and then quickly were able to come to a solution." Such a strategy might have turned Sophocles' tragedy into a comedy!

- *Leadership is, above all, about credibility.*
It's a relationship based on things like trust, confidence, even love. Jim Kouzes and Barry Posner, in their excellent book entitled *The Leadership Challenge*, found that credibility was the key to effective leadership. What makes up this illusive thing—cred-

ibility? Their research revealed four characteristics: (1) honesty—nothing is more important, (2) forward-looking—leaders are expected to know where they are going, (3) inspiring—they must enthusiastically involve their subordinates, and (4) competent—leaders must demonstrate the ability to get things done.

## Chapter 4

# But I Don't Want to Play Politics!: Willie Stark's Rise and Fall

*There is always something.*
— Robert Penn Warren

**Key Points**

- Changing yourself to fit the situation
- Misuse of power
- Ethics and corruption

Like it or not, "playing politics" is a part of any organization. And Willie Stark, protagonist of Robert Penn Warren's novel *All the King's Men*, can teach you everything you need to know and more about the sometimes seamy side of managing and leading.

From his profoundly philosophical belief that good can "only come from the bad" to his practical penchant for "giving 'em what they want," Stark's story is, at least to some degree, the story of every effective leader.

And it's not the least bit unrealistic. In fact, the political methods used in *All the King's Men* are similar to those used by Ross Perot in his failed 1992 presidential bid and by the man who has been called "the last great pasha of American business," the late Steve Ross of Time Warner.

You probably know the stories. Like Willie Stark, Ross Perot was, as one reporter put it, "... an incurable conspiracy monger who espies plotters in every thicket and easily persuades himself that some of his wildest suspicions are true."

You may recall the ostensible reason he gave for pulling out of the 1992 presidential race: the noble concern that his continued candidacy might result in an electoral college crisis. Yet the night before the election, he was moved to tell the world the real reason he ended his candidacy. It was, he said, fear that operatives of the Bush campaign were about to besmirch his daughter by publicizing a damaging, but fraudulent, photograph of her.

He went on to predict illegal phone taps and assassination attempts, earning the label—given to him by a Bush insider—of a "paranoid personality who has delusions."

We also see shades of Willie Stark in the actions of the late Steve Ross, *née* Rechnitz, who was the archetypal corporate hustler and ace salesman. Raised in Brooklyn, he struggled throughout his life to distance himself from his humble beginnings. His career path took him quickly from New York's garment district to the funeral business, then to parking lots and finally the big time: Time, Inc., cable TV, sports teams, and video games.

Then it was on to CEO of Warner Communications, where he became the consummate Hollywood schmoozer. He was on a roll, living grandly with a 172-foot yacht, a palazzo estate in Italy, and a fleet of jets (one of which he is reported to have sent from the Caribbean to New York just to buy hot dogs for his beach house guests).

But as it always seems, power corrupts and absolute power corrupts absolutely. When Gulf + Western tried to buy Time, Ross blocked the deal and instead orchestrated the takeover of Warner Communications by Time. Many were not amused.

As Connie Bruck, author of *Master of the Game: Steve Ross and the Creation of Time-Warner*, put it: "[Ross's] crucial role in keeping Time's stockholders from getting the best price for their stock is one of the low points of investor abuse in the postwar period."

Like Robert Penn Warren's Willie Stark, Steve Ross was a dreamer and a builder. Stark's passionate understanding of what the voters wanted was matched by Ross's virtuosity with numbers and what Donald Trump often calls the "art of the deal."

Yet, as one observer described it, "Steve Ross' life would seem to many like a success, but his real story is failure." The same might be said for the "hero" of this chapter, Willie Stark.

### Robert Penn Warren: Art Imitating Life

Stark's story is told, as we've said, by one of this country's truly great writers. Robert Penn Warren's list of literary accomplishments is mindboggling; his ability to write in several forms, including fiction, literary criticism, historical criticism, and poetry, yielded over fifty published works, including children's books and a play based on *All the King's Men*.

Penn Warren holds the distinction of being the only American writer to win the Pulitzer Prize for both fiction (*All the King's Men*) and poetry (*Promises: Poems, 1954–1956*). And in 1980, he won America's highest civilian award, the Medal of Freedom.

Born in 1905 in Guthrie, Kentucky, Robert Penn Warren had a father who was a businessman and a mother who worked as a schoolteacher. A bright and well-educated child, Warren moved through public school quickly and graduated from high school at sixteen. In the fall of the same year, he entered Vanderbilt University in Nashville, Tennessee.

His interest in his college studies was surpassed by his new-found passion for English and, in particular, poetry. His association with several professors and students who also shared his love for writing and studying poetry led Warren to see his first poems put into print in two of Vanderbilt's literary magazines.

After graduating college with honors, Warren moved to California for his graduate study at University of California at Berkeley in 1925. With his master's degree in hand, Warren moved on to Yale for his doctoral study and later became a Rhodes Scholar at Oxford, where he earned a degree in 1930.

Marrying in 1930, Warren returned to Vanderbilt and began teaching and writing in earnest. But while his teaching career may have been bright, his first two novels were rejected by several publishers.

Seeking a change of scenery, Warren and his wife moved to Louisiana in 1934, where he took a teaching post at Louisiana State University. It was during this critical eight-year period in his life that Warren was able to witness firsthand the life and work of the consummate Southern politician, Huey P. Long. Long, also known as "The Kingfish," served as governor of the state from 1928–1930 and senator from 1930–1935. He was assassinated in 1935, as he was preparing to run as a third-party presidential candidate against Franklin D. Roosevelt.

*All the King's Men* is a kind of "docudrama" which closely follows the life of Huey P. Long, with Willie Stark playing the life of the famous politician. Published in 1946, it would win the Pulitzer Prize the following year and become one of the leading American novels on power, leadership, politics, and corruption. In many ways, it serves as a model for what *not* to do as it tells the tale of one man's struggle for glory and the tricks and tactics he uses to get to the top.

There is more to Robert Penn Warren's *All the King's Men* than might appear at first. Critics were quick to characterize the novel as a story of a southern political boss in the 1930s. They saw it as the tale of one man's rise to power from obscurity and the events and actions that changed his personality along the way.

While the book is all of that, it also looks at the relationship between Willie Stark, the flawed pol, and his confidant, former newspaper reporter Jack Burden, who narrates the story and reveals Willie to us. As much as the story is about Willie the political wheeler dealer and leader, it is also about Jack, where he has gone, and how he finds himself at Willie Stark's right hand. Although the story appears to be all about Willie Stark's rise from the bleak farmlands of Louisiana to the Governor's office, it also shows how Jack Burden, college-educated, former reporter, and son of a judge, sees his life view change as he moves from a sheltered existence into the real world of back room deals, money-lined arrangements, suicide, and even assassination.

Even more than a story about specific people, however, *All the King's Men* is about a kind of mesmerizing leadership that harnesses the power of the average person. The result is an extremely effective, as well as powerful, leader. And examining the use and misuse of that power can help us understand its corrupting influence.

The novel opens with Governor Willie Stark speeding along a new highway on a trip back to his hometown, the fictional Mason City. Early on, we discover two sides of Willie: down home, "aw-shucks" country boy and skilled politician, speaker, and crowd-manipulator. Stark is a master of both.

It is the former that the crowd of people who follow Willie and his entourage into a soda fountain see and it is the latter who appears on the steps of the county courthouse. When an onlooker yells for Willie to give a speech inside the shop, the Boss (as he is called by all), shrugs it off. "My God, I didn't come here to make a speech. I came here to go out and see my pappy."[1]

Yet it *is* a speech—not social chit-chat—that Willie intends, and he has chosen the courthouse steps, a favored location of any political speaker, as his venue. Jack Burden knows exactly what is going on, and that these country folk would follow Willie wherever he led them:

> He walked straight across the street and across the patch of grass roots and up the steps of the courthouse. Nobody else followed him up the steps. At the top he turned around, slow, to face the crowd. He simply looked at them, blinking his big eyes a little, just as though he had just stepped out of the open doors and the dark hall of the courthouse behind him and was blinking to get his eyes adjusted to the light.

Is there any doubt what will happen next? Like all good speakers, Willie is using time and his apparently infinite patience to create tension in his audience. Jack Burden narrates:

> Then he gave his head a twitch, and his eyes bulged wide suddenly, even as if the light was hitting him full in the face, and you could see the glitter in them. It's coming, I thought. You saw the eyes bulge suddenly like that, as though something had happened inside him, and there was that glitter. You knew something had happened inside him, and thought, It's coming. It was always that way. There was the bulge and the glitter, and there was the cold grip way down in the stomach as though somebody had laid hold of something in there ...

This build-up is excruciating, and Willie knows the crowd is now completely in his capable hands. Next, he uses a salesman's oldest trick: Put the idea in the customer's mind of what you want him to do by telling him, "I'm not going to ask you to ..." (Such marketing shenanigans are not limited to fiction. American Express used this technique with its premium gold and platinum credit cards. The advertisements read: "This item is reserved for our best customers. It's not for everybody. It's only for those who qualify. We don't give it to just anybody.")

So what does Willie do? As we've suggested, he tells the crowd he's not going to do what in fact he *is* going to do—give a speech. And then he tells them he's not going to ask them for their vote—he acts like he doesn't even care about that—when clearly their vote is exactly what he wants.

> *And I didn't come back here to ask you to give me anything, not even a vote.... I'm not a politician today. I'm taking the day off. I'm not even going to ask you to vote for me. To tell the God's unvarnished and unbuckled truth, I don't have to ask you. Not today. I still got quite a little hitch up there in the big house with the white columns two stories high on the front porch and peach ice cream for breakfast.*

Here, master orator Willie, without seeming to, has emphasized several points he wants to get across to his audience: "I am your leader, but I'm also just like you are. I've come to visit my father and reflect upon the nature and wonders of my life. Since I'm already your leader, I don't need to ask for your vote today."

The implicit message is clear: "No vote-mongering today, but tomorrow, when I will need them, I want you to remember that we had this little chat on a hot afternoon in your town, where you got to stand near an important man such as me." On the surface, Willie is easygoing and gracious; he is a man of the people, a simple politician with only his motto (which accompanies his photograph all across the state) to guide him: "My study is the heart of the people." Could there be any better advice for any leader?

Willie (he'd like his audience to think) has become suddenly and blissfully unaware of politics. Yet it is, in fact, political "showtime." Like other leaders, both in the public and private sectors, he knows the value of acting as though he is apolitical; for him "politics" is a dirty word.

Don't get us wrong. Savvy leaders understand that, like it or not, politics is critical to success. A fascinating study of female executives recently completed by organizational behavior guru Lisa A. Mainiero at Fairfield University belies Willie-like protestations of political naiveté. Arguing that political skill is a necessary, even vital, aspect of career advancement, Mainiero's research confirms what we might have guessed: successful leaders are anything but apolitical. They are, in reality, consummate deal, alliance, and partnership builders.

The women who were the subjects in her study displayed such well-known political skills as developing an awareness of their organization's corporate culture, working with the system, delegating and team building, using personal influence, and mentoring others.

They were, in two words, masterful politicians, whose careers progressed through four predictable stages of political development. The first, which Mainiero calls "political naiveté," corresponds nearly perfectly to Willie Stark's early and manifestly unsuccessful political life which is described later in this chapter.

The second stage, "building credibility," occurs in the novel after Willie realizes his drab speeches and downhome idealism are hurting his campaign. Political savvy, it seems, can be vastly improved once you make a serious blunder, thereby learning volumes about the shifting sands and subtleties of the corporate culture.

The key to building credibility is to demonstrate to others your potential by outdistancing your peers. This Willie began to do masterfully when he positioned himself as a "man of the people"; someone who would forever change politics as usual. He then progressed nicely to Mainiero's third and fourth stages of political development—"refining a style," during which he served in office long enough to begin to reflect on his own leadership style and approach to managing others; and "shouldering responsibility," when he became, like Mainiero's study subjects, a fully seasoned leader.

Such growth along the political learning curve delivers Willie home to confront Judge Montague Irwin, a political sidekick who has inexplicably endorsed a rival candidate for the Senate. Willie pulls no punches. He orders Jack to dig up as much dirt as he can on the judge. When Willie learns that the judge took bribes years before, he makes plans to use this information to his political and personal advantage.

What we know of Willie Stark before his days as governor we learn from Jack Burden, who began covering Willie's rising political career when Willie was campaigning for county treasurer. In those days, as was common in many small towns, the political major domo, the person who called all the political shots, was the county commissioner. It was he who awarded building contracts, settled disputes, and chose the "winners" of the local elections.

Willie fails to understand the power of the commissioner. When he first arrives on this small-time political scene, he sincerely believes that by being honest and ethical, forthright and dedicated, he can make changes for the better. As happens in political life at many levels, this is far from reality. Running for county treasurer, against the party's candidate, he is soundly defeated. Honesty and truth, it seems, are no match for party graft.

Later, when the commissioner awards a contract to build a new schoolhouse to his brother-in-law, Willie howls in idealistic protest, unaware of the power of leverage and favors. He can't get anyone to listen. When the new school collapses due to poor workmanship, three children are killed and several others injured. Angry with politics as usual, the townspeople elect Willie as treasurer in the next election, voting not for Willie, but against the status quo.

Still, Willie feels he can make a contribution, and his soaring naiveté and idealism makes him easy fodder for the state's Democratic party machine. The party leaders draft him as a candidate for governor and assure him they will do everything to help him win. In reality, they have thrown all their resources and support to another candidate. It appears Willie is to play the part of the rube at a carnival.

Although he doesn't realize it, Willie is at a crossroads. After giving the same fact-filled speech over and over again, with the same less-than positive results, he finally realizes he is being duped. When he discovers he's been manipulated, he becomes a changed man. Realizing that he's been treated like a country hick, his anger motivates him to campaign. He loses the election battle, but not the war. He develops his speech-making talents into a cross between homespun homilies and solid political rhetoric. Mixing that with his natural affinity for people—the common man—and reminding them that he is one of them, he becomes a force to be reckoned with. His second bid for the governorship is successful.

It is while he is preparing his second campaign that Willie finally meets reporter Jack Burden personally and offers him a job. Burden, finding Willie enthralling and dynamic, quits his reporter's job and accepts.

One of Jack's strengths, which probably came from his reporter's background, is his ability to uncover incriminating information about Willie Stark's rivals. Willie quickly becomes adept at using that information to his advantage: when, for example, foes try to impeach his State Auditor, Byram White, for taking bribes; and when later they try to impeach Willie for condoning White's behavior, a new—and considerably nastier—Willie goes on the offensive. He will fight fire with fire.

Armed with Jack's damning information, Willie does two things to guarantee his survival. First, he goes straight to the people of his state, telling his side of the story. Second, he goes after his political enemies, blackmailing them into submission by threatening to expose their own dirty tricks. The expected happens: just as quickly as they began, the cries for White's and Willie's impeachments die out.

But Willie doesn't stop there. After the impeachment proceedings are quashed, he goes again to the people, and convinces them that the attempt was really an effort to deny them, the common people, what is their right:

> He said, "They tried to ruin me because they do not like what I have done. Do you like what I have done?"
>
> The roar came, and died.
>
> He said, "I tell you what I am going to do. I am going to build a hospital. The biggest and the finest money can buy. It will belong to you. Any man or woman or child who is sick or in pain can go in those doors and know that all will be done that man can do.... Not as charity. But as a right. It is your right. Do you hear? It is your right!"
>
> The roar came.
>
> He said, "And it is your right that every child shall have a complete education. That no person aged and infirm shall want or beg for bread. That the man who produces something shall be able to carry it to market without miring to the nub, without toll. That no poor man's house or land shall be taxed. That the rich men and the great companies that draw wealth from this state shall pay this state a fair share. That you shall not be deprived of hope!"

He'll soon trade that hope for votes, and it is no wonder. Willie has again positioned himself on the side of the people and, at the same time, reminded them that he is responsible for all the improvements they've enjoyed.

### Willie Transformed

We have witnessed a political transformation. Willie Stark is no longer the back-country hack he once was. He has tasted power. Power that he will never relinquish. And, whether by legal and ethical means or the converse, he will vanquish his enemies.

Willie chooses Dr. Adam Stanton, son of the state's former governor Joel Stanton, to head the new hospital he promised. This is a bold attempt at political peacemaking, since Stanton and his sister, Anne, despise Willie for all the things that he stands for that are so different from the ideals held by their beloved father. But Willie wants Adam because he is the best man for the job. It makes sense. The more successful the hospital, the more votes Willie will garner next time around.

He tells Jack to persuade Adam Stanton to run the hospital. The reporter takes a familiar tack: "Don't think of Willie. Think of all the good you'll be able to do as a doctor there." Stanton reluctantly agrees, but it's because he really does believe that good can come from his decision, despite the fact that he abhors the man responsible for the hospital.

Willie arranges a meeting to talk with Stanton, and it is during this encounter that he best describes his political philosophy and his assessment of humanity: If you want goodness, he tells the doctor, you have to produce it yourself.

> "You got to make it, Doc. If you want it. And you got to make it out of badness. Badness. And you know why, Doc?" He raised his bulk up in the broken-down wreck of an overstuffed chair he was in, and leaned forward, his hands on his chair he was in, and leaned forward, his hands on his knees, his elbows cocked out, his head outthrust and the hair coming down to his eyes, and stared into Adam's face. "Out of badness," he repeated. "And you know why? Because there isn't anything else to make it out of." Then, sinking back into the wreck, he asked, softly, "Did you know that, Doc?"
>
> Adam wet his lips and said, "There is one question I should like to ask you. It is this. If, as you say, there is only the bad to start with, and the good must be made from the bad, then how do you know what the good is? How do you even recognize the good? Assuming you have made it from the bad. Answer me that."
>
> "Easy, Doc, easy," the Boss said.
>
> "Well, answer it."
>
> "You just make it up as you go along."
>
> "Make up what?"
>
> "The good," the Boss said. . . .

Hardly an anthem for the "trust and empowerment" nineties, but Willie's view of human nature does provide justification for his actions: In order to make some good out of the bad, a leader may control and manipulate people in any way required. What's more, the leader can change the rules as needed to accomplish his goal.

As with other leaders we have studied, Willie Stark knows that to bring about change, you sometimes have to step on some toes, or challenge the status quo. But what if, in order to accomplish anything, a leader has to act illegally or unethically? If the outcome is for the good, does that make it acceptable to break the law or do something clearly wrong?

If this is becoming uncomfortable, stick with us. It's a question all leaders face at some time in their careers. Willie, it seems, would argue for that which is hugely politically incorrect these days: that the end *does* justify the means.

And what about Adam Stanton? He would probably argue the opposite. Yet as much as he hated Willie and all that he stood for, he was willing to overlook the "bad" in order to achieve some good—running the new, modern hospital. Stanton had two character flaws that ultimately destroyed him: he worshipped his father to such a degree that it clouded his judgement, and he hated Willie Stark with a passion. Both would ultimately spin Stanton's—and Willie's—worlds out of control.

First, Stanton learns that his father once aided and abetted a bribery, making him no "better" than Willie! Second, one of Willie's enemies tells him that Willie is having an affair with his sister. That's all he needs to hear. The world as he once knew it is over. Willie Stark—and what he stands for—have invaded every corner of his life. He must be stopped.

Stanton, pistol in hand, waits for Governor Stark to make his way across the capitol rotunda. Two shots ring out and Willie Stark falls to the floor, mortally wounded. His bodyguard shoots Adam Stanton, who dies at the scene. Willie dies from his wounds two days later.

This may sound like fiction, but—as we've already suggested—it is not. Stark's life closely parallels that of Huey P. Long. Both had roots in the Deep South, both were perceived by their political opponents as country bumpkins early in their careers, and then, later, as ruthless dictators. Both went through a sea change from idealist to realist, and both went to extraordinary, and sometimes controversial, lengths to stay in power. Both acquired many enemies and were killed in the same way, by medical doctors as they walked to their statehouse offices.

Willie's story is a cautionary tale. Leaders find themselves always trying to balance the requirements of practicality with the need for fairness and justice. The bottom line on all this is to be sure that your use of power is for the benefit of the organization, and not solely for yourself.

## Stark as the Flawed Leader: He's Not Alone

A scan of the newspapers—and not just the business pages—shows us that Willie Stark is not the only leader whose meteoric rise is followed by a precipitous fall from grace. Consider the usual suspects:

- *Leona Helmsley.*
  At one point in her life, she and her husband controlled acres of high-priced New York real estate. And for a time, her name was synonymous with hotel luxury and first-class service. But the imperial nature of her hotels was equally matched by her imperiousness as a leader. Stories of petty and mean-spirited treatment of her employees abound. And in the end, she tried to tangle with the one entity that had even more power than she—the Internal Revenue Service. It must have been quite a long walk from her place as the high-flying "queen" of one of New York's most lavish hotel chains to $8 million in fines and restitution and eighteen months in a federal prison cell.
- *Charles P. Keating.*
  Few men are so linked to one national event as Keating, whose very name is synonymous with the savings and loan industry debacle that is still firmly attached to the government coffers like a limpet to a shark. His is an example proving Lord Acton's aphorism that absolute power corrupts absolutely. His utter disregard for rules and ethics is matched only by his well-organized flimflam of thousands of investors.
- *Michael Milken.*
  Like Keating, Milken is also attached to an event—or in his case, an era—by name. When most people look back at the slash-and-burn economic environment that was the 1980s, his

name comes to mind immediately. Like his cohorts, Keating and Helmsley, Milken thumbed his nose at everyday people and at the government. The Milken lesson is similar to theirs: If you're making scads of money, best not irritate the people at the Securities and Exchange Commission.

- *Donald Trump.*
Say what you want about "the Donald," you have to admire his *chutzpah*. Can't make your bond payments? Renegotiate with the banks and blame it on them if they won't lend you any more money! Having trouble in Atlantic City with your casinos? Stall your investors off and point your fingers at the economy, the banks, and the government. Donald's philosophy seems to be one that says, "You people keep forgetting who I am. I'm Donald Trump. That means something." Like Willie Stark, Donald knows what it's like to be very rich and he knows what it's like to be not-so-rich; he'd rather be very rich and if you don't agree with his fiscal niceties, it must be your fault.

- *Frank Lorenzo.*
Is there one man more despised by the entire airline industry and its unions? There are Wall Street airline analysts, airline pilots, and machinist union members who turn purple at the mere mention of his name. Like Trump, Frank Lorenzo liked to blame everyone around him for his own failed management practices. Unions and pilots won't take pay cuts? Their fault, not mine. Eastern Airlines stock is in the dumper? Not because of me. Eastern is out of business? Gee, then how about I take a look at Continental?

- *Jim Baker.*
Here was a man who demonstrated the domino theory in action. Topple my house of cards and each one will do damage some-where else as it falls. After his Heritage Park Christian theme *divertissement* cum sideshow went bankrupt, a well-respected national accounting firm followed suit. Laventhol & Horwath (R.I.P.) had the misfortune to accept Baker, et al, as a client. Outside auditors say L&H made hash of Baker's books. True or not, the resulting law suits, fines, and other nightmares forced the firm to turn to its partners and say, "Pony up your share of our losses, folks. We're all going down with the ship." And so

they did. Baker spent the money his followers sent in by the handful and went to jail for his efforts.

If these stories of victory followed by the agony of defeat have a familiar ring, they should. It's part of human folly that many lives—and careers—follow the sigmoid curve, that S-shaped line symbolizing beginning, rapid growth, achievement of a great height or zenith, followed by stagnation, and then fall. For some the rise and fall is caused by external forces—the economy, foreign exchange rate fluctuations, and so forth. For others, the cause is more sinister, and much closer to home: overweening ambition. We call such Willie-like changes in fortune "the Icarus imperative."

It's a phenomenon as old as mankind, brought home to us recently by a story a colleague told. For forty years he had worked for a company that had been a leader in its industry, commanding respect, high prices, and even higher margins. Yet sales and profits suddenly began to plummet. Increasingly, smaller, more agile companies started to capture market share from our friend's company. The firm's long prohibition against layoffs was lifted. Plants were being closed. He had even heard rumors of a hostile takeover. Whatever happened, he wondered, to those halcyon days when his company seemed nearly invulnerable.

Welcome to the mythic world of Icarus, whose overconfidence led him to fly so close to the sun that his wings melted and fell into what is now called the Icarian Sea. So common is it in today's corporate world for success to engender overconfidence, disregard for ethics, carelessness, and other bad managerial habits that Icarus' unfortunate tale has become alarmingly modern.

*All the King's Men* can serve as an antidote to such seemingly ineluctable disasters. It is (or should be) a cautionary tale about the corrupting influence of power. It's clear that being a leader also means having the power to influence events and people's lives, for good or bad. How a leader uses that power, and justifies its use or misuse, is one of the central issues of leadership raised throughout the book.

## Speechifying: The Willie Stark Method
Willie Stark possessed a skill that is palpable in all effective leaders—the ability to "work the room," to gather a crowd, hold them spellbound, to tell people what they want to hear.

His methods bear examination:

- *Build dramatic effect.*
  "Take your time, don't be in a hurry, wait a minute" is advice that sounded good when it came from our parents and it works equally well when talking in front of groups. The sign of an inexperienced, flustered, or unsure speaker is to rush the news out and then go sit down. Remember, too, that the tension that occurs when you wait to speak is not always a bad thing. (Recall Willie on the courthouse steps?) What may seem like hours to you is, in reality, only seconds to your audience. Savor the moment, build anticipation, let the group focus in on what you are about to say, then say it.
- *Use pauses.*
  If you've ever seen Reverend Jesse Jackson speak, you can't help but notice the way he puts beats or measured pauses into his talks. You can almost count "one-two" between each of his ideas. i.e., "My friends (one-two), I come before you today (one-two) to speak of an important national issue (one-two) ..." This is a habit Jackson no doubt acquired during his days as a church pastor. His rhythmic, almost sing-song style of speaking is captivating to his audiences. It can be for yours, too.
- *Look, talk, and act like a person of the people.*
  There's a reason why many male executives appear in front of their managers, supervisors, and employees with their shirt-sleeves rolled up and their ties askew and why their female counterparts "dress down" a bit on such occasions. They want to convey a certain image that says, "I'm not just a 'suit,' I'm a regular person."
  Wearing a thousand-dollar suit, French cuffs, and a Hermes tie is not the best attire for a speech to those folks down on the assembly line. Like Willie, you must know your audience and its needs and match your presentation and your appearance to them. It's an effective way to get the audience on your side.
- *Create a bit of ceremony before you speak.*
  A professional public speaker offers this advice about using "ceremony" to spice up your talks. Mary-Ellen Drummond, of Polished Presentations in Rancho Santa Fe, California says,

"Whenever you speak in front of a group who does not know you, always have someone introduce you. Write out a simple paragraph for this person to read and put your name as the last two words. He or she can say, 'Your speaker today comes to us from ...' and then finish with "so please join me in welcoming ...'"

Your introduction can help establish your credentials (why they ought to listen to you). And the information you include in the introduction can help position you as "one of them" just as Willie Stark was clearly "of the people." Speaking to a group of middle managers? Mention something about when you held such a position. Speaking to assembly line workers? Recall how you earned money for college by working summers in your hometown factory. (This very basic technique is known as establishing empathy.)

- *Control the crowd using different speaking positions.*
  Mary-Ellen Drummond puts it this way, "Divide your audience into thirds—the left third, the middle third, and the right third. Then, address each third with a different point and move a bit as you do. If you're up on a platform speaking to a group, make a point to the center third, move to your left third, and make another point. Move back to the center third as you make another point, and then move to your right third as you conclude." Believe it or not, such perambulations can help make you a more effective communicator.

- *Take them where you want them to go, show them what you want them to see, and tell them what you want them to hear.*
  Speaking to groups, as Willie Stark knew, is all about controlling the message. Weak and ineffectual speakers can't hold their audience, lose their train of thought too easily, and can instantly make a crowd restless, bored, or both. Plan what you want to say and be dynamic when you say it. As Willie Stark knew so well, it's not just your message you want them to remember; it's you too.

## Good Advice from Popeye: Don't Put on Airs

*I y'am what I y'am and that's all that I y'am.*
—POPEYE THE SAILOR

As our cartoon hero attests, it's always best to be yourself. It was only after Willie threw away the canned speech and spoke "from the heart," as he would to one of his small-town neighbors, that people began to listen to him. They listened because they were frustrated with the status quo. The gap between the "haves" and the "have-nots" was growing, and the have-nots wanted their voices heard. Willie capitalized on this. In so many words he said, "Vote for me and you'll have one of your own working to make sure those big-time politicians don't cheat you out of what's rightfully yours."

Even after he became governor, he reminded people of his humble background. He knew that the "hick vote" was what got him to the governor's mansion and that, if he treated these voters well, they would propel him to even higher office. So he continued to use his "I'm one of you; it's us versus them" message whenever possible.

It works. In the airline industry, for example, few leaders have taken this idea—just "be yourself"—to heart more than Herb Kelleher, CEO of Southwest Airlines. He is well known as a hands-on leader/innovator and a super aggressive marketer of his services and his people. What started as a struggling Texas airline is now nearly twenty-five years old. And when it comes to people-skills, he makes Willie Stark look like a rank amateur. Here's how Kelleher was described in a recent profile:[2]

> He's known as outrageous, off-the-wall, even a wild man. Now 63, he continues to impersonate Elvis and dress up as a leprechaun to amuse customers on St. Patrick's Day. He smokes five packs of cigarettes a day, likes to drink and party all night and relishes a bawdy joke. On a moment's notice, he might take off on a hunting trip with employees who never thought he'd accept their last-minute invitation.

More importantly, listen to what Kelleher himself has to say about the importance of simply "being yourself":

> There's a lot being said about the importance of communication. But it can't be rigid, it can't be formal. It has to proceed directly from the heart. It has to be spontaneous. "Communication" is not getting up and giving formal speeches. It's saying, "Hey Dave,

*how you doing? Heard the wife's sick—she okay?" That sort of thing. Our annual report emphasizes getting back to basics. Business has gotten so complex that we've forgotten the basics. Do what your customer wants, be happy in your work. All these little things. The way I dignify it is to say, Remember Einstein's criteria: If you've got a choice between two theories, neither of which is overtly provable, pick the simplest one. Later, when the means are available to prove them, the simpler one will inevitably prevail.*

(Such esprit de corps was nowhere to be seen in the organizations run by the likes of our "gang of six"—Trump, Helmsley, Milken, Baker, Lorenzo, and Keating.)

### Situational Ethics: The Chameleon Approach

*All the King's Men* is a classic study in situational ethics. Willie could bend himself to play whatever role the situation, the crowd, or his enemies demanded. When it was time to appear pure of heart, clear of eye, and strong of will, he could deliver. And when it was time for a take-no-prisoners approach, which called for him to be hard-hearted, remorseless, even down and dirty, he could play it that way as well.

His ethical "convictions" were adaptable to the situation at hand, and he did what he thought was right for the moment, even though it wasn't always ethically "right." In many cases, it wasn't even legal. But that was all right, claimed Willie, because that's how things got done. "How they had always gotten done," he tells Adam Stanton, as he talks about how you make up the good as you go along:

> *"So you make it up as you go along?" Adam repeated gently.*
> *"What the hell else you think folks been doing for a million years, Doc? When your great-great-grandpappy climbed down from out of the tree, he didn't have any more notion of good or bad, or right or wrong, than the hoot owl that stayed up in the tree. Well, he climbed down and he began to make Good up as he went along. He made up what he needed to do business, Doc. And what he made up and got everybody to mirate on as good and right was always just a couple of jumps behind what he needed to do business on. That's why things change, Doc. Because what folks claim is right is always just a couple of jumps short of what they need to do business. Now ... folks*

*in general, which is society, Doc, is never going to stop doing business. Society is just going to cook up a new notion of what is right."*

The problem, Willie explained earlier to Stanton, is that a lot of people want "everything two ways at once." They want the benefits—the good—but don't want to have to do whatever it takes to get those benefits. Like his Attorney General, Hugh Miller, says Willie:

> *"He resigned because he wanted to keep his little hands clean. He wanted the bricks but he just didn't know somebody has to paddle in the mud to make `em. He was like somebody that just loves beefsteak but just can't bear to go to a slaughter pen because there are some bad, rough men down there who aren't animal lovers and who ought to be reported to the S.P.C.A."*

Willie's message is clear: " Somebody has to do the dirty work and if, sometimes, I'm the one, so be it." This sentiment is not unique, nor is it modern. It is, in fact, the theme of Machiavelli's 16th-century *The Prince*, a best-seller today. According to Machiavelli, since the world is already a bad place, a great man cannot also be a good man. It's just not possible, he counsels, to be both. So if you can't be great and good, is it not far better to be great?

Sometimes such hard-nosed leadership seems to be badly needed. Speaking to the National Press Club two days after he left his job as President Clinton's chief of staff, Mac McLarty remarked, "I think what this White House really needs is a chief of staff who can read Machiavelli in the original Italian."

Yet the kind of situational ethics that appealed so much to Willie Stark can send the wrong message to the people around you. "This person, who is supposed to be our leader and set the right example, bends in every wind, whatever the situation is, and creates an ethical stance so that he or she appears to come out smelling like a rose, while someone else gets the blame or takes the fall."

Obviously politics is not the only arena where questionable ethics come into obvious play. It certainly happens in business as well. Cheating, lying, theft, putting out false information, gaining at the expense of others, taking credit when it is not due, passing the buck, creating scapegoats, throwing people to the wolves, developing hidden agendas, and sabotaging programs, products, services, and people's careers are all a part of the "ethics-most-foul" side of our corporate world.

**Avoiding Executive Derailment: Keeping Your Career on Track**
At first glance, it's easy to look at the saga that was Willie Stark's life and say he got what was coming to him. The important question for you to ask is: Is it necessary to be a Willie Stark if you want to make it to the top? Or is it possible to make it to the top and remain a moral and ethically honest leader?

As you think about your own career, keep the following "right way" indicators in mind. They can serve as guideposts, allowing you to check to make sure you're on the "right road" and using your skills, knowledge, and experience in ways that will benefit your organization and its people.

- *Know the difference between sympathy and empathy.*
  This is a critical distinction, especially when it comes to dealing with your employees and their work or personal problems. When you *sympathize* with someone's problems, you have a tendency to get caught up in them or want to take on those problems yourself. When you *empathize* with the person, you can avoid getting personally attached to the emotional side of the problems and can be a bit more objective, which is why most employees look to you in the first place.

  In conflicts, people look for allies who will see their way and even take up their cause. As a leader, it's not your job to become embroiled in every personnel problem that sweeps through your office. It is your job to listen to all sides, ask appropriate questions that show you have been paying attention, and then render a fair decision. This is what leaders do: act, react, and then act again.
- *Know the definitions of integrity, honesty, and correct, ethical behavior.*
  Now more than ever, these abstract but essential qualities are important to your growth and development as a leader. Further, your understanding of them is important to the economic health of the organization where you work.

  In this era of employee "entitlements," (e.g., "They won't

miss one little copy machine" or "Since I didn't get the raise I expected I'm going to start submitting false expense claims," etc.), it's critically important for every company to create written policies about what is and what is not acceptable ethical work behavior.

Courts have held that off-the-cuff discussions about work behavior for new or current employees is not enough; you need well defined, well thought-out, and well written policies and procedures to explain what people can and cannot do.

- *Become known as a team player.*
This trait is so hard to win and so easy to lose. You should know, even intuitively, what this concept means and how to make it work. Most people in organizations don't like "lone wolves," especially if their operating philosophy tends to be, "If I want something done right, I'll do it myself."

Your bosses and your employees are looking for you to take control of projects and guide them with the good of everyone in mind. They all want someone they can trust, not just when times are good but in a pinch too.

And it's not just about taking over, it's also about delegating and guiding people and teaching them to work together as a team. Since this is not typically a concept we learn formally, for example, in business school, it's more of a skill that is either learned, developed, or taught to you by those who know how to work effectively with and for teams.

- *Be willing to share the limelight or even take a lesser role.*
Sometimes, quiet leadership is more powerful than basking in glory. In these cases, it's not always who's right, but what's right. Taking all of the credit is perfectly acceptable in certain situations, especially if you did all the work or took a project from start to finish. In other cases, it might be best to fall back on a more humble stance and let your employees get the praise.

One of the elements of real leadership is your ability to empower other people so that they can feel more of a sense of achievement. Just as you don't always have to win every battle, you don't always have to take the credit. If your bosses are sharp people, they will know who did what and you can often earn more points for leading from the rear rather than trying to hog the glory. (In chapter 11, we will look at Castiglione and the concept of "followership," i.e., letting your people go forward and win while you lead them from behind.)

- *If you can't be nice to everyone, be courteous to all.*

It's not necessary to love everyone you work or deal with as a part of your job. We all have personality clashes and conflicts with co-workers, employees, superiors, and even customers. Part of human nature is that different people will see and do things in different ways. Understanding that is part of the process; accepting that you can't always change people or make them be more like you is another.

One of the ways true leaders deal with these facts is to develop a general practice of being at least courteous to everyone. This is not a forced process where you fake sincerity or talk through your teeth, but rather, a policy of treating everyone with decency.

- *Don't hold grudges; toss your enemies list.*

Unlike Willie Stark, Richard Nixon, and other political leaders who devised written lists of their enemies, real leadership is not about scorekeeping, revenge, or uncovering dirt. Let other people have their hidden, covert, or even overt agendas. Concentrate your efforts on working hard and developing successful relationships with people.

The hard-hearted types who spend much of their time searching for conspiracies, creating payback schemes, and holding people accountable for past indiscretions usually burn out before too long. It's just not possible to function effectively at that level.

Paybacks and other revenge-oriented maneuvers are for schoolchildren. Be adult enough to admit that you won't necessarily get along with everyone in every situation and then move on.

- *Protect your flanks.*

Having said all this, you should still keep a careful eye on the people in your organization who are out to sabotage you or your programs. As the end of the Cold War has proved to us, sometimes the best offense is a strong defense.

You don't need to create a bunker mentality where you look upon everyone as a potential hostile force, but you do need to protect yourself from the few unscrupulous people who may want to see you fail.

This can include everything from making backup copies of your important computer files and keeping them in a separate place, locking your desk, and calling people on their negative, or self-destructive behavior if it affects the organization or your place in it.

- *Give more than is expected of you to your boss.*
  Be willing to work harder than might be required, if not all the time, a least as much as you can. This doesn't mean you have to put in 100-hour work weeks, just that there is a big difference in your boss's eyes between the employee who packs up and heads for home at the stroke of 5:00 P.M. and the one who stays until the job gets done, no matter the hour.

- *Give more than is expected of you to your employees.*
  Similarly, your employees expect you to be there to go to bat for them, either with senior management, problem customers, or just problems on the job. Nothing is worse than an absentee manager who should be handling things in his or her department and yet wastes valuable time in other areas of the organization.

  And like the hard-working manager who stays late to complete an important project, your employees expect you to walk your talk. If they have to stay late to work, in most cases you should volunteer to stay late and work with them as well. As King Henry V showed, sometimes it's the time spent in the trenches with the troops that reveals your true leadership qualities.

In *All the King's Men*, Willie Stark's score on the above indicators of leadership was more than a bit uneven. As happens with many flawed and failed leaders, Willie started out with the best intentions but somewhere along the road to power his values shifted and his commitment to them faltered.

Your mission—in growing as a leader—is to watch for these obstacles as they appear and use your own beginnings and experiences as your moral guideposts.

## Chapter 5

# Beating Them at Their Own Game: Cleopatra versus Caesar

## Key Points

- Alliance building for survival
- Female leadership in a male-dominated world
- Dealing with other cultures on their terms

If you believe that Cleopatra's historic success with Mark Antony and Julius Caesar was merely a matter of sex and seduction, think again. There is much more to this remarkable woman than that. She is history's first truly transformational leader: a ruler who, unlike many of the male leaders of her day, learned eight languages in order to gain the respect, support, and loyalty of her subjects; successfully overcame internal rivalries that seemed certain to destroy her realm; and forged alliances which would prove the power of cooperation over competition.

Much of this woman's remarkable story is told in Plutarch's *Parallel Lives*. Cleopatra, of course, was not Plutarch's only subject. He wrote about many leaders, including Julius Caesar and Mark Antony, who would both enjoy immortality when Shakespeare later wrote of their lives and times in his play *Julius Caesar*.

Plutarch, who lived in Greece from 120–50 B.C., wore many hats. He was an author, a scholar, a philosopher, and a priest. He penned a series of biographies about famous leaders largely in order to highlight their leadership styles and make critical or supportive comments about their successes or failures. And since his subjects were exclusively male leaders, Cleopatra appears as only a "bit player" in his biographies of Caesar and Mark Antony. Still, because she was such a charismatic leader, her actions (buried as they are in the biographies of others) make her hard for Plutarch, or for any student of leadership, to ignore. Indeed, as you'll see, Plutarch grudgingly recognizes many of her accomplishments and forward-thinking qualities in his book.

Like Antigone, whom we profiled in chapter 3, Cleopatra is an example of a woman battling for her beliefs in a male-dominated environment. That she succeeded so well is a tribute to her savvy. Cleopatra was a visionary. She was able to see the future of her organization—Egypt—and the need to build a working political relationship with one of her competitors—Rome.

Scholars who have studied Cleopatra have described her complex nature. In her best moments, she was compassionate, intelligent, dedicated, cooperative, and forward-thinking. In her worst, she was cunning, manipulative, seductive, and even murderous.

### Lessons in Alliance Building

To understand who Cleopatra was and what she did, you'll first need to know something of Greek, Egyptian, and Roman politics. Cleopatra was the last ruler of what was called the Ptolemaic dynasty, the royal family from which she was descended. The Ptolemies ruled Egypt, under one king or another, for more than three hundred years. They were known for their diplomatic ability to coalesce diverse groups into a coherent whole. When meeting with Egyptians, Ptolemaic rulers were famous for presenting themselves as being Egyptian, and when dealing with Greeks and Macedonians, they acted as if they were Macedonian kings. Cleopatra, who apparently inherited this important leadership ability from her forebearers, was blessed with the ability to deal effectively with different ethnic groups.

Still, the Egyptian ruling class considered itself to be Macedonian Greek by birth and, as such, did not bother to learn to speak Egyptian, the language of the land they ruled. Indeed, to speak to a Ptolemy, an

Egyptian would have to rely on a Greek interpreter or learn to speak Greek. Cleopatra's rule changed all of that; she became the first Ptolemaic leader to learn to speak Egyptian. It had a great effect, as Plutarch reports:

> [Cleopatra] had a melodious voice and she spoke in whatever language she wished, effortlessly using her tongue as if it were a many-stringed instrument, so that when she conferred with (non-Greeks) on very few occasions did she need an interpreter, but she answered most of them on her own accord.... She also learned the languages of many other peoples, although the rulers before her did not even attempt to master the Egyptian language.... [1]

These early rulers may not have tried to master the Egyptian language, but they did try to master those who spoke it. Not surprisingly, conflicts between these two different ethnic groups caused a number of palace revolts throughout the duration of the Ptolemaic rule. The solution? In order to keep things literally "in the family," the Ptolemies encouraged intermarriage between relatives, even brothers and sisters. Further, although everyone in the family had tremendous power, those who were female were not allowed to reign alone. The arrangement was that a queen must have a king so that in appearance at least, she was not the sole decision-maker. To deal with this onerous protocol, the eighteen-year-old Cleopatra did something chracteristically brash: she married a male much younger than she, her half-brother Ptolemy XIII. She knew that her mate would have no real power, little experience, limited authority, and no influence over her.

Increasingly, Egypt captured the attention of Rome because it was rich with agriculture, minerals, and precious metals. And the Roman *realpolitik* was simple: a land so full of these resources should not be allowed to rule itself. An historic die was cast—Rome would keep a careful eye on its southern neighbor.

When Cleopatra's father died, she and her younger brother were appointed the new Egyptian queen and king. But, to her great surprise, her brother and his advisors soon expelled her from the throne so that he could rule alone. Since he was too young and inexperienced to rule on the day-to-day political issues, the Roman Senate sent a general, Pompey the Great, to be his "guardian." Pompey's interest was Rome, not Egypt.

His mission was to insure that Egypt (and its untold wealth) did not fall into hands unfriendly to Rome.

Here, the story gets truly fascinating. At the time of his intervention into Cleopatra's reign, Pompey was embroiled in a fierce competition with his rival, Julius Caesar, a fact not lost on the ever-watchful Cleopatra. When Caesar defeated Pompey in the Grecian battle of Pharsalus, Pompey fled back to Egypt seeking protection. It was an idea that failed miserably. Upon arrival, he was murdered by aides to Cleopatra's brother.

With Pompey dead, Caesar took a renewed interested in Egypt, thanks largely in part to Cleopatra's alluring attention toward him. Cleopatra's brother would have no part of this shared kingdom and fought against Caesar's request for unity. The rebellion failed. Ptolemy XIII later drowned in the Nile River.

One year later, Cleopatra joined Caesar in Rome as his mistress. In Rome, Cleopatra lived the lush life befitting a queen. While Roman politicians revered Cleopatra for her beauty, wit, and wealth, they would never accept her as an equal. In short, women in Rome—queens or not—could not actively participate in politics, hold office, or even vote in elections. But while Cleopatra could not visibly move about in political circles, she was able to watch Caesar from afar and learn a great deal from his leadership style. For his part, Caesar prepared a treaty to protect Cleopatra's future rule of Egypt.

Caesar made quite a mentor. He was, of course, a brilliant general and an extraordinary politician. One story dramatically illustrates Caesar's ability to turn seeming catastrophe into victory: Leaving Rome to study in Rhodes as a young man, his ship was captured by pirates. He quickly obtained the necessary ransom, hired his own mercenaries, found and captured the ill-starred thugs, and had them immediately executed.

And he knew how to keep the troops happy, combining successful military operations with splendid celebration parties and games paid for out of his own pocket. Cleopatra, among others, must have been impressed by his ability to turn a phrase. His most famous boast "Veni, vidi, vici," (I came, I saw, I conquered) could be the rallying cry of any modern day takeover artist or merger specialist. And his last words, "Et tu, Brute" uttered as he lay dying on the steps of the Roman senate after his assassination, indelibly remind anyone who leads that power is often stunningly transient.

When Caesar was suddenly stabbed to death by Brutus and his band of henchmen on the famous "Ides of March" in 44 B.C., Cleopatra lost more than her lover; she also lost her political adviser and teacher, the man who had taught her much about Rome's Byzantine politics and the skills of leadership.

Upon Caesar's death, Cleopatra knew her influence in Rome was on the wane. She wisely decided to return home to Egypt and regain her throne. During this time, she clashed frequently with another brother who had ascended to the throne, Ptolemy XIV. This troublesome impediment to her career she dispatched quickly. Ptolemy was poisoned and replaced by Cleopatra's son by Caesar, Ptolemy Caesar.

Thus in one swift move, Cleopatra removed a key rival, replacing him with her own flesh and blood. With Caesar gone from her life, Cleopatra settled into her rule of Egypt. In a few short years, however, she would encounter another Roman leader, Mark Antony, a man, like his predecessor Caesar, with more than politics on his mind.

While living in Rome with Caesar, Cleopatra had met Antony briefly, when he was a military commander and politician of some repute. After Caesar died, Antony tried to take over the throne and found his way blocked by Octavian, the nephew and adopted son of Caesar. Since neither man would give up his desire to take total control of Rome, they built an uneasy alliance wherein they would share power. After defeating Caesar's murderers at the Battle of Philippi, they divided Rome and her territories. Antony took control of the Roman-backed territories of the eastern Mediterranean. As fate and geography would have it, this included Egypt and, of course, Cleopatra.

During an inspection of his lands, Antony met Cleopatra again and fell madly in love with her. Plutarch describes her famous arrival to meet Antony at Cilicia, which is in what is today southeastern Turkey:

> ... she ostentatiously displayed a mocking contempt for [Antony's] orders by sailing up the Cydnus river in a barge with a gold poop, flying purple sails, while the rowers plied the waters with silver oars in harmony with the music of the flute, complemented by pipes and lutes. Cleopatra herself reclined beneath a golden canopy, adorned as if she were the goddess Venus, while boys dressed as Cupids, standing on either side, fanned her, as if in a painting. Her most beautiful handmaids, dressed as [sea nymphs]

*and Graces, stood at the rudders and the ropes of the sails. Marvelous fragrances from the burning of incense spread from the barge to the river banks.*

Cleopatra, it seemed, knew how to make a grand entrance. But in her era, such female showiness was unheard of. Men made the decisions—and the conspicuous appearances; women were expected to fulfill whatever role was required of them, be it housewife, slave, worker, or courtesan. Cleopatra changed all that. Her grand entrances (and exits) were not accidental. Nor were they unimportant. Leadership, after all, is—to some degree—about appearances.

Antony spent the winter months with Cleopatra in her capital city of Alexandria. One year later, Antony returned to Rome in an attempt to reconcile and rebuild his fragile working relationship with Octavian. To cement their leadership agreements, Antony agreed to marry Octavian's sister, Octavia, and keep control of his half of the Roman empire.

But the bereft Antony discovered that he could not live without Cleopatra at his side. Less than three years after his marriage to Octavia, Antony left her and returned to be with Cleopatra in Egypt. As you might imagine, this abandonment of his sister by Mark Antony did not sit well with Octavian. He had sent his sister and a legion of troops to meet with Antony in Athens, but the latter decided not to come. At this point in his life, Antony had all but decided to stay with Cleopatra and establish himself as her co-leader in Egypt.

At a huge royal "coming out" party in Alexandria, Cleopatra named herself and her children the rulers of a newly expanded Egypt which included territories once held dear by Octavian. Enraged by this political slap in the face, Octavian called Antony a traitor and Cleopatra a foreign seductress who wanted to destroy Rome.

Within two years from this opening salvo, Octavian had Antony stripped of his Roman political powers, ran his supporters out of Rome, and declared war on Cleopatra and her country. Interestingly, Octavian did not mention Antony in his declaration of war. He knew his supporters would not agree to a war that included Antony, who was still a Roman in the eyes of many.

Antony quickly marshaled Cleopatra's own naval forces to battle Octavian's troops. But since many of Antony's Roman supporters could not support a woman (even one as forceful as Cleopatra), they had a difficult time rallying behind her as the commander of Egyptian military forces. Further, they questioned her motives and felt sure that she was far too influential. Although Cleopatra had a powerful navy and other soldiers at the ready to battle Octavian, her forces were defeated, forcing her to retreat back to Egypt. During a bold (but ultimately flawed) effort to move her wooden navy ships overland to the Red Sea, Cleopatra was finally betrayed by an outraged Arabian king who burnt her fleet to cinders. Cleopatra soon found herself increasingly vulnerable as Octavian's ground forces moved in to destroy her.

Even Antony, a brave warrior in his own right, could not stave off Octavian's troops as they pressed in from all sides. Certain that the end was near, Antony chose death before dishonor, using a sword to kill himself in Alexandria before Octavian could capture him. Despite this final ignominy, he had, according to Plutarch, lived well:

> *Lastly, he entreated her not to grieve over his misfortunes, but to remember that he had won the greatest renown and power of any man in the world and that these accomplishments brought him happiness.*

Eleven days later, her life wrenched by the violent deaths of the two rulers she loved, Cleopatra also took her own life.

For all her faults—she was a demanding, difficult leader—Cleopatra chose to die with all the dignity she could muster. As was common in the ancient eras, suicide was more acceptable than capture, imprisonment, or subsequent capital punishment. The import of this ultimate sacrifice was not lost on her rival, Octavian. As Plutarch put it:

> *Although Cleopatra's death angered Octavian, he was impressed by her noble spirit, and decreed that her body be entombed with Antony's in a royal fashion.*

Following his victory, Octavian spared the lives of the twins born of Cleopatra and Antony, but had Ptolemy Caesar, the son by Cleopatra and Caesar, quickly killed. Octavian's position as the new ruler of both Rome and Egypt was now secure.

### Charisma 101: Who Has It, How to Get It

Cleopatra was, as Plutarch makes clear, a charismatic leader—a person who grabs the soul, the attention, the imagination of her followers. Sure, her considerable power came from her vast wealth and her membership in a family of great power. When all this was not enough to enable her to achieve her goals, she resorted to the creation of what could only be called magnetic charm. She relied, as Plutarch put it, "most of all on herself and on the magic and spells created by her charm."

Does this mean that charisma can be learned? Perhaps. Some, not surprisingly, believe that leaders are born with it: you either have it or you don't. After all, the word charisma derives from the Greek word for *gift*. Others, however, argue that, as in the case of Cleopatra, charisma can be learned.

One expert has even suggested that leaders short on charisma use his four-step model to increase their "charisma quotient." First, he recommends a thorough assessment of followers' needs, accompanied by the development of goals and a vision aimed at meeting these goals. Second, the leader must develop a change strategy and share these goals with other members of the organization. Third, commitment to the vision must be engendered. And, finally, the leader must convince everyone involved that there is a good chance that the vision can be attained.

Lest you think that this kind magic is limited only to ancient characters, consider the career of a modern-day Cleopatra, Mary Kay Ash. How did she build a $600+ million company? She identified the needs of constituents (followers, stockholders, suppliers, etc.), developed a clear vision, and convinced thousands of female sales consultants that her vision was attainable.

But part of charisma is, of course, magical. Certain leaders in business and in politics possess the Cleopatra-like effect of lighting up a room or drawing attention to themselves in a positive way every time they enter the building. They have developed a positive posture, a way of carrying themselves, and a sense of magnetism that draws people to them.

Have you ever noticed how differently you feel about movie stars, TV celebrities, sports stars, and politicians when you see them in person, as opposed to on TV, on the movie screen, or in the newspapers? Even if you don't care for the person's acting abilities, status, personality, sport, or political values, there's something about seeing them live that sweeps you up in the moment. *That's* charisma.

Most of these people have learned to play to the crowd and give the people what they want—a chance to be in the same room or area with someone well-known, famous, or even infamous. (As you might recall, we pointed out Willie Stark's masterful ability to "play the crowd" in chapter 4.) There is a groundswell of excitement that surges through a meeting hall whenever the president of the United States comes in to speak. Whether you like his politics and policies or not is usually beside the point. For that brief moment in time, you get caught up in the pomp and circumstance that surrounds his appearance in front of you.

During these times, it's hard not to feel a swell of pride as you look upon someone famous who, like you, is a human being, but somehow vastly different. Cleopatra knew about this charismatic power and its effect upon the people she led. It helped her to sway her followers to her side and give them the strong sense that she was in charge and capable of handling anything.

Many well-known business leaders have this same sense of charisma. They know almost instinctively how to make the "grand entrance". Can you imagine Creative Artists Agency head Michael Ovitz or Disney CEO Michael Eisner walking into a room crowded with supporters and shareholders and going over to sit in the corner? Of course not. As we've suggested, personal charisma is a learned skill in many and inborn in a lucky few. What some dynamic business, professional, and political leaders lack in physical beauty, handsomeness, or good looks, they more than make up for with an inner strength or an inner power that says to all who encounter them, "I am somebody with important ideas and I want you to listen to them." Attention must be paid.

Charisma is not something you can order by mail, buy in a shop, or borrow from someone else. It is inside you and you must work hard to develop it. Think of charisma not as a showy or over-practiced flamboyance, but as a sense of great internal strength, balance, and what writer Ernest Hemingway called when he spoke of bullfighters who entered the ring with only a bull, a cape, and a sword, "grace under fire."

And charisma is not just empty flash and hollow outer beauty; it's much more internal. All great leaders in war have had it: George Patton, Douglas MacArthur, Winston Churchill, Ulysses S. Grant, Confederate General Robert E. Lee, Dwight D. "Ike" Eisenhower, Alexander the Great, Napoleon, Charles de Gaulle, and scores of others who lived and sometimes died on history's battlefields.

John Kennedy definitely had it, Golda Meir clearly had it, Ronald Reagan certainly had it, as did Margaret Thatcher; even Richard Nixon showed flashes of charisma on occasion. People want to be led by charismatic leaders, especially in business, where, somewhat like war, the risks are great and the rewards unpredictable.

Cleopatra used her natural and well-developed charisma to complete advantage. With it, she managed to lead a nation of disparate followers and successfully become an equal with two of the most powerful leaders of her era.

### Buffing the Fruit: Getting ahead by Knowing Your Audience

In the September 1994 issue of *Vanity Fair*, Contributing Editor Marjorie Williams writes, rather derogatorily, about the rise of former *New York Times* columnist and author Anna Quindlen:

> *When the 24-year-old Anna Quindlen first interviewed for a job at The New York Times, she followed a simple strategy: she told them what they wanted to hear. Specifically, when managing editor Seymour Topping asked her what her ultimate ambition was, she told him that she hoped to be a foreign correspondent—preferably with a posting to Germany. And when she reached the office of executive editor Abe Rosenthal, she said she yearned to cover Poland. Topping, she had learned from reading up on him, had been a correspondent in Berlin, and Rosenthal had won a Pulitzer Prize for his dispatches from Warsaw. This classic bit of apple-polishing paid off well: today, as the only woman to write a regular column on the op-ed page of the* Times—*and only the third woman ever to be assigned that plum—Quindlen is among the paper's stars, and one of a handful of candidates to manage the newspaper of record into the next century.*[2]

What's so wrong with that? Does this not sound like something Cleopatra would have done to improve her station in life? Since when is "apple-polishing" the same as doing careful research about the leaders you will meet, especially when they have something you want?

Where is it written that you should not use career-enhancing information to your competitive advantage? Isn't it reasonable to assume that in Ms. Quindlen's case the other applicants for the job also had access to the same information she did? It was certainly no secret that her prospective bosses had worked in Poland and (then) East Germany. She merely told her interviewers what she thought they wanted to hear. Her knowledge of their backgrounds tells us and them: "I've done my homework on you. I know where you have been and I know where I want to go."

## Cultural Diversity: Knowing It and Respecting It

As a leader, Cleopatra was unique in her understanding of the diverse cultures around her. We think, in fact, that she was miles ahead of many of today's mere managers who still rely on a cookie cutter approach to handling people from different ethnic backgrounds. Cleopatra's take on embracing, even celebrating, ethnic and cultural diversity was indeed prescient. For one thing, she knew that diversity was good for her "organizational bottom line." Thousands of years later, this bit of "Cleopatra culture" has been proven at scores of companies.

At a recent management get-together at chemical giant Hoechst Celanese, for example, a training group was split into teams (some made up of only white males, others composed of different races and sexes) to discuss ways in which the company might improve productivity and profits. The CEO, reported an article in *Fortune* magazine, was astonished. As he put it, "It was so obvious that the diverse team had the broader solutions. For the first time, we realized that diversity is a strength in problem-solving." [3]

The result of all this is that Hoechst Celanese is now recognized as a pioneer, doing exactly what Cleopatra would have recommended thousands of years ago. Recruiters at the company have since begun to search for, hire, and train women and a wide range of ethnic groups as part of their recruiting programs.

Business professors, too, are getting Cleopatra's message. At the University of North Texas, teams made up of diverse racial groups competed with more homogeneous teams in business simulation problems. The more alike teams performed better early on in the project, but the diverse teams consistently produced more innovative solutions to difficult problems.

Larry K. Michaelsen, one of the professors in charge of the project, said that "Cultural diversity in the U.S. workforce has sometimes been viewed as a dark cloud. Our results suggest that it has a silver lining." [4] Cleopatra would have been delighted, and not at all surprised.

If you are part of an organization of any size in a large to mid-size city, you will, in fact, come across ethnically or racially diverse groups of employees, managers, customers, vendors, and related people who interact with your company. Regardless of your own ethnic or racial background, part of good leadership is being sensitive enough to recognize and, more importantly, respect the diversity of these groups. Insensitivity, as almost everyone knows, can result in some truly embarrassing faux pas.

We recall, for example, a wire service story and photo in the newspapers many years ago where a politician demonstrated his complete lack of awareness for cultural taboos. In the photo, then-Speaker of the House Tip O'Neill is seen in China, with each of his big arms wrapped tightly around the shoulders of two young Chinese women. The photo shows O'Neill with a large grin on his face and the Chinese women grimacing politely on either side of him.

While we're sure O'Neill meant well, this photo example illustrates classic American ignorance about East Asian culture. As a general rule, Chinese people avoid public displays of affection and most forms of touching altogether. Chinese women are especially careful about touching other men and for O'Neill to wrap his arms around their shoulders must have caused them great embarrassment and discomfort. Better for O'Neill to have posed adjacent to the women and kept his hands at his sides.

Some western managers have a difficult time communicating with foreign-born employees, especially when it comes to the issue of eye contact. In many third-world and Asian countries, making direct eye contact is a sign of disrespect, especially where one person of power (the boss) is talking to a person of lesser power (the employee). So what some managers take as arrogance, inattentiveness, apathy, or disrespect is actually a cultural trait.

Putting your arm around certain foreign-born employees, making hard eye contact with them, raising your voice loudly, or otherwise showing no respect for their cultural practices is a sure way to cause communication problems on both sides. Any improper, impolite, or culturally ignorant action on your part can make their encounters with you difficult.

And while it's not necessary for you to learn eight languages like Cleopatra, it will certainly help your career if you have at least a familiarity with one other language besides your native tongue, especially if your organization does business on a global level. Ask yourself, "What new foreign language skills can I bring to my position and my company?

And more importantly, what alliances will these skills allow me to create on my own?"

Examples abound of executives who have improved themselves by learning the foreign languages of their customers, vendors, colleagues, and employees. We have a colleague who travels four times per year to his American company's French-owned manufacturer, where he spends up to two months working with French-speaking customers, assembly employees, and, of course, his executive counterparts. Although he hails from Texas, he learned to speak better-than-average French, and it has paid handsome dividends in terms of his worth to his company. Thanks to his language skills, it's he who gets to spend his summers in Paris, and not someone else from his office.

Maybe you'd prefer "south of the border"? It's possible. With the 1993 passage of the North American Free Trade Agreement (NAFTA), many companies have started to reevaluate their own labor, production, and manufacturing costs with an eye toward opening new plants in many parts of Mexico. A number of *Fortune* 500 companies already have *maquiladoras* or manufacturing plants in Mexico. This alliance with Mexico requires Spanish-language fluency of many executives who travel to Mexico. This is especially true of executives and managers whose parent companies are in border states like California, Arizona, New Mexico, and Texas.

Other savvy business leaders have tackled Japanese as their second business language of choice. With so much activity going on in the countries that make up the Pacific Rim, a solid grasp of Japanese can help western business people build a stronger position in the region. Other U.S. firms have looked to Taiwan and Hong Kong for new opportunities, where some knowledge of several of the difficult Chinese dialects is required. German has long been known as "the language of money," thanks to its use in Germany, Austria, Switzerland, and other European countries where so much international banking, finance, and currency trading takes place. Other more inventive entrepreneurs have tackled Russian as their second business language. With the need for new capitalistic businesses in the former Soviet Union, there is room for many new possibilities, as companies such as Pizza Hut, Pepsi-Cola, and McDonald's have so dramatically demonstrated.

As Cleopatra shows us, if you want to make friends rather than enemies, create new partnerships and build strong alliances, learn how to communicate well with your global audience.

## Using Shared Fate as a Problem Solver

As history has shown so clearly, as long as there have been people and land and strong feelings about ideas, there has also been conflict. The business world has not been immune. Since the dawn of commerce, there has always been competition, economic challenge, and internal and external warring going on at all levels of every marketplace.

Companies face their own battles for power, influence, and control, especially those where the established culture seems to promote conflict. Some organizations seem to thrive in a world of disharmony rather than harmony. Its leaders tend to be aggressive, control-oriented, and even egotistical enough to ruin good ideas and good people so that their own ideas win out. As you can attest if you've ever worked in a place where helmets and flak jackets are issued at the door, this kind of environment is hardly conducive to good business, happy employees, or organizational success in the long run.

Cleopatra and her allies Julius Caesar and Mark Antony also dwelled in a world plagued with turf battles, conflict among nations, and disharmony. Yet their efforts to strike a balance between dictatorship and laissez-faire benevolence helped them rule with more success than their less flexible and more autocratic counterparts.

For her part, Cleopatra offers us a good example of a coalitional leader; that is, she created like-minded groups around her to support her interests, plans, and goals. Whether it was with her brother as co-king, or Caesar as mentor/mate/leader, or Antony as mate/co-leader, she knew how to appeal to different people and groups in ways that made them see the wisdom behind her ideas.

This type of leadership is often identified with the idea of a "shared fate" between the leader and his or her people. In organizations, this leadership concept can best be illustrated through the "greater good" idea, which says in essence, "When you win, I win, and when you win, we all win, and when our group wins, the whole company succeeds." Some business people have a rare gift for distilling this broad and often abstract concept down to more concrete terms. By explaining that working toward common goals, first within your own area, and then for the rest of the organization, everybody benefits.

People won't work productively for you over the long term if they think you don't care about them, don't have their best interests at heart, and aren't on the same level with them. Being on the "same page," as it were, requires that you make it clear that you are working for them just as much as they are working for you. (The old saw "There is no 'I' in the word 'TEAM'" is true.)

### The Power of Vision: How to See in More than One Direction

Part of Cleopatra's strength as an alliance-builder came from her ability to see further into the future than her counterparts, especially the other Egyptian leaders. She was better able to consider the fate of her nation, knowing from early experience that her rule would be tenuous at best unless she developed relationships with people who shared her ideals and her vision.

In our continuing search for the characteristics of leadership, Cleopatra-style vision is certainly a powerful weapon. As a leader of your group or unit, you need to be able to see what others might miss. Much of what takes place in organizations, both the good and the bad, gets lost in the hustle and bustle of trying to complete daily work. Problems with systems, customers, products, deliveries, employees, and the like can prevent good leaders from looking ahead. "How can I look past today when my desk is filled with 'must-do' projects?" goes the common complaint in many fast-paced organizations.

"Visioning," therefore, is not easy. If you don't think you have the time to look ahead a bit, make it. The time to steer the boat away from the rocks comes long before they're ten feet ahead of the bow. Start with the following vision-based "scans" of what's going on around you.

- *The crows' nest view.*
  From here, you'll need to look all around your organization for what works and what clearly does not. Part of the art of management is about adjustment, especially timely adjustment. Be ready to look hard at the departments, services, and systems that flow around you, not just at your specific area. If you are in a position to make changes, make them. If not, get your ideas to someone who is.

- *The battle field view.*
  This requires some outside work. Get up from your desk, pack your briefcase, and leave the building. (Earlier we referred to this as getting out of your comfort zone.) Go out into your market and start asking questions—of your customers, of your vendors, of your suppliers, and of your business partners. Try to

make it a point to make a trip outside your office at least twice per year, just so you can get an idea of what is going on in your industry. Shop at your competitors, try new brands, and collect lots of feedback from all kinds of people.

- *The desk level view.*
  Start with your office, your unit, your team, or your department. How well do you all do things now and what changes or improvements will you need to make to keep on doing them right in the future? Which of your employees are "doers" and which are merely "watchers"? How do the policies and procedures in your company affect your group? How do things look from where you're sitting?

- *Look backwards.*
  Consider things from the customer's viewpoint. How easy is it to do business with your firm? Are your service systems and procedures set up to help or hinder the efforts of your front-line service providers? Start at the end of the customer's encounter with your firm and work backwards to the beginning. What and who works and what and who does not? Part of vision is making changes, especially when the feedback is not glowing.

- *The moccasins' view.*
  Walk a mile in someone else's shoes if you can. Test yourself and your abilities. Do the work that your people do. Serve customers, meet with vendors and suppliers or other people who come into contact with your company and whom you might not know otherwise. Introduce yourself to new customers. Change your perspective by seeing how other people come into contact with the many parts of your organization.

Cleopatra's ideas of leadership, as scholars Thomas R. Martin and Richard Larson have put it, added a fascinating alternative to traditional Roman rule. For us, her story offers insight into leadership development in the face of such obstacles as gender discrimination. Clearly, Cleopatra's tale is full of the same kind of problems and challenges that confront today's organizations and the people in them. When you consider the fact that leadership, above all else, is a process of influencing others, you begin to understand why the life of Cleopatra is so instructive. Consider these lessons:

- *Connecting is everything.*

  The operative word is, of course, *networking*. At this, Cleopatra was without equal. Her formula was simple. She could best meet her leadership needs by connecting with the needs and desires of Caesar and Antony. Such ability to discover, embrace, and enthusiastically support key players' goals and aspirations is as much a part of successful leadership today as it was in Cleopatra's time. And, you'll be happy to know, females seem to be better equipped for this sort of thing than males. In her breakthrough book entitled *The Female Advantage*, Sally Helgeson pointed out that, in many ways, women have an edge on leading. They disdain traditional organizational structures like the hierarchical ladder. Instead, they place themselves at the center of things and "connect" to all those around them as if by invisible strands or threads.[5]

- *You are a "transformer," not a "transactor."*

  Transformational leaders, like Cleopatra, promote new ideas and inspire change. Mere transactional leaders, on the other hand, maintain stability and the status quo. In the language of Plato's "Allegory of the Cave" (chapter 1), they hugely enjoy staying in their comfort zone. As a transformational leader, you have four jobs to do: (1) recognize your colleagues' and subordinates' unique abilities by reinforcing their key roles in your organization, thereby moving them beyond self-interest to self-sacrifice for the good of the organization; (2) build feelings of trust and loyalty, thereby achieving higher levels of productivity; (3) use charisma and shared vision rather than position power to get your team to reach and exceed its goals; and (4) inspire and energize team members to exceed their (and your) expectations.

- *Know your position.*

  We all have different sources of power which give us the ability to influence others. Cleopatra's intially came from her position as a member of the Ptolemaic family. As we saw, however, this was not enough. Cleopatra then developed an additional power base by carefully constructing a kind of charisma. Modern organizational theorists would have been impressed. Two of them, J. R. P. French and B. Raven, have discovered five classic interpersonal sources of power. Check the list to see what your power (and that of your boss) is based on: (1) Expert power is based on high status or access to key information, (2) Referent power (charisma) results from attractiveness (appearance, fame, respect, etc.), (3) Reward power goes to those who control rewards like salary, promotions, etc, (4) Coercive power is based on the ability to punish others, and (5) Legitimate power comes from the leader's position to give orders. Careful here. If you seem to score high on such bases of power as "coercive," "legitimate," and/or "reward," watch out. You badly need an infusion of referent power or expert power if you are to truly form your group into a committed team. By the way, studies have shown that women tend to use personal power (based on expert and referent power) while men prefer a "command and control" style of leadership.

- *Construct your own charisma.*

  Charisma is capable of grabbing the souls of your followers, giving you a powerful hold on their emotions and feelings. Cleopatra, as Thomas R. Martin and Richard Larson have pointed out, realized that "... the charisma of a leader was a learned skill, not a gift that one either enjoyed or lacked by sheer dumb luck or divine favor. That one should construct his or her own charisma is one lesson that Cleopatra's career teaches."

- *Build coalitions.*

  Cleopatra was a great alliance builder, using heartfelt appeals to develop coalitions with her friends and her enemies. Her technique was simple. She connected with supporters of her vision for Egypt and she created a sense of obligation in others to repay her favors. She even resorted to trading something she had in exchange for what she desired from others.

## CHAPTER 6

# GETTING THE REALLY BIG ONE: CAPTAIN AHAB'S QUEST FOR MOBY DICK

*Swerve me? Ye cannot swerve me... The path to my fixed purpose is laid with iron rails, whereon my soul is grooved to run*
—CAPTAIN AHAB

**KEY POINTS**

- TEAM BUILDING
- OBSESSIVE FOCUS
- THE LEADER AS MONOMANIAC
- THE QUEST

Someone once said that Al Neuharth, founder of the *USA Today* newspaper, was the kind of guy who would go after Moby Dick with a knife and a jar of tartar sauce. Like many entrepreneurs, this modern-day Captain Ahab truly was and is a monomaniac on a mission.

You may remember reading about his literary counterpart in Herman Melville's great novel. And if you're like many people, you probably wondered then why you were forced to slog your way through this classic, yet seemingly irrelevant, book. But as you'll discover, this story contains superbly relevant connections to managing and leading. Ahab's ship, the *Pequod*, is after all, a business, with a clear objective to search for whales whose blubber can be made into oil to light the lamps of New England. It's owned by a group of shareholders and its motive is profit.

Indeed the *Pequod* is a replica of any organization. And Melville's *Moby Dick* is one of the best books ever written on goal-setting. It chronicles how its central character, Captain Ahab, transforms a group of rag-tag sailors into a committed team by using several important, but frequently overlooked, goal-setting secrets. Melville wrote other books before and after this one, but it is primarily for this tale of men going down to the sea in ships after whales that he is remembered. (Our enthusiasm for the leadership wisdom conveyed by Herman Melville is unallayed, however. In chapter 9, we tease out the leadership lessons contained in another of his works, the novella *Billy Budd*.)

Melville began his story of Ahab and his quest for the white whale when he was thirty years old and had already written five novels. Like *Moby Dick*, the other five books all centered around sailing ships and sailing men, drawing on the author's experience working on ocean vessels. Although his novels are not strictly autobiographical, it's obvious from a review of each of them that much of what Melville knew about life aboard ships influenced much of what he wrote. Authors like Melville, writing before the turn of the nineteenth century, frequently relied on a popular device: a tale about the "big adventure," an epic literal or figurative journey that took the main character from one set point in his or her life to another, and changed that person forever. For Melville, the journey was Ahab's quest for the great white whale Moby Dick. And while his tale did not necessarily break new ground in terms of its "epic proportions," his was the "big book" of its day about man versus beast.

If the language of *Moby Dick* sounds a bit stilted or archaic, keep in mind that Melville's writing style was influenced by what he knew of Shakespeare and what he saw in the work of his friend and literary boon companion, Nathaniel Hawthorne. In addition, in his era, it was common to write about people, places, and things in such a way as to try to divine the symbolic truths behind them. Therefore, a sailing ship wasn't just a sailing ship. It represented a collection of men put together to test the ocean and its creatures. Whales weren't just whales, but rather mythical leviathans, embodiments of evil, who roamed the seas at will. In this respect there was always more to a Melville story than "just the story."

That doesn't lead to brevity. As director-comedian Woody Allen once said, "I took a speedreading course once. We read *War and Peace*. It's about Russians." And looking at the text for Moby Dick, a book of 135 chapters and nearly 500 pages, it's tempting to summarize the story by saying that it is "about a big whale." It is that, of course, and more ... much more. Melville's *Moby Dick* is about a leader, his quest, and the effects of this quest on himself and the people in his organization.

## Ahab: Obsessive-Compulsive Behavior at Work

If you don't remember Moby Dick too well from school, or if you were never asked to read it, it's important to know that the book is narrated not by its central character, Captain Ahab, but by Ishmael, one of the sailors on the *Pequod*.

Indeed, the first three words of the book, "Call me Ishmael," are among the most recognizable in literature. Melville chose to use a third party, an objective voice, to tell the tale of a captain's hunt for the great white whale. Ishmael was a natural, offering a contemplative voice of reason in the book.

Whale hunting was big business in the years before the U.S. Civil War. Whaling ships left from both coasts in search of whales of all types, with the sperm whale a favorite target because it yielded so much oil. Syndicates, groups of individual investors who owned shares in ships, paid the bills for the captains and their crews to ply the oceans in search of as many whales as they could harpoon, slaughter, render, and store before returning home. These investors succeeded or failed along with the captain and his shipmates. No whales meant no money for the investors, the captain, or the crew. It was with this apparent mission that Captain Ahab and his crew sailed the *Pequod* out of Nantucket harbor in search of Moby Dick.

But Ahab has a hidden motive, one quite different from the pursuit of whales and the collection of their oil for manufacture. Narrated by Ishmael, who has signed on as an able-bodied sailor on the *Pequod*, we learn that Ahab has lost his leg in a battle with a whale. (It is not until much later, in chapter 36, that we officially learn from Ahab that it is Moby Dick who has "unmasted" his limb.) One of Ahab's business associates, Captain Peleg, briefly tells Ishmael how it happened:

> *I know that he was never jolly; and I know that on the passage*
> *back home, he was a little out of his mind for a spell; but it was the*
> *sharp shooting pains in his bleeding stump that brought that about,*

*as anyone might see. I know too, that ever since he lost his leg last voyage by that accursed whale, he's been a kind of moody—desperate moody, and savage sometimes; but that will all pass off.*[1]

And even before he ever meets the man, Ishmael senses there is something evil about Ahab. Melville's superb foreshadowing tells us that this will be no ordinary whaling voyage. Its purpose will be to seek and destroy the source of Ahab's past and present pain and the object of his unrelenting revenge, Moby Dick.

As the book opens, Ishamael makes his way on a rainy December day to a boarding house in New Bedford. He is given a room to share with another sailor, Queequeg, a huge, tattoo-covered South Sea Islander whose specialty is harpooning whales. While Ishmael may be an adventure-seeking young man hoping to make his living on the open seas, his mate Queequeg is nothing less than a whale warrior. He carries his razor-sharp harpoon everywhere with him. Appallingly, he even uses it to shave.

As Ishmael and Queequeg make plans to travel to nearby Nantucket to get on a whaling ship, a heavy rainstorm sends them looking for shelter and they end up in the Whaleman's Chapel. In the church, Father Mapple gives a somewhat Biblical, hair-raising sermon about Jonah and the great whale who swallowed him.

Arriving later at Nantucket, Ishmael searches for a proper whaling ship and chooses the *Pequod*. Seeing that Queequeg is an expert harpoon man, the ship's fitters hire him as well. Soon after, Ishmael asks to meet Captain Ahab, only to be told he is staying in his quarters—a place he will remain until the *Pequod* is far from shore.

On Christmas morning, the men of the *Pequod* set sail for what they believe will be a business-as-usual whaling cruise. But their leader has other ideas: to find and kill one whale in particular.

During the cruise, Ishmael is startled one day to find Captain Ahab out on deck, enjoying a rare moment of warm weather and calm seas. The effect of seeing Ahab disturbs Ishmael:

*He looked like a man cut away from the stake, when the fire has overrunningly wasted all the limbs without consuming them, or taking away one particle from their compacted aged robustness. His whole high, broad form, seemed made of solid bronze, and shaped in an unalterable mould.... Threading its way out from among his grey hairs, and continuing right down one side of his tawny neck, till it disappeared in his clothing, you saw a slender rod-like mark, lividly whitish.... So powerfully did the whole grim aspect of Ahab affect me, and the livid brand which streaked it, that for the first few moments I hardly noted that not a little of this overbearing grimness was owing to the barbaric white leg upon which he partly stood.*

Ishmael is completely unnerved by the sight of Ahab, from the vivid scar on his face to the polished gleam of his ivory-carved artificial leg anchored firmly into a hole drilled into the ship's deck. His evil countenance sends chills through Ishmael's soul.

Later, we—and the crew—learn of Ahab's monomania: they will search the Seven Seas for the whale with the crooked jaw and the white skin known as Moby Dick. Ahab promises a reward of an ounce of Spanish gold to the first man who spots the whale and he tells them they cannot rest until this whale is caught and killed. His speech is unforgettable:

*Aye, aye! It was that accursed white whale that razeed me; made a poor pegging lubber of me for ever and a day!...and I'll chase him round [the Cape of] Good Hope and round the [Cape] Horn, and round the Norway maelstrom, and round perdition's flames before I give him up. And this is what ye have shipped for men! To chase that white whale on both sides of land, and over all sides of earth, till he spouts black blood and rolls fin out. What say ye, men, will ye splice hands on it, now? I think ye do look brave.*

Not surprisingly, the members of the *Pequod's* crew, excepting Starbuck, Ahab's first mate, enthusiastically embraced their captain's challenge. The men cheer in unison; they have all sided with Ahab, save Starbuck, who warns:

*I am game for his crooked jaw, and for the jaws of death too, Captain Ahab, if it fairly comes in the way of the business we follow; but I came here to hunt whales, not my commander's vengeance. How many barrels will thy vengeance yield thee even if thou gettest it, Captain Ahab?.... To be enraged with a dumb thing, Captain Ahab, seems blasphemous.*

Starbuck, it seems, is the lone dissenter, the one voice of reason. He is, of course, correct; going after one whale merely for revenge seems foolhardy; it puts the entire enterprise at risk and it deters the *Pequod* from its original mission and responsibility, to hunt whales, fill the hold with oil, and then head for home and market.

Yet the crew of the *Pequod* takes to searching for the elusive white whale with reckless abandon. As they sail through different oceans, catching, slaughtering, and storing whales and their oils, they encounter other whaling ships hard at the same task. Each time they meet a new ship, Ahab's request is the same: "Have ye seen the White Whale?"

But Ahab is not out to exchange pleasantries with passing ships. He is on a quest and time is wasting. He must know exactly where Moby Dick is so he can head toward him straightaway. Soon the *Pequod* meets the ship *Enderby*, and when Ahab asks of Moby Dick, the *Enderby* captain shows him his ivory arm. He has lost the limb in a recent battle with Moby Dick. While the *Enderby*'s captain feels strongly that Moby Dick should be left alone because he is so dangerous and so adept at killing and injuring crewmen, Ahab thinks differently. Nothing the *Enderby* captain can say will dissuade Ahab. He leaves quickly for the *Pequod* so he can begin the chase anew.

But there seems to be a delay. First mate Starbuck tells Ahab that several huge whale-oil casks are leaking. He wants Ahab's permission to heave to and have the crew search for the leak and make the repairs. Ahab, poring over charts in his obsessive search for Moby Dick, will have none of it. He raises his musket and orders Starbuck back to his assigned task—finding Moby Dick as quickly as possible. So much for delays.

Even after suffering through a severe typhoon which nearly destroys several parts of the ship, Ahab vows to continue on. The *Pequod* comes across another ship, the *Rachel*, whose captain tells Ahab that they have just finished a battle with Moby Dick and that his son was lost in the fight. When the *Rachel*'s captain asks for help searching for survivors of the encounter, Ahab refuses and presses on with his search.

All this nearly ends when Starbuck considers killing Ahab and freeing the crew from what he understandably sees as a dangerous, foolhardy voyage. But he decides not to act, leaving Ahab to his own devices. (Ahab later admits his quest for the white whale is maniacal and that he is so driven by the thought of victory he can do nothing to stop himself.)

Finally, the *Pequod* sights Moby Dick and the chase begins. On the first day, the harpooners hit the whale which angrily capsizes Ahab's small whaling boat. All the crew is rescued and make it back to the *Pequod*. On the second day, the harpooners hit him again, and once more, Moby Dick sinks Ahab's small whaling boat and again Ahab is rescued. This time, however, several *Pequod* crew members in other whaling boats lose their lives. On the third and last day, Ahab drives a harpoon into Moby Dick and the crazed mammal goes on a rampage. Ahab orders the other small whaling boats back to the *Pequod* so that he can fight the beast himself.

He heaves his last harpoon into the whale just as the animal smashes its huge forehead against the *Pequod*'s bow. As the harpoon hits its target, the rope catches Ahab around the neck and he is pulled into the sea to drown. The *Pequod*, badly damaged by the whale's crushing blows, sinks with all hands, save Ishmael, who clings to a coffin made during the trip by his friend Queequeg. After floating for nearly a day, Ishmael is rescued by the crew of the *Rachel* who are in the area to look for their own missing mates.

As you can see, Moby Dick is a big book because it tells a big story. The members of the *Pequod* are an ensemble of diverse characters, each with their own goals for life, each with their own duties aboard the ship, and each with their own reasons for being on the ship in the first place.

Some have gone to sea for the money; others, like Ishmael, for the adventure; and others, like Queequeg and Starbuck, simply because it is what they do, they are whalemen. But for one man, Ahab, the trip is an unstoppable journey that will finally pit him against his great nemesis, Moby Dick.

### The Sins of Single-Mindedness

For leaders, Melville's story of Moby Dick suggests a very common problem: putting all your eggs in one basket and becoming so obsessed with an idea that requires such a tremendous use of capital, assets, and people that, if it fails, it does irreparable damage to the organization. Such nasty things *do* happen. Take the case of Borden Inc., the home of a bovine icon, Elsie the cow. As a scathing report in *Forbes* recently put it, the troubled firm is "overmilked, underfed and abused, Elsie is one sick cow."

Borden's precipitous downfall is a story of near-Ahab dimensions. The company's debt recently sank as fast as the *Pequod*, from A+ to BBB. Its stock plunged to a ten-year low. It had to pay junk bond rates to borrow. In 1994, the $5.5 billion business struggled unsuccessfully to raise cash and pay down its Brobdingnagian debt, even resorting to the doomsday factoring of its accounts receivable to put a little money in the till.

What happened? According to the *Forbes* report, Borden's downward spiral began in the 1980s when its CEO went on an Ahab-like hunt for acquisitions, purchasing nearly one hundred companies. So mesmerized were Borden executives by the thrill of the hunt that they forget to manage well what they'd already captured. Ice cream, where Borden was once a leader with its Lady Borden brand, is a case in point. Not paying attention meant that the company missed out almost entirely in the high-margin, premium ice cream segment of the market. And in pasta, a dynamic and profitable market, management's inattentiveness meant that Borden still sells low-margin spaghetti while competitors like Lipton and Rice-a-Roni market hugely profitable specialties like fettucine Alfredo.[2]

The lesson in all this is, of course, that monomaniacal attention to distant goals, no matter how laudable, can lead precipitously to horribly fouled-up management of the business today.

### Going on "Nantucket Sleigh Rides"
Herman Melville gives us the name of this unpleasant phenomenon: a "Nantucket sleigh ride." In the case of the whaling business, it was the men in the small whaling boats, lowered into the water from the mother ship, who did the real work. Filled with tillermen, harpooners and oarsmen, the boats rowed out into harm's way, the men speared huge whales with as many harpoons as they could toss and then held on for dear life as the animal thrashed, twisted, and dove for the bottom of the sea. The phrase describes this operation, the most hazardous moment in the hunt.

Put simply, when you're on a Nantucket sleigh ride, you can win big, or you can lose everything. Ahab wanted to confront the mighty white whale more than anything else in his life. He was willing to risk everything—the lives of his crew, the safety of his ship, the value of his whale oil cargo, and the money invested by the syndicators who owned the *Pequod*. He got his chance to battle with Moby Dick once again and it finally killed him.

How many "Nantucket sleigh ride" projects have you seen your organization or others tackle with this same obsessive sense that says, "We will fail or die trying"? Have you been so committed to an idea, a project, a policy, or an approach that you failed to see the impact on your division or work group? Did you ignore the warning signs that told you, as Starbuck tried to warn Ahab, "Turn back! Stop! Go no further!"?

One of the main themes that emerges from our discussions about *Moby Dick* is the need for balanced leadership. This could be best defined as the ability to see the big picture, to keep your eye on your main goal, but to not go overboard (literally or figuratively) in your quest to achieve it. There is a fine line between being committed to an idea and being obsessed with it. There is an even finer line between risking it all and taking calculated risks. The annals of corporate history are filled with stories of leaders who grabbed the dice, blew on them for luck, rolled them hard, and lost it all.

And yet for all his faults, Ahab was a great team builder. He managed to motivate a ragtag group of sailors, ranging from journeymen whalemen to novices, toward one cause: "Let's find the white whale and kill it." And for their part, the crew looked at this battle-scarred veteran of the whaling wars and agreed. They worked with renewed vigor, even in the face of difficult odds, bad weather, rough seas, a three-year trip away from their home port—and only Starbuck "challenged the boss."

## Leader as Quasi-Maniac
With his missing leg, his scarred face, and his brooding outlook, Ahab's demeanor told everyone who met him, "I mean business. If you expect to make it with me, you need to show me you mean business too." Such a "this-is-serious-stuff" persona is not altogether inappropriate in today's—and yesterday's—competitive business world.

Take the case of Henry Ford, for example. During his earliest days as the premier American automobile manufacturer, Henry Ford was known as a hard—even Ahab-like—taskmaster. Once he got his mind around an idea, he simply would not take "no" for an answer. His quest was a simple one: make a low-priced, mass-produced, and mass-marketed automobile. As the father of the auto assembly line, Ford employed hundreds of technical experts who helped him make his cars better, smarter, and, most importantly, faster.

One story describes his monomania. It seems he once ordered his mechanical engineers to build him an eight-cylinder engine block. Away the engineers went, armed with their papers, models, tools, and prototypes. They returned and said, "We're sorry, but it just can't be done."

"Go back and try again. This time, think harder about what it is I want you to do for me and then do it."

So the engineers returned to their offices, labs, and test sites and puzzled over Ford's challenge once more. And again, they could not come up with an effective design for an eight-cylinder engine block. "We're sorry, but we're positive this time that it's just not possible."

And again, with Ahab-like obstinacy, Ford stood his ground. "I want it. I need it. It's part of what will make this company great and you will build it for me. I will not be denied. You *will* go back and create this engine for me." And so they did. After countless hours, the designers came back to Henry Ford with the complete design for what is now known as the in-line V-8 engine.

The difference, of course, between Ford and Ahab, is that Ford didn't risk the health and safety of his entire organization on this one engine design. He wanted it and he wanted it badly, but not at the expense of everything he had worked so hard for up to that point. Too, the eight-cylinder engine was only one of many of Ford's big goals.

Ahab, though, made the slaying of the great white whale his one and only unwavering quest. His monomaniacal obsession drove him and his crew to their deaths. And it was no wonder. For all his strengths as a leader, Ahab lacked what we call "controlled charisma." What Ahab failed to see was that leaderly obsession must be tempered with a sense of reality. That old saw, "All things in moderation" applies here. Ahab's major fault was that he didn't pay enough attention to the warning signs around him; he refused to take the advice of his closest associate (the first mate Starbuck); and he let his emotions interfere with good judgement.

The secret of balanced leadership, we think, is to be a "controlled" monomaniac with a mission, to have a plan to harness your positive obsession, and to set attainable goals couched within realistic and acceptable limits.

### The Whale as Quest: Every Organization Needs a Big Goal
Every good leader needs a figurative "great whale" to chase from time to time. The need for a grand goal is what drives people and their organiza-

tions to new heights. It's important for you and your people to break a sweat—physically, mentally, psychologically, and even spiritually—from time to time.

What we're saying here is that every organization needs a quest and questor. That old bromide, "management by objectives," has a venerable and long history. Part of this, of course, is that it's disarmingly simple. It makes good sense: "Set a goal for yourself. You may not reach it, but you'll go a lot further in life than if you don't know what you want to achieve."

In an organizational setting, MBO boils down to this: The head honchos set the overall strategic goal for the organization. Then the subordinates set their goals and are given wide latitude on how to achieve them. Chaos is contained by the simple expedient of frequent performance appraisals. However, things are not that simple. It should come as no surprise that MBO has failed more times than it has worked, due, no doubt, to the mountains of paperwork it generated and the cumbersome review process it required.

But there's more than bureaucratic make-work that's wrong with MBO. Its lockstep "You-will-achieve-X-by-Y-date-or-suffer-the-consequences" dictum does nothing less than diminish the human spirit. And its insistence on controllability and quantifiability assumes an elegant simplicity that just does not exist in the real world. Furthermore, its fixated notion that there is only one best way to arrive at a desired result encourages what in today's management world is a very dangerous malady known as tunnel vision.

What we call managing-by-*quest* is rapidly replacing management-by-objectives in corporate America. MBQ demands not a simple quantifiable goal, i.e., "Sell 2.5 million widgets by June 30," but a near-transcendent, overarching organizational purpose. Sound impossible? Instead of the 2.5 million widgets goal, try saying, "We will change the way the world does business by making and successfully marketing a revolutionary, earth-shattering new widget! We will become the masters of the widget universe!"

Too lofty? Too crazy? Perhaps. But going on a quest, as opposed to merely "managing by objectives," is as old as mankind. If you doubt this, think of how great quest stories have permeated all of history. Recall Joan of Arc, who led France to a victorious quest over its British invaders; King Arthur's quest for the Holy Grail; Moses's quest for the "promised land"; Odysseus's quest for his return to Ithaca; and finally, Captain Ahab's quest for the great white whale.

The point is that organizations, like these mythic characters, have an innate need for the quest. "Questing" elevates mere goal-setting by encouraging circular, rather than linear, thinking; that is, you might actually learn some things as you meander for a bit. It stimulates exploration and curiosity (while MBO can easily blind you to the possibilities); it promotes intuitive as well as rational thinking; it suggests that process is often as important as the end itself; and it embraces the reality of our highly unstructured world. Put simply, questing can transform you and your team into a learning organization.

But just saying, "We ought to do something around here to raise sales" won't do it. Your company's big goal, or your big quest has to be something specific, definable, and slightly out of reach.

### Mission Statements and Marching Orders

While Ahab may have been an enigmatic man, he was upfront and straight to the point when it came to setting goals. He communicated his ideas and thoughts to his shipmates in nothing less than concrete terms. He didn't say, "Let's go look for whales and if we stumble onto Moby Dick, we might take a shot at him." He said, "The sole purpose of this voyage is to catch and kill Moby Dick." And, importantly, he waited until the *Pequod* was already well underway at sea before he made this big announcement.

Put simply, he picked his moment: He knew when to call the big meeting and how to deliver the big idea. You need look no further than American politics for many good examples of similar "stretch" goals. Consider President John Kennedy's Ahab-size quest in 1962, "We will put a man on the moon by the end of this decade." In the summer of 1969, we did just that. Or recall the message President George Bush used to motivate the country to support Operations Desert Shield and Desert Storm, "We will free Kuwait." Even though he had a problem with the "vision thing," he was able to rally a nation behind his quest in the Persian Gulf.

Such grand goals are not the sole province of politics or, for that matter, great literature. "Stretch targets" are increasingly replacing business-as-usual incremental objectives in businesses across America. And "doing the impossible" is the anthem heard throughout firms whose bosses are asking employees to jump over seemingly impossible goals in a single leap. As GE's Jack Welch recently told a reporter, "We used to nudge the peanut along, moving from, say, 4.73 inventory turns to 4.91. Now we want big, stretch results like ten turns or 15 turns."[3]

It's catching. CSX, the $9.5 billion railroad and shipping company, recently challenged a tiny unit of its railroad business to move from breakeven to big profits in one year while at the same time eliminating rail cars, locomotives, and coal hoppers. "I thought the goals were impossible," said the hapless executive sent to run the business. Yet the impossible *did* happen. Twenty percent of the rail cars and 25 percent of the locomotives are history, depreciation and operating costs are down, and—get this—profits, as well as sales volume, are up.

And at 3M, an outfit already renowned for innovation, the CEO recently ordered that no less than 30 percent of revenues must come from products introduced within the past four years. Such an Ahab-style goal not only sent tremors throughout the company, it also got things galloping along in R&D and new product development. One notable result? Scotch-Brite Never Rust soap pads, designed to put an end to those nasty rust-laden scouring pads we're all used to. Introduced at a record clip, this unlikely revolution in scrubbing (they're made from recycled plastic bottles, not from steel wool) has already achieved a 22 percent share of market.

But, while accepting the challenge to take on stretch goals, 3M didn't stop with their new fangled Brillo Pads. They've also recently introduced a sponge containing an agent that stops bacteria before they can cause odor; a brightness-enhancing film that ends up on the screens of portable computers, thereby cutting the energy required to light the display; and a whole new line of coated abrasives. This corporate stretching is having superb results. After lackluster revenue growth of 1–2 percent in 1991–1993, 3M recently posted a 10 percent increase in revenues and an 8 percent increase in profits.

Even Boeing, long number one in its industry, is putting as much stretch into its management as it is in its stretch jets. There, management recently has insisted on (a) reducing the cost of manufacturing a plane by 25 percent in six years, and (b) reducing the time it takes to manufacture a plane from eighteen months to eight months in less than four years. The results so far are impressive: 747s and 767s get built in ten months.

Like CSX, 3M, Boeing (and the *Pequod*), every organization needs a grand goal—an operating plan for success. Leaders *know* that their grand goal is achievable; they're absolutely fixated on it. Leaders can come with one dozen reasons why they can achieve their goal. Mere managers can come up with one million reasons why trying to achieve the big goal is unworkable, a bad idea.

### Away All Boats: Preparing for Your Quest

"Questing"—especially during those first tentative steps—is a lot like house painting; it requires 80 percent preparation and 20 percent actual painting. And so it goes in business, where the necessity for plenty of pre-work and sweat equity can scare many mere managers away from committing to a big goal.

As you plan your quest, whether it involves changing the way the company serves its customers, developing new products or services, or opening an office overseas, realize that it will follow several predictable stages. In their engrossing article, "Corporate Change and the Hero's Quest," management gurus Robert J. Holder and Richard McKinney describe the three stages of the corporate, as well as the mythic, quest.

First comes separation and departure, stepping into the unknown, responding to the call of adventure. And if you think this is just mythical hocus-pocus, talk to any wily entrepreneur.

This is followed secondly by trials and victories of initiation which transform both the individual and the group into a team. This is not "initiation-as-usual"; it is initiation out of the past and into the future. And it involves countless trials. The bad news is that all this can hurt. The good news is that going through these trials together builds a sense of community, and a notion that "we're all in this together."

In the third and final stage of the quest, called "return and reintegration," the leader shares the vision, via rituals, with the larger community. This is what GE's Welch has done by introducing the concept of "work out," a ritualized process in which all employees discuss ways to improve productivity and quality, thereby transforming the culture of the company.

Do the article's authors believe that managing in today's environment is like white water rafting? You bet. Write Holder and McKinney:

> *Traditional planning is a dead end! Planned change has been the process for moving organizations into new conditions. It assumes that the future is predictable and there is an end state to be reached. The last ten years have shown us that these assumptions are no longer valid. Firms which acknowledge that new assumptions are needed have entered into adventurous change.*

So welcome to the daring new world of management-by-quest. As you examine the many intricacies of your quest, you can keep everything together by brainstorming, either alone or in groups. Start thinking big and don't scrimp on the paper you'll need to capture all your ideas and plans. Get some large pieces of paper, tape them to the walls, and hunker down. This technique is especially helpful in groups where everyone can contribute his or her ideas and then see the finished product on paper in front of them.

Think big, talk big, and write big. After all, this is not planning as usual—it is a quest. Now is the time to plan for every contingency, every detail, and every potential problem. The more you do at this stage and the harder you work before you take the big plunge (and leave your home port, or—need we add?—your comfort zone) the better. No one ever spent too much time planning, as long as they took action after they created those plans. After all, you've got to leave your office and start the journey sometime, otherwise it's not much of a quest, is it?

Ahab offers us a classic example of what it's like to be a relentless planner. He knew everything about the great white whale, where it would be, where his ship would find it, and what he would do when he came face-to-nose with it. Nothing was ad hoc for him, and nothing should be for you either. Just as Ahab knew what he wanted and, more importantly, what he needed to do and where he needed to go to get it, you should make the same commitment to planning.

Part of that is, of course, preparation. And clearing the decks. Before you begin your quest, be sure that you and your organization have jettisoned overboard everything that might get in the way. Here's the way Ishmael describes Ahab's process of deck-clearing:

> ... Some moments passed, during which the thick vapor came from his mouth in quick and constant puffs, which blew back again into his face. "How now," he soliloquized at last, withdrawing the tube, "this smoking no longer soothes. Oh, my pipe! Here have I been unconsciously toiling, not pleasuring,—aye, and ignorantly smoking to windward all the while; to windward, and with such nervous whiffs, as if, like the dying whale, my final jets were the strongest and fullest of trouble. What business have I with this pipe? This thing that is meant for sereneness, to send up mild white vapors among mild white hairs, not among torn iron-grey locks like

*mine. I'll smoke no more—" He tossed the still lighted pipe into the
sea. The fire hissed in the waves; the same instant the ship shot by
the bubble the sinking pipe made. With slouched hat, Ahab lurch-
ingly paced the planks.*

Ahab's pipe, clearly, represented peace, contemplation, comfort, and
relaxation. But his plans were made. It was the time for action, the time
to move forward. As he jettisoned this needless cargo overboard, the
*Pequod*, not surprisingly, surged forward. It, and its captain, could no
longer be burdened by such preoccupations.

This metaphor for jettisoning your corporate and personal deadwood
is a strong one. Too many companies cling to their flotsam and jetsam,
no matter how out of date, infeasible, or irrelevant it appears.

Whether it's unprofitable divisions, unproductive people, bad products or services, bad policies, or bad systems or strategies—if it's not
working, or if it gets in the way of your quest, or if it keeps you from
achieving your big goal—learn from Ahab: throw it overboard.

## Becoming Goal-Specific

Just as putting the big goal or the next quest into your sights puts a premium on careful planning, it also requires help. The bigger the goal, the
more help you'll need, now, later, and throughout your quest. Go out and
talk to people—those who work for you, those who work with you, and
especially senior executives, who may be in the position to approve or
disapprove your attempt at a big project. Now is not the time to hole up
in your office and wait for them to come to you. Get out, communicate
your big idea, gather feedback and advice, marshal help from various levels and departments in the organization, and continue to talk it up.

The result of all this is simple. People who participate in defining a
goal buy into that goal. Best to emulate Ahab here. He didn't simply
announce that the *Pequod*'s goal was to get Moby Dick. He talked with
his crew, asking them about the great whale, and got them to specify
the goal.

*"Captain Ahab," said Tashtego, "that white whale must be the
same that some call Moby Dick."
"Moby Dick," shouted Ahab. "Do ye know the white whale
then, Tash?"*

*"Does he fan-tail a little curious, sir, before he goes down?" said the Gay-Header deliberately.*

*"And he has a curious spout, too", said Daggoo, "very bushy, even for a paracetty, and mighty quick, Captain Ahab?"*

*"And he have one, two, three—oh! good many iron in him hide, too, Captain," cried Queequeg ...*

There's little question that anyone who participated in this dialogue had not only helped to specify but had also "bought into" Ahab's quest.

Like Ahab, you should be unrelenting in the pursuit of your goal. It helps to write it down and, like Ahab, post it in a place where you and everyone else can see it. If it's "We will build 2,500,000 widgets in thirty days," don't leave this message on your desk or in a file folder, get it out there! Let the assembly workers see it, show it to the plant managers, post it in every hallway and help people to believe in it.

### Electrifying the Troops

Jack Welch has put it this way: "You're either Number One or Number Two in your respective market, or you're dead." Like Ahab, he leaves little question about where his people and his company should be in this electrifying statement.

One of the things that helped Ahab on his quest was the enthusiasm from the majority of his crew. You can't tackle the big goal alone, so you'll need to do your best to breed enthusiasm as fast as you can. While you'll never get 150 percent commitment from everyone, you can do a lot, as Ahab did, with committed, motivated, dedicated, hardworking people.

Getting people to buy into your quest can happen in three distinct ways: immediately, gradually, or never. Focus your efforts and energy on the first two groups and skip the last one. Some of your people and the people around both you and them will buy into what you say right away, offer their help and support, and get busy trying to catch your whale. Others will jump aboard your ship more slowly, and probably only after they see what's in it for them. If they don't know what benefits they'll receive, tell them. And since the it-won't-work group has already made up its collective mind, and there is probably very little you can say or do to help them buy into the project, devote your time to the people who will help and skip the naysayers.

As a rule, people in organizations like quests, but only if they're visible and viable. There has to be some light at the end of the tunnel, otherwise, it's like climbing a mountain with no hope of ever reaching the summit. Your big goal can't be a pipe dream; there has to be a strong sense that although it might be difficult to achieve—rewriting the company's policies and procedures manual, changing the way the sales force gets compensated, bringing a new product to market, opening a new division in another state or country, etc., given the right mixture of hard work and energy, and some luck, the end can be in sight. Money and benefits are not the only motivators for employees in organizations today. There is still something to be said for the company and its leaders who create a dynamic, positive, and humane work environment, and then give the employees constant challenges, lots of feedback, and big rewards.

If you're in charge, consider creating an "Ahab Division" of people who want to think up new quests for your organization and its different divisions, units, or teams. And if you're unfortunate enough to be saddled with a band of idea-killers who constantly dash cold water on every new quest that comes along, get rid of them. People who say "no" to everything, no matter what it is, are a psychic drain on organizational energy that disrupts the kind of positive culture you want to create. Vince Lombardi said it best: "If you aren't fired with enthusiasm, you will be fired with enthusiasm." If you can't get a willing crew to help your quest, either change your quest or change your crew.

## Leading by Asking Questions

Captain Ahab was anything but talkative. When he did speak, his words usually boiled down to one and only one question, "Where can I find Moby Dick?" He led by asking questions.

One way to motivate and communicate is to use rhetorical questions; that is, those that you want your people to ask and that you or they already know the answers to. "What can we do to change the way our customers perceive our products?" is a good example. This starts the ball rolling and gets people to think out loud as they try to answer a question they know has many possible answers.

As a leader, it's your job to come up with these kinds of questions, put them to your people, and step back and watch them come up with solutions, new and creative ideas, and answers to the problems these questions raise. Managers tell. Leaders ask questions, lots of them.

Consider these questions as examples that can encourage your people to think, act, react, and problem solve:

What do we do with the feedback we gather from our customers? (This may lead to an answer that says, "But we don't get feedback from our customers!" This response will point you in another obvious direction toward solving that problem.)

What opportunities are there for us to create new partnerships or business alliances with our suppliers?

Which of our products or services would sell best overseas?

How can we change the working hours here so that our employees have more freedom?

What are our customers telling us they want most from us, in terms of new products or services?

How can we cut costs in each department without resorting to downsizing?

What products or services should we be selling five years from now?

As you can see from this short list, there are a number of Ahab-type questions that have a multitude of possible answers. That's what you want and that's how you should phrase them to your people. "Tell me how you would answer this question and give me a number of different solutions. Show me how you can think a bit outside the envelope. Be more creative than usual. Come up with something novel, unique, and thought-stopping for me."

Unfortunately, Captain Ahab was a bit of a one-trick pony. His obsession was both a blessing and a curse. It's fine and necessary to talk about your quest and be committed to it, but you've got to let some other kinds of lights shine in; otherwise, you'll get a bad case of tunnel vision.

## The Value of an Occasional Failed Quest

Another Ahab flaw was that his ego constantly got in the way of his capacity for rational thought. Most leaders are slightly ego-driven; that's what helps us all get out of bed in the morning and go to work. But letting your ego get in the way of your good judgement—as Ahab did despite repeated pleas from Starbuck to give up his foolhardy hunt—can lead to disaster.

Many companies have had their leaders say, "Only I know what's good for my company. Only I know what's good for our customers and I'm gonna give 'em what I think they want." And as history shows us from time to time, when the big quest is tied to an even bigger executive ego, it is doomed to failure.

Recall the recent corporate ego problem at Coca-Cola. The company made the mistake of tinkering with its century-old soda formula with near-disastrous results. Consumers hated the new Coke, screamed for the old one, and left a seemingly intelligent, well-run organization with egg on its face.

How many times have we seen companies try to fix what was not broken? "Here's a new product we're sure you'll love as much as or more than the old one," they crow to their customers. And when that product "tanks" in the marketplace, they're left to scramble for their now dwindling market share. "Come back!" they plead with departing customers, as they lurch back in the original direction, desperately trying to find the magic formula, when perhaps they had it all along.

As singer Kenny Rogers so aptly put it in a country song about living as a gambler, "You've got to know when to hold 'em, know when to fold 'em, know when to walk away, and know when to run." Best to employ, in such situations, the "tactical retreat," and follow this old military dictum: "When the game is up, hustle back to safety, reevaluate your position, and wait for another opportunity."

It's hard to understand why this concept has not caught on in business, since many leaders have taken their people and their firms down a difficult and expensive path only to find a dead end. And instead of admitting, "I may have made a mistake" and going back to the drawing board, too many of these ego-driven leaders keep plunging down the same dead end, hoping more time, more money, and more pushing and shoving will cause it to become something it's not.

If you have lost your opportunity, blown the one chance you need to succeed, or misunderstood some segment of your marketplace, industry, or even your organization, know when to give in. And giving in is not the same as giving up. In the first case, you simply retreat, rethink, and regroup. In the second, you throw in the towel. While Coca-Cola made a big mistake and proved that their quest was flawed, they at least had enough sense to say, "You know, we messed up. Let's leave well enough alone and go back to giving our customers what they want, instead of what we think they want."

It's called learning. While these kinds of experiences are certainly painful, ego-bashing, and expensive, they serve a purpose. No matter what went wrong for your own big quest, some things probably went right. And no matter how painful it is to say, "It's time to call it a day," these lessons can motivate you and your people to improve, regroup, and get it right the next time.

Of course, no leader is perfect. Ahab was so driven to destroy Moby Dick that he ultimately confused his need for revenge with what was good for his organization. The lesson, of course, is not to emulate Ahab, but to learn from him. And when it comes to goal-setting, this talented but deeply flawed man has much to teach. Ahab could have benefitted from such wisdom. No wonder his story offers a great deal of leadership wisdom. Bear with us as we try to summarize some "Ahab lessons" from a very lengthy book.

- *The more specific the goal, the better.*
  Captain Ahab's goal was marvelously detailed. That wasn't just any whale he was after. It was Moby Dick, a very particular whale, as we've learned: a white albino with an oddly shaped tail, a crooked jaw, three holes in its starboard fluke, and an unusual spout. Cork-screw shaped harpoons—grisly evidence of previous unsuccessful attempts to capture him—bristled from his body. Simply put, there was no other whale like Moby Dick and there was no confusion. Everyone in the organization, from foretopman to ship's carpenter, knew exactly what the *Pequod*'s mission was.
- *Question. Don't Tell.*
  Too many managers simply announce goals to their employees. Big deal. It's a monologue, a top-down game that few listen to and fewer buy into. But Ahab knew better. He got his men to commit to his goal not by telling but by asking. Sure, the most famous line in the book, as we've said, is its opening three words, "Call me Ishmael." But the real magic starts when Captain Ahab asks, "What do you do when you see a whale, men?" And he doesn't stop there: "What do you do next, men?" he asks. Then, "What tune is it ye pull to, men?" The effect of this barrage of questions was as dramatic as it was immediate: The crew, because they participated actively in the process of setting objectives, quickly made the boss' goal their own.
- *Timing is everything.*
  In goal-setting, as in all of leading, synchronizing things adroitly

can have more to do with getting people's agreement than any-thing else. At this subtle art, Ahab—and Herman Melville—were masters. The literary technique is called "delayed emergence of character." But to Ahab, it was just good leadership. By remaining below decks for weeks, emerging only late at night when the crew was asleep, he heightened the men's curiosity. Ironically, when finally he did appear before them, he was able to control them better by having remained at a distance for so long.

- *Every goal requires an incentive.*

Ahab's was an ounce of Spanish gold, worth about $16. It does-n't seem like much, but that isn't the point. Ahab knew how to turn even the most niggardly bonus into a valuable and highly visible symbol of a job well done. He did it by shining the gold piece to heighten its luster and then nailed it to the mast. Whoever spotted Moby Dick first, he announced, would collect the reward. It only needed to be said once. Every time a member of the crew walked by the mast, he was unmistakably reminded of the organization's overarching goal: to capture Moby Dick.

- *Know your employees.*

Ahab knew every member of the crew intimately, from Starbuck, the first mate, to Pip, the cabin boy. He was passionately inter-ested in what made them tick. And he used this knowledge to motivate them to join him in the chase. No wonder he was able to say, quite rightly, about his relationship with the crew, that "... my one cogged circle fits into all their various wheels, and they revolve." Those thirteen words teach more about the art of leading successfully than scores of textbooks on the subject.

- *Try a little monomania.*

Peter Drucker's definition of a successful entrepreneur is "a monomaniac with a mission." It's also a remarkably apt descrip-tion of Captain Ahab. For him nothing much mattered except plunging ahead from sea to sea until he could capture Moby Dick. When Starbuck urges him to give up his "madness" and get back to the business of routine whaling, Ahab's single-mind-edness emerged like granite.

- *Do your homework.*

Most people think of Ahab simply as an irrational leader rushing mindlessly, and disastrously, toward his goal. Wrong. He was extremely well prepared. His superb spadework for the cruise of the *Pequod*, as we've seen, could provide a model for many a corporate planning department. Ahab poured over countless sea charts and piles of old logbooks showing in what season and places sperm whales had been captured or seen. He calculated tides and currents. He estimated the driftings of the sperm whales' food. He constructed elaborate migratory charts of their movements. These intricate computations had but one purpose: to plot the place where Moby Dick might be found.

- *Forget whales; remember the geese.*
If you're trying to build a team, as Ahab was, a very memorable story comes from an unlikely source: the study of geese. Flying in a V-formation, these birds travel many thousands of miles each year, with ease and great navigational accuracy. There are a number of memorable reasons for this. First, as each bird flaps its wings, it creates an updraft for the birds behind it. The result of this teamwork? A 70 percent improvement in flying efficiency! Then there's the willingness to accept and to give help that characterizes the formation. If a bird falls out of the formation, it quickly feels the increased drag and resistance that comes from "going it alone," and immediately rejoins the flock. What's more, leadership is shared. As we've all noticed, there seems to be a single leader—that bold bird at the apex of the formation. Yet, when the leading bird tires, it drifts back into the formation. Almost imperceptibly, a fresh bird takes the lead. But what's a team without encouragement? Scientists studying geese have learned that, amazingly, they seem to understand motivation. The geese honk from behind to boost the morale of those up in front. Finally, there's help whether things are going well or not. If a member of the flock gets sick or is wounded by a gunshot, two geese leave the formation and join the wounded bird as it floats to earth. They'll stay with it until it either rejoins the flock or dies. Ahab's crew, once mesmerized by his quest, would have done no less.

## CHAPTER 7

# FROM DREAM TO REALITY: HOW MARTIN LUTHER KING CHANGED AMERICA

*When you are right you cannot be too radical; when you are wrong you cannot be too conservative.*
— MARTIN LUTHER KING

## KEY POINTS
- CHANGE IN THE FACE OF ADVERSITY
- CHANGING THE CULTURE AROUND YOU

It's an unfortunate truth that many leaders who have tried to bring about change in an organization have failed, not for lack of a vision, but because they didn't know how to implement that vision. Fortunately for America, Martin Luther King, Jr., was a leader who understood the importance of both. He compellingly articulated his vision of a more just American society in his famous "I Have a Dream" speech; more importantly, he clearly spelled out his techniques for implementing that vision in his less well-known "Letter from Birmingham Jail."

The "Letter," written while he was incarcerated for leading protest demonstrations in Birmingham, turns out to be a veritable primer on how to make change happen in your organization. In it, you'll find such never-mentioned-in-a-management-textbook secrets of leadership as the need for "constructive tension," the efficacy of—stay with us here—"self-purification," and, perhaps most importantly for anyone trying to quell organizational turf battles, King's notion of "inescapable networks of mutuality."

## A Modern-Day Paradigm of Leadership

For today's business leaders too young to remember firsthand the news accounts of the civil rights movement and Martin Luther King, Jr.'s, role in it, let us provide a bit of historical context. It was a time of turmoil, of national soul-searching, as the government, business, and ordinary people were forced to wrestle with questions and accusations about the treatment of blacks in America. Martin Luther King, Jr., who was very much a part of this dialogue and this seaching, found himself in the forefront of the movement demanding equal rights for all people.

King died fighting for what he believed in. His assassination in 1968 sparked race riots across America, as people reacted in grief and anger to his death. Yet nearly thirty years later, his teachings on nonviolence and his vision of a fully integrated society where the worth of all individuals is recognized continue to influence thinking not only in America but in nations around the world.

Martin Luther King Jr., was born in Atlanta, Georgia, on January 15, 1929, the second of three children. His was a close-knit, middle-class, southern Baptist family in which respect for the family unit and the importance of spiritual and moral values were emphasized. His youth was relatively comfortable and secure: Besides growing up in a stable and loving family, he lived in a neighborhood filled with other successful middle-class blacks whose values and aspirations were similar to those of his parents. It was a community in which respect for each other and pride in each other's achievements were paramount. It was an environment which not only shaped King's values but also contributed to his self-esteem, helping to counter the effects of racial discrimination which intruded on his life.

Clearly, his was not the environment of poverty and ignorance so often depicted in studies of the black community. Yet regardless of the fact that they enjoyed a more comfortable lifestyle than many blacks, King and his family and friends encountered the same racial attitudes and prejudices and had to follow the same humiliating Jim Crow laws as the less affluent members of the black community. Later, as King's prominence brought him "privileges" the average black did not enjoy (when he was jailed in Birmingham, Attorney General Robert Kennedy made sure local authorities knew he was watching their treatment of the civil rights leader), King repeatedly reminded his followers that he was still "one of them."

King was a precocious child who, even in his youth, demonstrated the ability to speak eloquently and extemporaneously that later played an important role in his emergence as a civil rights leader. Moving rapidly through the public school system, he graduated from high school and entered Atlanta's Morehouse College at the age of fifteen. Although he initially planned to become a doctor or an attorney, King eventually decided to become a minister, following in the footsteps of his father and grandfather.

After graduating from Morehouse in 1948, he enrolled in the Crozer Theological Seminary in Chester, Pennsylvania. It was here that he discovered the writings of two individuals whose thinking was to greatly influence his work as a minister and civil rights leader.

One was Walter Rauschenbusch, a leader of the "social gospel" movement that began in the early 20th century. Rauschenbusch believed that religion "must be relevant to real world problems and that the church should be actively involved." This belief not only influenced King's actions as a minister but became part of his argument refuting a charge by white clergymen that racial and economic injustice were social issues "with which the gospel has no real concern."

The other political and spiritual leader whose work so dramatically influenced King's thinking was Mahatma Gandhi, whose concept of "Satyagraha," or the use of nonviolent protest and resistance, was used to encourage political and social reforms in India. (We will study the life and work of Gandhi in chapter 12.) By the time he wrote "Letter from Birmingham Jail," King had seen, over and over again, the power of nonviolent tactics in bringing about change.

When he finished his coursework at Crozer, King entered the School of Theology at Boston University to complete his Ph.D. program and, early in 1954, at the age of twenty-five, became pastor of Dexter Avenue Baptist Church in Montgomery, Alabama. From his pulpit, he urged his parishioners to embrace the concepts of love and justice for all people, concepts strongly embedded in the Judeo-Christian tradition, and taught in the Bible's New Testament.

Although efforts by blacks to challenge segregation occasionally made the news, two events, in 1954 and 1955, helped move the fight for desegregation into the forefront of American consciousness. The first was the 1954 Supreme Court decision in Brown versus the Board of Education, which was a unanimous ruling calling for the end of segregated schools. The other was the arrest of Mrs. Rosa Parks on December 1, 1955, for refusing to give up her seat to a white man on a Montgomery, Alabama, city bus.

Montgomery's Women's Political Council had been trying to organize a bus boycott prior to Mrs. Parks' arrest. Outrage over her arrest and subsequent humiliating incarceration not only strengthened the council's desire to target the transit company but also galvanized support from the black community for such action. Community leaders quickly formed the Montgomery Improvement Association, elected the twenty-six-year-old King as president, and adopted the idea of a bus boycott. Initially, King had a number of doubts about his ability to lead the organization: his age and newcomer status in Montgomery, concern for the safety of his family, and fear that he might fail as a leader. Above all, he was concerned about the sacrifices he would have to ask of Montgomery's black bus patrons.

It was during these difficult times that King, filled with tremendous self-doubt, experienced what he later called a "profound spiritual transformation." While praying for guidance, King said he heard an inner voice that he believed to be Jesus' telling him to continue the fight. For King, it was a moment of transformation, strengthening his sense of purpose and dedication to the fight for equality for all humankind.

With new self-assurance, King began planning for the boycott in earnest. The black community embraced the action, willingly walking miles to and from work while enduring taunts and jeers and threats along the way. And the longer the boycott lasted, the stronger and more united the black community became in its determination to force change.

The boycott, begun in 1955, lasted for 382 days. The economic impact on the bus company and on local business was significant, and the city was finally forced to repeal its segregationist policies. It was a step, small as it may seem, toward King's notion of the "beloved community"—his vision, we'd argue—in which the oneness of humanity and the dignity and worth of all people would be recognized.

King's stature as a proponent of nonviolence continued to grow as he became deeply involved, as president of the Southern Christian Leadership Conference (SCLC), in the organization of civil rights protests throughout the South. In 1963 he was invited by black leaders in Birmingham, Alabama, to come and help them plan and implement a direct action program of sit-ins and marches to protest treatments of blacks in that city. While many other southern cities were making slow but steady progress toward racial equality, Birmingham was well-known as a hotbed of continuing segregation, police brutality, and white-led vigilantism.

Nonviolent protests in Birmingham, with King as one of the leaders, began on April 3, 1963. Eight days later, King was served with an injunction against further demonstrations. Undeterred, he and his demonstrators gathered the following day, Good Friday, prepared to ignore the injunction. Local authorities responded by arresting King and putting him in solitary confinement in the Birmingham Jail.

Alone and unable even to talk with his attorneys over the weekend, King spent the time working on a response to criticism from liberal white clergy leaders who had called his present activities "unwise and untimely." Using a pen smuggled in by a black trustee and writing on the margins of a newspaper and scraps of paper, King began his "Letter from Birmingham Jail." In it he answered the charge that anti-segregationist activities hurt the civil rights movement and that the protesters ought to rely on the courts to bring about change.

But even more, King's "Letter" is a concise lesson on how to write a successful plan for implementing change. He stated clearly, and in no uncertain terms, the problem (discrimination), the goals of the organization (to bring about change), and the methods by which they planned to achieve those goals (direct action which would force change to occur).

King knew that relying on challenges in the courts to bring about change would be a slow process, and he believed that black nonviolent protests were a better way to call attention to racial policies and practices in the south. In addition, he knew that if white attackers retaliated against the protestors, the federal government would be forced to step in and enforce the new laws against discrimination and segregation.

Eventually, King was released on bail, and his "Letter," intended as a public document as well as a message to the white clergy, was widely circulated and read. Not only did it clearly define the goals of the civil rights movement and the method of nonviolence as a way to achieve these goals, it has become accepted as a monumental work on the philosophy of nonviolence.

Later that same year, King gave what would become his most famous discourse, his "I Have a Dream" speech, to a crowd of 250,000 civil rights marchers in Washington, D.C. In it, using eloquent and unforgettable phrasing, he reiterated his vision for America.

In 1964, King was awarded the Nobel Peace Prize. But as he continued his efforts on behalf of the poor and disenfranchised, threats of violence against him increased. And on April 14, 1968, while in Memphis, Tennessee, to help lead a strike by black sanitation workers, King was assassinated. His death, however, did not stop the demands for equal rights, nor did it destroy the power of his ideas or his vision of a brotherhood of mankind where love and justice would prevail.

### The Letter: Lessons in Leadership

King's "Letter from Birmingham Jail" is a powerful and persuasive argument for the right of citizens to engage in civil disobedience in order to bring about change and a clear and comprehensive explanation of the role of nonviolence in this struggle.

As such, his "Letter" served two distinct purposes: it answered his white critics and it clarified his position as civil rights leader. The "Letter" clearly delineated his goals and the methods by which he hoped they would be achieved. It sought to encourage white moderates and church leaders to join the struggle for human rights. It warned of what might happen if this nonviolent quest for change was ignored. Finally, it appealed to what King believed was the fundamental decency of Americans and urged reconciliation between the races.

This is leadership at its best. Like Captain Ahab in his quest for the white whale (chapter 6), Martin Luther King, Jr., had a clear goal in mind for his "organization" and was able to articulate that goal so that others agreed to join in the quest. Even more important, like Captain Ahab and other great leaders, King had a well-defined plan for reaching his goal and would let nothing (being beaten, jailed, threatened) deter him from that goal.

King well knew, from his studies of Gandhi and other nonviolent protesters, that to fight brute force with passive resistance, to counter antagonism with nonviolence, was an effective way to bring about change. His "Letter" was not the overly aggressive, hostile, or argumentative missive that his critics (or even his followers) might have expected. Rather it opened on a conciliatory note:

> I feel that you are men of good will ... I will try to answer your statement in what I hope will be patient and reasonable terms.[1]

His technique is one you might want to remember the next time you need to confront someone in your organization about a problem. King clearly disagreed with his critics and certainly with the practices they had done nothing to change. Yet he made it clear that he respected them and that he wanted to begin a dialogue that was thoughtful and reasoned.

Having established the tone of his "Letter," King then addressed the accusation that he was an "outsider" who had no business involving himself in the problems of Birmingham. He had the right to be there for several reasons, he said: an invitation from local leaders for assistance from SCLC, which operated in every southern state and, more importantly, "because injustice is here." And, as a leader of his people, it was his duty to be there:

> ... just as Apostle Paul left his village of Tarsus and carried the gospel of Jesus Christ to the far corners of the Greco-Roman world, so am I compelled to carry the gospel of freedom beyond my own home town.

No armchair leadership here. King knew how important it is for a leader to be visibly involved in bringing about the goals of his organization. Why should the rank and file care, if the boss doesn't care enough to make an effort? King was always active and visible in any nonviolent campaign in which he was involved, never asking his followers to do anything he himself wasn't willing to do.

Then, providing an excellent demonstration of the importance of making sure everyone understands the issues, King gave a frank assessment of the racial problems facing Birmingham and the country. He cited concrete examples of injustices and mistreatment endured by blacks and of the effects of prejudice and segregation on their lives. And to the argument that their action was not well-timed, he replied:

*We have waited for more than 340 years for our constitutional
and God-given rights.... There comes a time when the cup of
endurance runs over, and men are no longer willing to be plunged
into the abyss of despair.*

King calmly, but firmly, puts his opponents on notice. Yet the message is clear: "We've taken about all we can. The status quo cannot continue. Things have to change, and with or without your help, we're going
to make it happen."

Such sense of urgency is a universally important leadership tool.
Consider the impact it might have had on Apple Computer, which late in
1994 announced that it would allow IBM to duplicate its software. The
idea of cloning was anything but new, having been considered by erst-
while Apple CEO John Sculley back in 1989. And "making it happen" in
1989 would have given Apple a far better shot at surviving the computer
wars of the nineties which have fast made Apple a marginal contender.
Yet, for Sculley, the status quo, apparently, was good enough. Apple
would stay solely a computer maker, leaving Microsoft Corporation to
soar in sales and profits as the industry's major supplier of operating software. It was a disastrous decision, leading one industry observer to comment: "There's no question Macintosh could be where Windows is today
if they had done this [licensing] five years ago."[2]

Besides establishing a sense of urgency, King's explanation of why he
was in Birmingham served another purpose as well: to remind the city's
black community that he was "one of them," and that what affected
them affected him too. What it comes down to, suggested King to his
white critics, is that like it or not, we're all in this together. King called it
"the network of mutuality"—the idea that events, actions, and decisions
don't take place in isolation but in fact have an impact far beyond the
immediate point of action. In King's words:

*... I am cognizant of the interrelatedness of all communities
and states. I cannot sit idly by in Atlanta and not be concerned
about what happens in Birmingham. Injustice anywhere is a threat
to justice everywhere. We are caught in an inescapable network of
mutuality, tied in a single garment of destiny. Whatever affects one
directly, affects all indirectly.*

He was right, of course. Mutual dependency and cooperation have lately eclipsed dog-eat-dog competition as the anthem of our society as well as our economic order. The euphemism for all this is "strategic alliances," but whatever you call it, it means that "we're all in it together."

It's increasingly clear that to ignore or deny the idea of a network of mutuality can be as shortsighted in business as it can be for the nation. Watching out only for one's own welfare can be hazardous to your—and your organization's—health. Consider, for example, the problem faced by passengers on a sinking ocean liner. One group says to the other passengers, "Since the leak is on your side of the ship, it's your problem. We don't have to worry about it, because things are fine for us over here. So don't run around making noise just because there's a problem on your side."

We are, in other words, part of a greater whole. John Donne was right: no man is an island unto himself. Such interconnectedness has lately led to some interesting possibilities. Does, for example, the flap of a butterfly wing in Tokyo affect a tornado in Texas or a thunderstorm in New York? Can the falling of a leaf on some distant planet account for the motion of a billiard ball on a pool table on earth?[3]

King, who might well have answered "Yes," further reinforced his message that events are interrelated and that decisions, whether they are intended to or not, often have an effect beyond what was anticipated. "You deplore the demonstrations taking place in Birmingham," he wrote to the clergy.

> But your statement, I am sorry to say, fails to express a similar concern for the conditions that brought about the demonstrations ... It is unfortunate that demonstrations are taking place in Birmingham, but it is even more unfortunate that the city's white power structure left the Negro community with no alternative.

## Creating Social Change: A Four-Step Plan

Having justified his involvement in "local" affairs, and gently but firmly chastized his critics for blaming him for a situation that they allowed to continue, King seeks to educate them on the steps involved in a nonviolent campaign.

As a leader, he knows and understands the importance of making it clear to everyone what the goals of the organization are and how they're to be achieved. His explanation, therefore, is directed not only at his critics but also at the demonstrators, to remind them of the importance of what they're doing. But perhaps most important as a leadership ploy, one that's bound to make his opponents sit back and think, King's explanation puts everyone on notice that this is no half-baked idea that's bound to fail, but a carefully crafted, well-thought-out plan of action. Black community leaders had researched the problem, considered alternatives, decided how to proceed, determined beforehand what the consequences of their actions might be, and decided how they would respond to those actions.

Is there any better prescription for successfully managing change in an organization? King listed four steps for developing a plan for change:

1. *Collection of the facts* (to determine whether injustices exist).
   King is blunt here. "Birmingham is probably the most thoroughly segregated city in the United States. Its ugly record of brutality is widely known." He speaks of police beatings, bombings of black homes and churches, and the failure of the city courts or government to respond. He reports that black leaders had long sought an opportunity to talk with Birmingham's city leaders and merchants about unfair treatment of blacks, "but the latter consistently refused to engage in good faith negotiation."

2. *Negotiation.*
   It finally came. Black leaders were willing to end demonstrations that were hurting the merchants' trade in return for certain promises from those merchants—that they would, for example, remove humiliating racial signs found in their stores. Such promises were made and, in good faith, black leaders agreed to a moratorium on demonstrations. But, as King put it, "as the weeks and months went by, we realized that we were the victims of a broken promise." Nothing had changed.

3. *Self-purification.*
   What King had in mind here was nothing exotic, just *practice.* "We had no alternative but to prepare for direct action," he wrote. Yet mindful of the difficulties involved, the demonstrators undertook a process of "self-purification"—a series of workshops in which they simulated what might happen, much as you may have done in your own training programs. They asked themselves: "Are you able to accept blows without retaliating? Are you

able to endure the ordeal of jail?" Hence they became fully committed to responding to violent treatment with nonviolence.

4. *Direct action.*

King and his followers were now ready for direct action, a campaign that would serve "as a means of laying our case before the conscience of the local and the national community." They began a campaign of boycotts, protests, rallies, speeches, meetings, and other forms of civil disobedience in order "to bring pressure to bear" on the politicians, merchants, and justice officials of Birmingham. Wrote King:

> *Nonviolent direct action seeks to create such a crisis and foster such a tension that a community which has constantly refused to negotiate is forced to confront the issue. It seeks so to dramatize the issue that it can no longer be ignored. My citing the creation of tension as part of the work of the nonviolent resister may sound rather shocking. But I must confess that I am not afraid of the word 'tension.' I have earnestly opposed violent tension, but there is a type of constructive, non-violent tension which is necessary for growth.*

King made it clear that the purpose of the fourth step—direct action—was to "create a situation so crisis-packed" that city leaders would be forced to participate in the very thing his critics were calling for—negotiations. "I ... concur with you in your call for negotiation," he wrote. "Too long has our beloved Southland been bogged down in a tragic effort to live in monologue rather than dialogue."

But while indicating a willingness to negotiate, King made it clear that the black community remained committed to their plan of action until change actually occurred. He knew the importance of standing firm at this point; he knew, as any leader who has attempted to bring about change in his or her organization knows, that change isn't always comfortable, and that given a choice, most people won't change on their own. It was a fact King was all too familiar with, and one he reminded his critics of as well:

> *My friends, I must say to you that we have not made a single gain in civil rights without determined legal and nonviolent pressure. Lamentably, it is an historical fact that privileged groups sel-*

*dom give up their privileges volunarily.... We know through painful experience that freedom is never voluntarily given by the oppressor; it must be demanded by the oppressed.*

Finally, King addresses the question of whether or not the end justifies the means, especially if those means are illegal, go against the status quo, or bring possible harm to others. He solved this moral dilemma neatly by asserting that some laws are just, others unjust. Citing everyone from St. Thomas Aquinas to Jewish philosopher Martin Buber, and from the early Christians and Socrates to the Allies who fought against Adolph Hitler, King said:

> *There are two types of laws, just and unjust. I would be the first to advocate obeying just laws. One has not only a legal but a moral responsibility to obey just laws. Conversely, one has a moral responsibility to disobey unjust laws.*

And here, King has skillfully summed up the scope of his argument. "I would agree with St. Augustine that 'An unjust law is no law at all.'" It is from this ethical and spiritual posture that King could feel justified in developing and encouraging the nonviolent protest movement.

As he summed up his reasons for calling for this type of civil disobedience, King wrote:

> *Human progress never rolls in on wheels of inevitability; it comes through the tireless efforts of men willing to be co-workers with God ... "*

and then he sharply criticized white church "leaders" who were actually more like church "bystanders":

> *... I felt we would be supported by the white church. I felt that the white ministers, priests and rabbis of the South would be among our strongest allies. Instead, some have been outright opponents, refusing to understand the freedom movement and misrepresenting its leaders; all too many others have remained silent behind the anesthetizing security of stained-glass windows.*

And as he concluded, King reiterated what he had said from the beginning, that theirs was a just and true mission, and they would never stop demonstrating for what is morally right until all people were free.

## What the "Letter" Means to You as a Leader

Much is made of the fact that leaders need to have a vision for their organization, and need to be able to articulate that vision. But such a vision isn't worth much if there's no definitive plan for implementing it.

King's "Letter" was certainly that—a clear plan of action for bringing about change that would lead to greater racial equality. He told everyone what they could expect, step by step. But as a document, his "Letter" was more than just a description of how his vision was to be implemented. It established, in a precise and logical manner, why action was necessary at that time, the possible consequences if no action was taken, and the role white moderates and clergy could play in helping assure that the necessary changes were brought about without violence or bloodshed. As such, it stands as a classic model of augumentation—presenting reasons, drawing conclusions, and applying them to the case being discussed—that you would do well to study before developing your next position paper on changes you're advocating in your organization.

King's "Letter" did one more thing. He made it clear, throughout the document, that the plan wasn't just *his* plan, its goals not just *his* goals. Everyone involved in carrying out this plan, from community leaders to the average citizen engaged in a sit-in at a lunch counter, had had a part in its development. Every member of Birmingham's black community had a stake in its success. Not only was he putting Birmingham on notice that this thing was bigger than just one man or a small group of men and women, he was doing what any good leader does—reinforcing the idea in the minds of his followers that "we're all in this together."

The importance of a clear plan of action to bring about their vision for their organization is just one of the themes participants in our leadership seminars have identified in "Letter from Birmingham Jail." Other management and leadership themes noted during discussions about the "Letter" include the following steps:

- Taking risks alone
- Taking risks for your people

- Asking your people to commit themselves to a goal
- Asking your people to take on risks themselves
- Using charisma as a motivator
- Bending the rules or even breaking them
- Using powerful communication techniques to win people over to your side
- Managing conflict effectively; using conflict as a change agent
- Resolving conflicts; helping people to do it themselves

The lessons found in King's "Letter from Birmingham Jail" are as pertinent today as when he wrote it. His "Letter" and the success of direct action campaigns in changing the course of American history offer a powerful testimony to the need for a well-defined plan, as well as much practice, before you undertake a campaign of change.

**Constructive Tension: The Leader as Comfort Zone Mover**
If you remember our discussion of comfort zones in our examination of Plato's "Allegory of the Cave" (chapter 1), you'll remember that moving people out of their comfort zones is necessary if change is to occur. But as Martin Luther King knew, people often don't want to leave their comfort zones, because change can be uncomfortable, unfamiliar, or even scary. It's why challenging the status quo is often fraught with such difficulty—people will expend as much energy resisting change as would be required to embrace it.

That certainly appeared to be true among the white moderates in Birmingham, whom King denounced for their refusal to take a stand against racial injustice.

> *I have almost reached the regrettable conclusion that the Negro's great stumbling block in his stride toward freedom is not the White Citizen's Councillor or the Ku Klux Klanner, but the white moderate, who is more devoted to "order" than to justice: who prefers negative peace which is the absence of tension to a positive peace which is the presence of justice; who constantly says: "I agree with you in the goal you seek, but I cannot agree with your methods of direct action"; who paternalistically believes he can set the timetable for another man's freedom ..."*

King's message was clear. Their inaction, their refusal to push for change, was as destructive as the action of rabid segregationists. A harsh condemnation? Perhaps. But King knew that sometimes people have to be shaken out of their complacency, out of their willingness to accept business as usual.

And what he was telling white moderates was: You can't have it both ways; you can't acknowledge that change may be needed, but then protest that any change that occurs mustn't affect you. The desire to have it both ways is certainly as common in organizations as it was among white moderates in Birmingham. You've probably encountered it at one time or another in your own organization. Everyone agrees that change is needed, "but not in my department. It's the department down the hall that needs shaking up."

Shaking up is right, whether it's one department or the entire organization, if you're going to avoid what Judith Bardwick, former psychology professor and management consultant, says is a "psychology of entitlement" among some workers today. In her article, "Danger in Comfort Zones," Bardwick says that when people get too comfortable in their jobs, a kind of malaise occurs that has people believing their employer owes them a living, that it's okay to do mediocre work, and that it's not important to hold people accountable for their results.[4]

How can you prevent this illness from infecting your organization? Create the kind of constructive tension that King said was necessary to bring about change. To do that, Bardwick offers the following suggestions:

You might first try being sure your employees have real work to do, she says. Work that is rewarding and somewhat risky (she claims that motivation is highest when the odds of success are a rather uncomfortable 50–50). To add some get-out-of-your-comfort zone impetus, Bardwick recommends something truly Draconian: that each year, 25 percent of a person's job should become new.

Then there's the matter of increased visibility and peer pressure. There's nothing like knowing that four other members of your team depend upon your being there to start you earning your keep. Organizing work in small groups helps immensely, since people begin to feel more responsible for their performance when they realize the group won't tolerate goof-offs—that they will, in fact, quickly kick them out of their comfort zones.

This practice has worked at Nissan, where absenteeism is (to turn a phrase) largely absent, even though the company does not use time clocks. How and why? Nissan workers are organized into groups of about twenty members. Laggards are quickly noticed, particularly because the firm uses no relief workers. Fellow team members are forced to take up any slack. You can be sure that the rest of the team doesn't allow that to go on for very long before they begin making it very uncomfort-zone like for the laggard team member!

Incentive pay, too, can help get people out of their comfort zones. "People," writes Bardwick, "become apathetic when none of their pay is at risk." Maybe that's why about 75 percent of American employers have some kind of incentive pay plan today.

Finally, there's the simple expedient of termination. Call it what you will—downsizing, re-engineering, "You're fired!"—moving people out of their respective comfort zones can get nasty. But it's a necessary evil. Underachievers who have received ample evaluation, guidance, and support but still don't pull their weight must be let go. Everyone in the organization should know that firing is an option for change. "Make this," urges Bardwick, "indelibly clear." (Perhaps you could use the following statement in your internal company newsletter; it will do wonders to let everyone know exactly where you stand: "Seven people left through regular retirement, four left to join other firms, and six were fired for inadequate performance.")

It should be obvious that if you're going to create constructive tension that forces people to leave their comfort zones, then you'd better be ready, as a leader, to get out of your comfort zone as well. King certainly understood this necessity—he frequently left his home in Atlanta and traveled to troubled southern cities to provide leadership for a direct action campaign. And once there, he was on the front line. No "leading from the rear" as some might try to do. Rather he was where everyone could see him, encouraging and inspiring his people to do more than they thought possible.

Clearly, that ability to inspire and motivate people was part of what made King successful as a leader. It can do the same for you. Don't get us wrong. We don't expect that you will ever have to tell your employees that when they come to work tomorrow they're going to risk facing crowds who will spit on them and call them names, police beatings, riot squad dogs, tear gas, being sprayed by firehoses, and finally, being arrested. Nor will you breezily announce that, during all of this abuse they have to turn the other cheek and take it. You probably wouldn't have anyone show up for work if you did. But it does help to frankly inform your team of what they might expect when the going gets tough. King did it and still they came, because they believed so strongly in their cause.

But there was more. They also knew he'd be there in the midst of the battle. And that's another important lesson. As their leader, King endured whatever his followers did. For them, that was heady stuff, to know that he wasn't back where it was clean and safe and quiet, but beside them, pitching in, helping out, and dealing with the same risks, problems, and disappointments they were.

That kind of involvement suggests a certain empathy and humility on the part of King. He had firsthand knowledge of the conditions his followers were enduring, of their fears and concerns, and of when they needed a chance to recoup and refresh their spirits. He knew the human spirit could not take constant conflict, humiliation, and violence without any opportunity for rest and renewal. The evening rallies held in one or another of the churches offered that kind of solace and, perhaps more important, a sense of community that enabled demonstrators to be right back out on the streets the next day.

Although it's seldom that individuals working for an organization face the kind of physical, mental, and psychological abuse that King's followers endured, it is true that there can be periods of great stress in nearly any working environment. And if your employees are valued people you don't want to lose, it's important that you find ways to help them manage that stress.

### The Language of Leadership
Good leaders know how to use carefully chosen words to motivate people. It's not just the ability to talk extemporaneously in front of a group, it's the ability to use the spoken and written word in ways that motivate people to act. You don't want people to read one of your memos about an important project or idea and say, "Hmm, that's interesting. But I'm kind of busy right now, so I'll just put this in my in basket and think about it later."

You should always be thinking about ways to "ask for action," just as King did, in your written correspondence and your verbal announcements, presentations, or meetings. It's not enough to voice your ideas and hope for the best. Don't expect everyone to make all of the necessary key connections between what you've proposed and what needs to be done next. Sometimes you need to recap what you've said or written by adding, "Okay, so what's our next step?" or "Those are my ideas. Do any of you have some suggestions of your own?" or "How might we put these ideas into action?" Always, always move toward action.

Here are two communication methods which you can use to get your ideas across with more power and flair. (Notice how King used both of them.) Either of these formats will work well for you in writing or speaking.

*Problem-Solution-Justification*

Here, you'll first want to state the problem (or restate it if everyone already knows what you're talking about) in clear terms. Then, give your solution, going into as much detail as you think is necessary. Finally, justify or "sell" your solution to your reader or your audience by discussing its merits or the reasons why you chose that course of action.

This approach can help get everyone moving in the same direction, especially with complex, technical, or multifaceted problems. Using this three-step process ensures that you'll cover all of the cogent points. And the last step requires you to use a bit of salesmanship to promote your solution. You can use this method in a written outline form, in a short report, or on a whiteboard in a meeting room.

*Facts-Opinion-Conclusion*

The second method is similar to the first in that you give your reader or your audience the facts about a certain subject or problem area, thereby setting the stage for what follows—your opinion on how to tackle the problem. Follow this up with your conclusion based upon your understanding of the facts and your opinions as to how to solve the issue at hand.

This approach is often useful in situations where much of what you and your audience know (the facts) tends to be mostly concrete, definable, and tangible. Your opinion and the accompanying solutions, of course, follow logically from your research, planning, past discussions, and experiences.

## Some Thoughts on Conflict Resolution

Martin Luther King lived and worked in a time of great conflict. He faced turmoil on all sides: from his critics, many of whom wanted to see him dead; from apathetic government leaders who certainly wished he would just go away; from splinter groups inside his own organization who wanted to urge his followers to take up arms; and from racists everywhere who went out of their way to make his life hard.

Yet through all of this, he managed to keep his eyes squarely focused on his goals. He knew what all good leaders know: Conflict is inevitable in organizations and is almost always necessary to effect change. This means that rather than trying to avoid conflict, complain about it, or back off as things get uncomfortable, you've got to learn to manage conflict.

Here are some steps you can take to deal with the conflict that is bound to arise in your organization. Whether it's between individuals, teams, departments, peers, suppliers, or customers, keep the following ideas in mind as you seek to solve these problems in a way that keeps both sides relatively happy.

- *Get the emotional temperature down.*
  There's no use everyone yelling at once. Ask for quiet, enforce the rules that allow each side to tell his or her story first, and don't get caught up in the heat of the moment yourself. Stay impartial and stay in your role as mediator, or if you're one of the involved parties, take several deep breaths and try to stay calm.
- *Put a moratorium on posturing and theatrics by either side.*
  Make it a rule that you will not allow either side to engage in events that only serve to make the other person feel bad. If things have really gotten out of hand, encourage each side to take a five-minute break. Give off positive body language yourself—open posture, an unbiased, empathetic expression, gestures of calm—and ask the others to do the same.
- *Don't allow personal attacks or accusations.*
  This is especially likely to happen whenever the conflict at stake has been simmering for a long period of time, or when the participants in the conflict don't like each other, or both. It's up to you, if you're the mediator, to keep a firm hand on the resolution process. You should not allow ad hominem arguments with each person shouting at the other, cutting each other off, or making wild assumptions, accusations, statements, or demands.
- *Create a dialogue that focuses on interests.*
  Frequently, when there's a conflict, neither side knows what the other wants. Get out a pen and a piece of paper and ask each

person to make one list of their interests and another list which guesses about the other side's interests. (At least, this gets them both working and not shouting at each other. What's more, it clarifies each side's position without your having to act like an interrogator trying to extract information from disgruntled people.) Then have them exchange or explain their lists. Often, this step alone is enough to get them to start saying closure statements like, "You need that? Well, I can do that for you if you do this for me."

- *Look for options that can serve the interest of either party.*
There is always more than one way to solve any conflict. Unfortunately, in the heat of an argument or under the emotion of the moment, it's hard to see more than one solution (read "My way or I'm walking out."). If you're called on to counsel two people or two groups locked in a battle of who's right, remind each side it's better to concentrate more on what's right. Once each side has agreed that separate and mutual interests exist, urge them both to look for added value options that will fulfill these interests. Trade-offs, barter deals, and a realization that each side may be able to get more by giving more, can help to bring the matter to a close.

- *Create solutions and try to save the relationship using an added value approach.*[5]
If neither side can come up with an approach that serves their respective interests, encourage the process by creating some solutions for them. If you're in the position of mediator, you may have the proper perspective that allows you greater objectivity. And even if you have a vested interest in the outcome of one side over the other, try to remain as neutral as possible as you explore solutions and offer various ideas to the two sides.

In some instances, you may be called upon as a leader to facilitate a group meeting between two unhappy or even warring groups. These events call for tact and the leadership quality that compels you to keep your head while those around you are losing theirs. Follow these steps anytime you're trying to get two diverse sides to come to an agreement. And consider the process of conflict resolution as a managed event, not something that happens by accident, chance, or blind luck. It's up to you to guide people in a direction that helps them find solutions, save face, and come to an agreement that is balanced and fair.

Keep the following twelve steps in mind as you prepare for a conflict resolution meeting between two sides:

1. *Choose a mediator or facilitator who has no stake in the outcome and is not in a position of power over either side.*

   If this is not you, then have the group pick someone whom they can trust and whom they agree to work with as they try to solve their differences. In many cases, this responsibility of leading the group—especially if you're in charge of everyone in the room—will fall on your shoulders. If you're like most leaders, you'll welcome the opportunity to be the group's facilitator. That way, you can have some positive control over the outcome.

2. *Acknowledge past failures and move on.*

   Now is not the time to dredge up old problems, create bad feelings throughout the room, or otherwise jeopardize the resolution process. Keep the peace by saying, "We all know why we are here. There have been these difficulties in the past and instead of wasting a lot of time arguing over who was right and who was not, let's focus our efforts on what we can do today."

3. *Keep the group size at around ten to twenty participants.*

   Too few people and it's hard to get much accomplished; too many people and it can be hard to hear your own voice over the din. If you can keep the group size manageable, you'll get better results. You may want to include only department heads or several key representatives from each side instead of a whole roomful of people.

4. *Hold the meeting off site if possible and encourage people to roll up their sleeves and get comfortable.*

   In situations where there is deep divisiveness or a long-running feud between groups, it may help to leave the actual grounds of the company and regroup at a neutral site. Often, the walls of the organization can feel as if they're closing in and the company setting can inhibit creativity, free thought, or the need to seek real solutions. Some organizations use two-day retreats to look at corporate culture or other related personnel, service, or product problems they need to solve. Other work groups will go away for one day to a hotel or other conference or meeting room facility in an attempt to get away from the organization, at least for a bit. Here, they can meet, talk, eat, and even socialize in a more relaxed setting.

5. *Set a time limit. Make it no longer than two days; people will have a chance to sleep on their actions after the first day.*

   One of your roles as the group's leader is time management. Although it can be difficult, one of your principal tasks is to become a dedicated clockwatcher. Nothing is worse than two days of often-heated discussion and no solutions at the end of the encounter. As in any training seminar, encourage people to look for answers as the time spent together draws to a close.

6. *Start with a discussion of some human experience that can unite the group; don't focus on the actual issues right away.*

   These events can be extremely stressful for some of the participants. It's not unusual to see tears, anguish, or other expressions of emotion. You need to get the group off on the right foot. Develop some kind of icebreaker technique to get people on the same track and thinking of each other more as human beings rather than as adversaries.

7. *Tell the group that they must reach a decision; their participation should be seen as a requirement, not an option.*

   You need to stress that a fair and equitable solution to this problem is the most important goal of the encounter. Don't let the group or individual participants stray off on distracting tangents. Stay focused on one result or several key result areas.

8. *Set clear goals.*

   It can be as easy as saying, "By the end of this day, we will all leave here comfortable with our solution to this problem." Or you can be more specific and spend the initial phase of the meeting developing, extracting, and writing down what the group wants to do. Some of the issues may be quite concrete, others more abstract. In any case, it's important for the participants to see the reason for the meeting and to have some sense that it has a real beginning, a middle, and an end.

9. *Encourage brainstorming.*

   As we all should know by now, brainstorming is a highly synergistic process that allows you to come up with a lot of material in a short period of time. Don't be shy about explaining the rules for brainstorming, the first of which is "No initial criticism allowed." And the brainstorming process should not deteriorate into an immediate search for solutions. Your goal as a facilitator, and the group's goal, should be to come up with a list of ideas, suggestions, discussion points, problems, and conflict areas that will start the group off on the right foot.

10. *Weigh each option for its potential to help solve the problem at hand.*
    Once you've helped the group complete the brainstorming process, you can begin to look for common ground, areas of mutual interest, and other focal points that can bring the group closer together. Focus, focus, focus should be your chant, especially if the group seems willing to attack each other, bring up side issues, or discuss other irrelevancies that can waste valuable time or keep them from looking for solutions. But don't always be in a hurry to converge on the first solution that achieves initial group consensus. Sometimes the group process is like a stew pot; you have to let the ingredients, the people and the ideas, mix around for a bit before you can serve it up.

11. *Don't always insist on a public vote.*
    Depending on the issue at hand, you may want to allow group members to write their vote or their choice on a slip of paper. Sometimes, allowing the choice of confidentiality will actually enhance the solution to the problem. If most of the people in the room want to express themselves on paper, allow them the opportunity. Too often, "groupthink" will affect the outcome of a public vote. If less senior people see their colleagues voting for or against something, they may have their original choice swayed by the need to conform or the desire for consensus.

12. *Recognize the group's consensus when it appears.*
    And speaking of consensus, it's up to you as the group leader to know when to say "when." If the discussion is flowing toward a solution that seems perfectly acceptable to everyone involved, ask them to make their decision and then help them tie up the loose ends. Know how to balance the discussion so it doesn't appear that you are actively campaigning for your favorite choice. In rare instances, you'll notice that some people will take

the contrarian point of view just to be different (or difficult). Know how to let the power of consensus-building work to control any cranks, naysayers, and nitpickers who may inhabit the room. If the group wants to decide on a course of action, help them and then let them.

Martin Luther King offered a voice of calm and reason in a time of great turmoil. He had a tremendous capacity to persuade people, supporters and critics alike, to see his vision. Even more, he had the ability to marshal the energies of many people, bring them together in a cohesive group, and steer them toward the same goal. His use of the written word and, more noticeably, his capacity to encourage people through the breadth and depth of his speeches, made him one of the great communicators of our time. His innate leadership skills gave his people hope just as yours can for your team—a rare commodity when times are tough.

## CHAPTER 8

# BUSINESS AS CIVILIZED WAR: HOW TO BEAT YOUR BATTLE-READY COMPETITORS

*In war there is no substitute for victory.*
—GENERAL DOUGLAS MACARTHUR

## KEY POINTS

- THE LEADER AS WARRIOR
- BUSINESS AS WAR
- THE GLOBAL PERSPECTIVE CONCERNING YOUR JOB

Much has been made lately about business being like war. Military language regularly permeates articles appearing in business magazines, including terms like these: offensive, defensive, conquering, butting up against, terrain, staging, threat, targets, dead time, and struggle. In the life or death quest for strategic success, business people have much to learn from those who practice the art of war. Both share the same purpose: success against your competition. And at the core of true leadership in any field of endeavor is the ability to be bold, brave, and aggressive at the same time and in just the right places—clearly warrior-like traits. Such military analogies have fueled a burgeoning consulting industry that urges today's business leaders to adopt strategies and tactics—things like mass and surprise, painstakingly thorough planning, and concern for the troops that have worked so well for the great military leaders.

There's nothing new about this. Successful generalship has always taught much about leadership, both good and bad. There's Thucydides' account of the Peloponnesian War, for example, which reminds 20th-century leaders that small organizations short on resources yet sharply focused (Spartan-like start-ups, for example) can sometimes whip their larger competitors (those "Athenian" *Fortune* 1000). And Winston Churchill's massive history of World War II provides countless lessons in the art of effective decision-making in times of crisis, as we shall see in chapter 10.

And there was Lycurgus, the ancient Spartan lawgiver and general. Faced with a rebellion that threatened *his* organization, Lycurgus' turn-around strategy enabled Sparta not only to recover but to survive for centuries, a model of self-control, moderation, courage, and reverence for law.

Lycurgus used a strategy that boiled down to six very modern steps. First, he knew something that many unsuccessful turnaround managers miss. He started slowly. A successful turnaround, he realized, is a lot like painting a house. Careful preparation is the key. He listened. He knew that restraint, not impulsive action, was the key. He asked a few friends for help. And only after they pledged their support did he begin to lobby others. Gradually, he forged coalitions with others who shared his vision for a renewed Sparta.

Second, he got rid of the perks. Things like executive jets, fancy lunches, and stretch limos may be OK when things are going well, but they're death to a successful turnaround. After all, they symbolize the kind of physical and spiritual flabbiness that gets organizations into trouble in the first place. You should eradicate them just as Lycurgus did. He started by closing the Spartans' elegant board room. Worried that such fancy digs would divert his subordinates' attention, they all met outside instead, in the fields. Then he shut the executive dining room, forcing his executives to forego fancy meals altogether and eat with the employ-ees. Lycurgus was no less fanatical about drinking. He taught young Spartans the importance of sobriety by forcing slaves to drink vast quan-tities of alcohol to demonstrate how foolish drunkenness is.

Lycurgus' third turnaround strategy was more difficult, but just as important. He changed his organization's power structure. In his day, land equalled power. He changed all this by changing the basis for ownership. His land reforms put everyone on an equal footing. As you might expect, it upset the entrenched deadwood, but it quickly got everyone else on his side.

Fourth, Lycurgus knew that the Spartans could not be all things to all people. He focused their efforts on doing a few things very, very well. Nowhere was this truer than in their industrial policy. Spartan craftsmen concentrated on manufacturing staples and essential items, primarily furniture. One notable, and highly successful exception, was a drinking cup—an ancient version of the modern military canteen. It was ingeniously designed in such a way that it automatically filtered mud from the water before drinking. It was an instant success throughout all of Greece.

He also did something we've been longing to do for some years: He got rid of the policy manuals. He burnt the moutainous accumulation of rules and regulations that symbolized the mindless bureaucracy Sparta had become. He knew it was better to rely on good discipline and strong corporate culture than on a mere book of rules. For this reason, he never reduced his laws to writing.

Finally, Lycurgus was absolutely ruthless about getting rid of deadwood. The Spartans had always been brutal when it came to cleaning house. Healthy children were trained and then given a share of the enterprise. Weak ones were thrown off cliffs or left to die. It was called infanticide. Today we call it "outplacement." By any name, it's horribly cruel. Yet nothing gets the message across about a turnaround leader's seriousness of purpose more than a tough-minded personnel policy, one that carves out non-performers with Spartan ruthlessness.

Napoleon, too, offers today's leaders myriad leadership examples, many of which boil down to his genius for tricking *his* competition, the enemy. It paid off for him at Austerlitz, where he defeated the combined Austrian and Russian armies in 1805. He set a trap, the enemy fell into it, and by sunset the French artillery had finished things off.

The key was a swaggering ruse. Napoleon had placed a few troops at his center near a marshy field, as a mock defense. As he had hoped, the Austrians and the Russians quickly became bogged down in it. In a confused retreat, they swarmed onto an ice-covered lake. Napoleon was ready and waiting. Just as they were nearing the middle, he ordered his guns to fire. As the ice noisily broke up, thousands of enemy soldiers, complete with horses, guns, and wagons, could be heard screaming as they sank into the frigid water. Only a handful survived.

## Military Failures

And then, there's always the possibility that military leaders may set precisely the wrong example. Take the case of the architect of the Spanish Armada, Philip II of Spain. It was just over four hundred years ago that this leader, convinced that England should be liberated from the clutches of a heretic queen, attempted one of the boldest military maneuvers in history—and failed.

You've probably studied the defeat of the Armada in school. But what you may not have learned is that its demise had less to do with poor seamanship, bad weather, and clumsy galleons than it did with something much more damaging—bad leadership. It's all in a remarkable but little-known study of the battle written by the British scholar, David Howarth.[1] His report of what really happened turns the centuries-old episode into a pathetically real modern leadership disaster.

What happened?

Almost everything. Perhaps most important, Philip did not believe in his own plan. He said as much in a letter to the Duke of Parma: careful reading of the letter reveals a leader who expected failure. Not only was Philip willing to leave Elizabeth on the throne, he would even have considered negotiating the tricky matter of religion. "The more one looks at the letter," wrote Howarth, "the more outrageous it seems. In the end, not even [the king] could define in any reasonable words the motive for which the Armada was sent to sea...." So much for management by objectives!

Then there was the matter of personnel. The man Philip picked to lead the Armada was especially ill-suited for the job. He was the duke of Medina Sidonia, whom Howarth describes as "more gardener than seaman." When Philip appointed him Captain General of the High Sea, the duke was horrified. To his credit, he told the king so. "Sir," he protested, "... it would be wrong for a person like myself, with no experience of seafaring or war, to take charge of it. I cannot attempt a task of which I am sure I should give a bad account." Philip did not listen. He placed his Armada in the hands of an incompetent.

Even worse, he buried himself, and his organization, in an avalanche of paperwork. It choked the entire enterprise. No wonder history has labeled Philip "chief clerk of the Spanish empire," and that the term "red tape" comes from the brightly colored ribbons carefully wrapped around thousands of his memoranda. When it came to decisions, the king was glacially slow, a habit that led to another uncomplimentary nickname, "Philip the Prudent." He apparently believed that if he simply waited long enough, his problems would vanish.

Philip also tried to always avoid one-on-one meetings, which he found hugely uncomfortable. On those few occasions when he did allow subordinates into his inner sanctum, he would listen with royal impatience, then get rid of them as soon as possible. Days, weeks, or months later, a letter would emerge from his palace containing an astonishingly oblique and noncommittal reference to the long-forgotten audience.

Nor was Philip willing to delegate, overseeing himself the Armada's smallest details. There was the matter of the wine, for instance. Lisbon and Condado wines, he commanded, would be drunk first, then Lemego and Monzon. Sherry and Candia were to be saved until last, since, he earnestly explained, "they would survive the long sea voyage best."

Maybe all this had to do with smarts. The king had a knack for being monumentally wrong. His meticulous orders for the Armada's voyage up the English Channel are a good example. These instructed the fleet to "keep away from the French and Flemish coasts because of the shoals and the banks." There are no shoals and banks off the French coast, only rocks and salient promentories—just the kind of landmarks sailors love. Philip's hopelessly wrong order put the Armada precisely where it should not have been, hugging the English coastline. And his command that the Isle of Wight must be entered by the east side because it is "wider there than the west" was equally off base. True, the eastern entrance is wider, but it is also full of dangerous, hidden shoals.

So was the entire enterprise. Unfortunately, the more things went awry, the more Philip became hopelessly inflexible. When someone noticed during a brief port visit that the food had gone bad, Philip ordered the fleet to sea anyway. He could not tolerate bad news. It was God's will. His Armada would sail, food or not. And when it did, Spain's "Enterprise with England" would fail miserably. While the British lost no ships and only one hundred men, less than half the Spanish ships returned home and twenty thousand Spaniards died. Quite obviously, what happened in the English Channel four centuries ago had more to do with lack of leadership than it did with anything else.

## ... and Military Successes

Happily, the leader we review in this chapter provides an antidote to such military bungling and teaches lessons in leadership that you will find timeless. He is Carl von Clausewitz. To him, a daring offensive is the most brilliant aspect of an effective defensive move. What's more, winning, on both military and commercial battlefields, depends upon concentrating your forces at your opponent's most vulnerable spot, even if it means you become weaker at other points.

We're not stretching here. Von Clausewitz himself made it very clear that war and business were related. Here's how he put it:

> *War belongs not to the province of Arts and Sciences, but to the province of social life. It is a conflict of great interests which is settled by bloodshed, and only in that is it different from others. It would be better, instead of comparing it with any Art, to liken it to business competition, which is also a conflict of human interests and activities....*[2]

Von Clausewitz was right, of course. Business is a lot like war. And today's vast corporations are much like the nation-states exisiting during his (and even our) times. Like states, corporations are political entities preoccupied, as was Willie Stark in chapter 4, with the sources and applications of power. Both corporations and states go to great lengths to maintain order and security. A state may apply force to coerce its citizens into lawfulness; corporations can apply such powerful sanctions as transfers, demotions, even terminations. States defend their boundaries by military force; corporations by the weaponry of unbridled competition, industrial espionage, employee pirating, or predatory pricing. Corporations and states are equally territorial, each tenaciously defending its turf. And, perhaps most importantly, the fortunes of corporate giants, like those of nations, are frequently determined by those at the top.

Let's look at one parallel between the military and the corporate worlds, competitive intelligence. Nothing could be more important to the military commander than the ability to assess the enemy's strength, weakness, tendencies, and intentions. After all, success in war is dependent on one thing: the ability to anticipate the plans of the enemy and to be certain the enemy is unable to anticipate yours.

The same is true for business, where competitive intelligence is critical, even though it may have little James Bond or CIA cachet. Sometimes collecting it takes on near-hilarious dimensions, as in the case of six Marriott employees who once checked into a cheap hotel near the Atlanta airport. This bit of corporate sleuthing was reported not long ago in *Fortune* magazine. Once inside their room, the spying began. One member of the team called the desk to report that one of his shoelaces had broken—could a new one be sent up immediately? A sidekick checked soap, shampoo, and towel brands in the dilapidated bathroom. Another writhed on the bed and knocked loudly on the headboard as his compatriot listened next door. Marriott's secret agents continued for the next six months, collecting information on the hotel's rivals. The result? Fairfield Inn, a new hotel chain designed to beat the competition from "soap to service to soundproof rooms."[3]

There are other techniques in the corporate G2 arsenal. One frequently used is to glean information from unwitting recruits. The idea, it seems, is to turn the interview into an intelligence-gathering opportunity by getting potential employees who have worked for the competition to volunteer valuable, and competitively sensitive, information. Another is to hire management consultants to find out what the competition is doing. It's quite a scam: the consultants announce breezily that they're doing an industry-wide study and that they'll share information with everyone who participates. You, in fact, get only superficial facts back. The real client gets the inside dope. Then there's the "phony bid" request. A supplier gets a loyal (and willing) customer to submit a request for proposal to the suppliers' competition. He then sits back and waits to review the resulting mountain of descriptions and technical facts the supplier had hoped to keep confidential.[4]

But von Clausewitz offers more than advice on spying on the competition. Sounding like a harried manager rather than a military leader, von Clausewitz decries the "infinity of petty circumstances" (his early version of Murphy's Law) which cause organizations of any kind to go awry. As he put it:

> *Everything is very simple in War, but the simplest thing is difficult. These difficulties accumulate and produce a friction which no man can imagine exactly who has not seen War.... In War, through the influence of an infinity of petty circumstances, which cannot*

*properly be described on paper, things disappoint us, and we fall short of the mark.*

*This enormous friction, which is not concentrated, as in mechanics, at a few points, is therefore everywhere brought into contact with chance, and thus incidents take place upon which it was impossible to calculate, their chief origin being chance....*

In order to help you from suffering such disappointments, in this chapter we'll show you how von Clausewitz' maxims of leadership and strategy can be successfully used to deal with today's increasingly combative global business challenges.

## Von Clausewitz: Philosopher of War

Unless you're a military history buff, a former or current military officer, or a devout student of Prussian history, you're probably not familiar with the life and works of Carl von Clausewitz, whose magnum opus, *On War*, offers us a look at leadership on the battlefield (and, as we will show, in business).

In *On War*, von Clausewitz tells us why war exists and what soldiers do in battle. He offers a plan for success and explains how and why war is like no other human conflict—except, perhaps, business. Along the way, he details the need for leadership and the traits required of a leader in battle.

To understand von Clausewitz and his work, it's important to know the context in which he lived, wrote, led, soldiered, and died. His homeland of Prussia began as a Germanic state, a defensive post along the outermost boundaries of the Roman Empire. It was created to protect the Roman Empire from marauders and because it had no useable natural resources. As such, it was derisively called the "Sandbox of the Empire."

Prussia, therefore, was created to serve military convenience. Military minds built it, ran the region and, as you might expect, made their decisions from an entirely military point of view. All of this did not happen by accident. Prior to this strong military buildup, early Prussian leaders from the 1400s to the late 1600s had little control over the region. Roving soldiers of many nationalities used Prussia as a battleground and it was not until Frederick the Great took control in 1740 that this practice came to a stop. Frederick built the Prussian army into one of early Europe's strongest fighting forces. The nation's defense budget used over half of its resources to keep the army well-supplied and fit for battle. Not surprisingly, other nations were reluctant to fight this "20th-century Sparta."

In Prussia, being a military man was more than just an assignment, it was a calling. Carl Philip Gottfried von Clausewitz seemed destined from birth to be a soldier. Born in 1780 to a wealthy family, von Clausewitz was groomed for a military life. Following the death of Frederick the Great in 1792, he entered the Prussian army as a cadet at the age of twelve. By 1801, at age twenty-one, he enrolled in the Berlin War College where he began more rigorous army officer training. Three years later, he graduated at the head of his class and began his career as a leader and commander of men.

Fighting in the Battle of Auerstadt, von Clausewitz and his commander, Prince August, were defeated and captured. As prisoners of war, they were taken to France and held captive for ten months. Returning to his homeland, von Clausewitz felt strongly that his side had been vanquished for two reasons: Prussia had not used the act or threat of war as a tool of effective foreign policy, that is, to keep other countries—friend or foe—in line, and also because the Prussian people were passive, apathetic, and did not support the army's efforts.

Back home, a wiser von Clausewitz teamed with his mentor and teacher, Gerhard von Scharnhorst, to reform and rebuild the Prussian army. To achieve this end, he was offered a teaching position at the War College. And although his reform movements were meant for the good of the army, von Clausewitz' political views often clashed with the country's political leaders, who did not always take the military's advice as they formulated their policy decisions.

In 1812, von Clausewitz resigned his army commission and teaching post when he learned that Prussian politicians had agreed to let Napoleon use Prussia to stage its attack on Russia. Incensed, von Clausewitz (along with several of his colleagues) joined the Russian army, where he became a colonel. He helped to defeat Napoleon at the legendary battle of Waterloo and returned home again to become the director of the Berlin War College.

## Lessons in Leadership from a Military Man

As armies go, the Prussian military force was a paragon of strength, equipment, tactical knowledge, training, and muscle. Developed initially by Frederick the Great, the army owed its success to its use of constant drill to keep its soldiers focused and disciplined. Its officers were highly-motivated professional men who came from positions of stature, culture, and education.

It was not always that way. Prior to Frederick's reform movements (which began just before von Clausewitz entered the army), desertion, insubordination, and various forms of goldbricking, either from the rank and file or the officers' quarters, were quite common. Since the early officers tended to be aristocrats not willing to sully themselves with battle and the soldiers tended to be social misfits, drunken scoundrels, and common thieves, it was easy to see why this cross-cultural mix created a fairly pathetic fighting force. And because many of the enlisted soldiers were foreigners, it was hard for their officers, unschooled in the ways of military order and discipline, to communicate with them or exercise much control over them.

Frederick the Great, von Clausewitz' mentor, saw these inadequacies in his troops and set about to fix them. He increased the penalties for desertion, created a rank structure, and trained his officers to use the element of surprise to defeat unprepared enemies. He knew that the typical back and forth battles of the day were costly in human terms and required too much of the soldiers to continue for very long. Ambush and guerilla warfare-type tactics, therefore, were the skills he (and later, von Clausewitz) taught and urged upon the men.

To continue further this idea of unity of purpose, Frederick and his generals preached that military service, that is, the willingness to defend your nation, was the highest calling you could respond to. Like our own military personnel, Prussian soldiers thought themselves to be the best, the toughest, the bravest, and the most resourceful. This kind of thinking has filled the heads of nearly every soldier, regardless of country, for hundreds of years. "Courage, service, and integrity," it was said, "were important Prussian values" and Frederick the Great and von Clausewitz reinforced these ideals at every turn.

Following the defeat by France, Prussia's military leaders, including von Clausewitz, set about to create an army that could function effectively during both wartime and peacetime periods. They wanted to allow for the army to grow systematically and logically, using recruiting policies that told the common man what army life was all about. More importantly, von Clausewitz and his allies realized early on that the army thrived or failed on the shoulders of its officers. They created a system to attract and educate well-schooled citizens as officer material. Until then, receiving a rank and a command was more an accident of birth and breeding than proper military training and experience. The military schools, like our U.S. service academies, attempted to build well-rounded officers who knew as much about history and literature as they did about small arms tactics and strategic battle plans. Entry into these schools was difficult. Student officers were expected and compelled to show initiative, take responsibility, and be objective, flexible, and able to think clearly under pressure.

The Prussian army leaders saw that trench warfare and open-field warfare were both pointless; battlefield charges where men were cut down like high grass were ludicrous. The Prussians were the first army to regularly use the breech-loading rifle and this ability to hurl bullets great distances downrange at their sabre-wielding opponents made them a fierce adversary.

As the director of the War College in Berlin, von Clausewitz was able to bring his practical battlefield experiences to bear with his education, communication skills, and leadership abilities. He divided *On War* into eight sections. The first two looked at the nature of war in general; the third focused on ideas of military strategy; the fourth and fifth examined combat maneuvers and the proper use of military forces; the sixth discussed defensive strategies; the seventh discussed offensive strategies; and the last section spoke of war as a part of the political process.

What follows are some of the important themes von Clausewitz touches on during his discourse. As you review them, note the parallels between the traits needed to succeed in war and the traits you need to succeed in business.

As we mentioned earlier, von Clausewitz speaks of what he calls "friction," that is, those elements that get in the way of good communication, good relationships, and above all, good leadership. In his view, friction between people, nations, groups, or more abstract and less concrete entities like time, assets, or distance, is something that is inevitable in any organization. He understood, rightly, that anytime you put people, equipment, and services together as a unit, and then move those people, change their positions, or take them out of their comfort zones, you're bound to stir up some dust.

Since this is bound to happen, the mark of a good leader, according to von Clausewitz, is one who can deal with it and move on:

> ... but a [leader] must be aware of it that he may overcome it, where that is possible, and that he may not expect a degree of precision in results which is impossible on account of this very friction.

He also makes an important distinction between tactics and strategy. The first, he argues, are the methods leaders use to carry out their plans; the second is made up of the actual plans, policies, procedures, and operations themselves. You can't have one without the other, warns von Clausewitz:

> According to the notion we have formed of tactics and strategy, it follows, as a matter of course, that if the nature of the former is changed, that change must have an influence on the latter. If the tactical facts in one case are entirely different from those in another, then the strategic must be also, if they are to continue consistent and reasonable. Only great tactical results can lead to great strategic ones....

Von Clausewitz also lists the elements, ideals, and physical, mental, and psychological traits a good leader must have. They constitute the characteristics of true leadership.

*Indifference to danger.* When things get tough, the leader must know how to keep fear under control and show a brave face.

*Courage.* This comes with pride, patriotism, and unbridled enthusiasm for the cause. Its source is within.

*Physical fitness.* It's not just the battles that demand fitness, it's the preparation for them that many leaders find so trying. A strong body and a strong mind can be invincible together.

*Tolerance for uncertainty.* There is much in life that we can't predict. Many things are hidden at first and only appear after careful research, effort, other events, or just the passage of time.

*Understanding the presence of chance.* Von Clausewitz feels strongly that chance is a major factor in success or failure. You can plan for every eventuality, and yet, one unseen, unknown, or unplanned factor can still slip into the works.

*Intellect.* Having and using your intelligence is critical to your success as leader. Here von Clausewitz suggests that wise leaders must be able to know instinctively and almost immediately what will work and what will not. Those, he says, "who have little intelligence can never be resolute."

*Presence of mind.* Too often, events and episodes—and the people involved in them—can swirl around you like a strong wind. You must develop the ability to think on your feet, adapt to changing situations, and keep your head.

*Energy.* Related to physical and mental fitness, this trait is what causes people to go where others have not gone and do what others have not done. Energy gives you the drive and the reason to stick to your plans and see them through.

*Firmness.* Make your decision and stay with it, even in the face of seemingly long odds or when you're surrounded on all sides by idea-killers. Resist the temptation to take the easy way out or look for an escape route.

*Staunchness.* Stand firm and develop a reputation for completing your tasks, even when others have quit beside you.

*Strength of mind and character.* Be known as an ethical, honorable, and fairminded person who does not intentionally harm, manipulate, or deceive other people. Make your convictions known, invite others to challenge them, and then be ready to defend your position.

*Self-command.* This is a feeling of personal pride, passion, and desire to do your best.

*Avoidance of obstinacy.* In his view, von Clausewitz feels that those leaders who can't change or be flexible are far too egotistical to be very effective. Be willing to hear other viewpoints and, if the ideas are better than yours, accept them and implement them.

*Esprit de corps.* It's hard to get people to serve your ideas and help you complete your plans if they don't feel much loyalty to either you or their co-workers. Work hard to create a professional and personal bond between yourself and your people by modeling the traits of hard work you'd like to see. Roll up your sleeves; get into the trenches.

*Aptitude.* Here, a certain native intelligence shows itself. Play to your strengths, both as a leader and when completing tasks, and ask others to focus on what they do best as well. Even if you don't know all the answers, if you can devote more time to doing what it is that you do best, it will outweigh your deficiencies.

*Endurance*. This is the ability to keep on "fighting the good fight." Sometimes, it's easier to throw in the towel and give up, especially when a project is at its most daunting stage.

*Enthusiasm*. This can be a positively contagious disease that spreads through an organization if it's created in the right spirit. It can't be phony, contrived, or extracted from people; it has to come from the heart.

To summarize his discourse on battle and how to achieve victory in war, von Clausewitz offers four rules to live and fight by.

1. *Employ all your available forces with the utmost energy.*
   Von Clausewitz suggests that the harder you work and the more you plan, the better everything will run and, more importantly, the better everyone around you will feel. "The moral impression," he says, "produced by vigorous preparation is of infinite value; everyone feels certain of success." In our context, this means you'll need to plan, plan, plan, and then move out smartly, making sure everyone knows their role.

2. *Concentrate your force at the place where you're most likely to win.*
   Don't go into battle haphazardly. Study your plans, pick the enemy's vulnerable spot, and then target all of your resources (in our context, that means people, products, services, advertising, marketing, money, commitment, and time) right at it. You want to break through the opposition's lines and enjoy an immediate, swift victory. This strategy is correct, says von Clausewitz even if it forces you "to run the risk even of being at a disadvantage at other points, in order to make sure of the result at the decisive point. The success at that point will compensate for all defects at secondary points."

3. *Don't lose (or waste) time.*
   Sometimes you might want to wait. You may think that a short delay (when introducing a new product, for example) may be to your distinct advantage. Usually though, says von Clausewitz, "it is important to commence work as soon as possible." Time, unlike money or other seemingly replaceable goods or assets, is

always gone forever. By moving ahead when ready, you can often gain the element of surprise on your competitors. "Surprise," admits von Clausewitz, "plays a much greater part in strategy than in tactics; it is the most powerful element of victory."

4. *Follow up your success with your utmost energy.*
   Don't rest on your laurels. Continue to press on and see your efforts through to the end.

As he concludes *On War*, von Clausewitz offers a few last pieces of advice for the budding warrior/leader.

- *Create defensive strategies, not just offensive ones.*
  In other words, sometimes the other team is going to have the ball.
- *Attack, attack, attack.*
  Move forward as much as you can, take initiatives when they arise, and be ready to maneuver around obstacles of people and things when necessary.
- *Be bold.*
  He or she who hesitates is lost. The higher your position in the organization, the more your people look to you for examples of bold leadership.
- *Persevere.*
  Keep going, because things are not always going to go exactly as you planned. You have to be flexible, sidestep problems you can't fix, and focus on those ones you can do something about. You're going to run into problems with people, products, services, and relationships, especially when you least expect them or can ill afford them. Keep going.
- *Save your energy for another day.*
  The world turns. There are always going to be other battles to fight, or, more importantly, to prepare yourself and your people for. Don't use all your resources at once unless you have no other choice. The victory doesn't always go to the baddest, maddest, or toughest fighter; it goes to the one who can remain standing till the end.
- *Have a "tactical retreat" plan in place.*
  Unlike Captain Ahab, whose monomaniacal leadership we pro-

filed in chapter 6, sometimes you have to know when to call it quits and try again later. If you don't have the necessary support, tools, people, supplies, or other assets, and you can't win, gather yourself together and come back another day and try again. Although von Clausewitz' work focuses on the essentials of combat, his messages can easily be applied to today's business environment. By looking at his ideas and the way he perceived the learned skills of leadership, we can apply some of his methods to the way we organize people and projects, motivate our employees, solve tough problems, and vigorously go after our competitors with new products and services.

## Von Clausewitz and Staying Close to the Customer

We think von Clausewitz would have been wildly enthusiastic about one of today's most honored business principles: it's important to be "close to the customer." In military terms, this translates into spending more time at the front lines than back at headquarters. After all, it's in the heat of battle where we learn almost everything about warfare and strategy.

And, as marketing mavens Al Ries and Jack Trout pointed out recently, just as you can't learn about winning battles back at headquarters, you rarely find solutions to management issues locked in the board room. As in von Clausewitz's case, those solutions are much more likely to be found down at the front lines. Ries and Trout suggest that you show up at your "front" with an open mind and be responsive to spontaneous and often marvelously creative ideas that can only emerge when you're "on the line." Their point is persuasive and they remind us of a number of super-successful leaders who had a great deal in common with von Clausewitz:

- *William H. Gates III, Head of Microsoft Corporation*
  This Harvard dropout went from hot-shot programmer to the youngest CEO of a *Fortune* 500 company. Along the way he accumulated and dispensed invaluable insight into the ever-changing software industry.
- *Thomas S. Monaghan, Founder of Domino's Pizza*
  Monaghan learned about the pizza business in the trenches, then went on to build a company with some 6,000 outlets and almost $3 billion in revenues.

- *Frederick W. Smith, Founder of Federal Express*
  Smith built Fed Ex after learning everything he wanted to know
  about airplanes (and probably more) in Vietnam. He must have
  learned well; his firms' share of the overnight delivery market is
  now more than 50 percent.

What all of this boils down to, we're afraid, is more frequent flier
miles for you. You'll have to spend even more time in the field, away from
the "other world" serenity of corporate headquarters. As Ries and Trout
put it, "to become a great strategist, you have to put your mind in the
mud of the marketplace. You have to find your inspiration down at the
front lines, in the ebb and flow of the great marketing battles taking
place in the minds of your prospects." Our advice is to pack your briefcase and head directly for the airport.

As with anything, it's always important to keep things in perspective.
Sure, it's useful to think of yourself as a "warrior." But there's also the
matter of ethics. Ruthlessness as a leadership trait leaves a lot to be
desired. Resolving this apparent paradox depends on understanding
something very non-Prussion, the Japanese "scholar-warrior."

This idea relates two seeming opposites: the "scholar," who knows
literature, art, and has a certain educated grace, and the "warrior," who
knows strategy, tactics, and how to fight. The Japanese samurai of old
were masters of this duality. They could easily switch from one role to
the other, practicing their calligraphy in the morning and battling with
swords in the afternoon. While it's not necessary for you to learn origami
or become proficient at swinging a pair of *nunchakus*, you can, it seems,
be a tough businessperson without losing your humanity.

## Business as War: The Japanese Point of View

You don't have to look very hard at the Japanese—their operations,
approaches, and tactics to see that they have taken von Clausewitz and
his ideas to heart. In nearly every export product—from cars and light
trucks to electronic equipment to computer chips—the Japanese have
approached their entry into U.S. markets with Clausewitzian single-
mindedness.

The Japanese don't apologize for their view of business as war, with
the United States as the target. Interviews with Japanese CEOs from
large manufacturing firms reveal an attitude that says, "Business is war.

We're coming over, we're bringing better technology, cheaper products, and a more powerful work ethic. Deal with it, America, because no matter what you do, we're coming." It's not surprising that when Japanese executives were asked to comment about their representative portrayal in the film, *Rising Sun*, most agreed that it was accurate. Their comments? "We are at war with you, for products, services, trade agreements, exports, and whatever else we can make there and bring here."

### Frictional Losses: Mr. Murphy Comes to Town

We want to return to one of von Clausewitz's most important points. "When something can go wrong, it will" seems to be the anthem of business today, especially during any critical operation, manufacturing procedure, client meeting, overseas negotiation, or other life-and-death organizational event. Mistakes happen. This is the concept of "friction" that von Clausewitz spent so much time discussing in his book. A good leader always knows that even the best-laid plans can go awry and even the most well-intentioned people can make mistakes.

The point of all this is that the small stuff, the seemingly trivial, can easily become the big stuff: the newly arrived deal-killers; the contract breakers; the counteroffers thrown into the deal at the last minute that change the entire structure of the deal package you just spent weeks or months creating; the fuzzy contract language that spins both of you into civil court; the unforeseen industrial accident; the new design or specification changes that disrupt your production schedule; the firing of a key person who served as your guiding hand; a new buyout offer that suddenly looks so much better than yours; a crop failure that puts your supplier out of business; overdependence on one key inside or outside person; government interventions; new federal rules, laws, or tax consequences; problems with your bankers, insurance brokers or accountants; overseas supplier problems; shipping, mailing, or packaging snafus; a sudden change in the financial picture of your competitor, vendor, or partner; or any other large or small catastrophe that keeps you from achieving your goal. Quite obviously, it's endless.

So what was von Clausewitz' counsel to deal with these sources of "friction?" First, he said, understand that they exist and that in the heat of the battle, when things are going full steam ahead, change is inevitable. In fact, you should expect something to go wrong anytime you undertake a big quest or a large project.

Second, with the existence of these corrosive "frictions" already in the back of your mind, recognize that if you can't predict them, do the next best thing: plan for them. As the old airplane pilots' credo goes, "In God We Trust. Everything else we check."

Make and keep your backup and contingency plans handy. Practice if-then thinking that says, "If this happens, then we will respond this way." Encourage the people around you to do the same as well, e.g., "If our supplier falls through and can't deliver the parts we need, we will call this new supplier, whom we have already developed as a manufacturing contact in case of such an emergency" or "If five people from the dayshift catch the flu at the same time, then we will pull two people from the second and third shifts and ask a supervisor to pitch in as well."

This type of if-then thinking is all too rare in some organizations. As employees race around trying to either put out small fires or plan for the Next Big Idea, they take their collective eye off the downside potential. The solution? As you develop plans for any major project, you should always throw in some backup or contingency ideas. You don't have to be gloomy about it; you're not setting yourself up to fail, you're only creating backup systems, policies, procedures, and plans for those "just in case" times when Mr. Murphy (Clausewitz's "friction") comes to call.

It's perfectly acceptable to stay strictly focused on your goals. You can be wholeheartedly positive and still stay realistic about what might not work so well.

### The Pogo Theory: Knowing Your Enemy

As our own General George Custer found out at Little Big Horn, there is not much benefit to taking the low-ground position. As military strategists like von Clausewitz have attested, placing a skirmish line of your troops on a flat battlefield and lining them up to face your enemy's skirmish line is a sure way to induce high casualties. Worse yet, if your opponent sits on the high ground and you wait in an area below, your group will induce far worse losses.

From a business standpoint, the idea's the same. The strongest companies always try to operate from a position of strength. They've done their homework, i.e., they've asked the tough questions of their customers, employees, vendors, and business partners, such as "What business are we really in?" and "What do our customers tell us they want most from us?" They've done careful market research that shows their own position in the marketplace and that of their competitors. They've taken a hard look at their policies and procedures to see that they're both customer-friendly and employee-friendly.

And finally, they know their own weaknesses and their competitors' strengths. They work to maximize their strong points and minimize their competitors'. They make educated guesses about what to expect from their markets and industries and they keep pressure on their competitors by trying to stay one step ahead in products, services, and customer "intelligence," that is, what they hear or know their customers want from their mutual business relationship.

Von Clausewitz would surely agree, counselling that the way to win the high ground and stay there is to never let your opponent gather enough resources or momentum to knock you down. In business terms, this means preserving and expanding your market share.

## When Bad Things Happen to Good Companies: Believe It, Deal with It, Move On

Have you noticed that many people exhibit a common trait when something goes wrong? When their plans go astray or something significant happens to disrupt their activities, many people say, "I can't believe this happened!"

Are you one of these people who says these things? Do you rant and rave about your fate or about how unfair life is for you, either at that particular moment or in general? It's easy to feel this way when you have a flat tire on your way to an important sales meeting, when the airline loses your luggage before your big speech at a convention, or when your competitor comes out with your newest product two weeks before you do.

While this "I can't believe it" lament may be common amongst us, the leaders in the group will say something a bit different: "I do believe this happened. It's certainly unfortunate and it's going to make things a bit tougher on me or for the other people around me, but since it happened, it's over and done with. I need to reorient myself and move on."

See the difference? Your business, professional, and personal life is filled with these kinds of moments when something unpleasant happens. We would like to suggest you adopt this habit of saying "I believe it," rather than "I don't believe it." Leaders deal with problems and move on. They know there's no sense in whining and wailing about what can't be undone. It's better to accept it, not curse your fate, and get to work on solutions, alternatives, or new ideas.

Stay out of the "I can't believe it" syndrome. Believe it, admit that it happened, and then hitch up your belt and go and fix the problem, repair the damage, or look for another way around the obstacle. Don't dwell on things you can't change, and anyway, that's why you have a backup plan in the first place!

### Perspective: Winning the Battle yet Losing the War

When Adlai Stevenson lost the 1952 presidential election to Dwight Eisenhower, he made his now famous remark, "I'm too old to cry, but it hurts too much to laugh." Even in the face of a humbling defeat, Stevenson managed to be gracious, humorous, and even self-deprecating.

You can be gracious in defeat; there will be other chances with this idea, this competitor, or this project. Good leaders know there is no sense in burning all their bridges or leaving in a huff when you will have to do business with the same people on another day. And as von Clausewitz' life demonstrated, you can learn from your defeats. After his release from the French prison camp, he redoubled his efforts to make certain he never lost again. As head of the War College in Berlin, he spent his remaining years writing and teaching his soldiers how to win, but it was only after his loss that he could see the real path to victory.

There is often more to learn in defeat than there is in victory. History is full of examples of this. When Thomas Edison was working diligently on the filament material for his electric light bulb, he was said to have tried over seven hundred different elements, all of which failed to perform. When someone asked him whether he felt like quitting in exasperation (and there were just as many idea-killers around then as there are now), he replied, "Of course not, now that I know of seven hundred elements that won't work, I'm sure I'll discover the one that does." And so he did.

In his 1990 book *Getting It Right the Second Time*, author Michael Gershman tells stories of now well-known products that were miserable failures when they were first introduced.[5]

- Carnation's "Instant Breakfast" milk powders sold dismally in the diet food section of the store and like a champ once they were repositioned in the breakfast foods aisle.

- Instant coffee flopped when it was introduced in 1901 but, during World War II, workers and soldiers wanted fast coffee and it caught on.
- Raytheon lost $5 million on its first microwave oven. The company went back to the drawing board, made some design and customer-requested changes and put it back on the market with great success.
- Little Short Cake Fingers and I Scream sold poorly until they were renamed Twinkies and Eskimo Pies.

There is no shame in defeat if, of course, you learn from your mistakes and don't make them again. The old saying "Fool me once, shame on you. Fool me twice, shame on me," certainly applies to those people and companies who keep making the same mistakes over and over again.

Can von Clausewitz' military leadership genius be transferred to the executive suite? Certainly. But we live and lead at a time when cooperating may well become a more important leadership skill than competing; when "make peace," not "make war," may be the rule. In this "new world order," effective leadering may have more to do with trust, inspiration, alliance building, nurturing, involvement, openness, creativity, and even love than with battle.

Real leadership, whether on battlefields or in board rooms, may be about setting people free, not conquering them. Even the inscription on the bronze bust of MacArthur by Japan's leading sculptor attests to this possibility. It reads: "General Douglas MacArthur—*Liberator* of Japan."

Even so, who would disagree with the assertion that business—at its best and at its worst—is much like war? And among the injunctions that von Clausewitz leaves with us are these:

- *Think strategy.*
  Strategy is to the leader what an income statement and balance sheet are to the accountant. Strategy is a road map that shows you where you are going. It is an overall plan. And strategy in business is similar to strategy in war. It is long-term. It is determined by top management. It provides general goals toward which the organization should strive. And, perhaps most importantly, strategy must match resources and skills found within the organization with the task at hand. Simply put, if you don't have

the resources and skills necessary to achieve your goal, you badly need a new strategy.

- *Strategy is like a magnet.*

As case writers Wendell Frye and Michael K. Green have pointed out, any organization is made up of vastly different parts and constituencies. The environment provides different opportunities as well as risks. There are, as pointed out above, real limits to resources. What's more, each of the organization's leaders may have different values. Finally, ethical standards impose limits on the organization. The purpose of strategic planning is to align these disparate parts so that they work together in a kind of synergy, much like the force a magnet creates when it is dragged across a collection of tiny bits of metal.

- *Goals need to be precise, measurable, and fixed in time.*

This is just as fundamental in business as it is in war. Lest goals become organizational laughing-stocks, make certain that there is broad "buy in" among the troops. Be sure that goals are consistent with each other (We recently became aware of a near catastrophic inconsistency in a small college's goals: accept students with lower than average grades in order to meet the school's financial plan and at the same time, reduce attrition—students failed for poor academic performance—by 10 percent!). Install a reward system that reinforces the actions needed to make goals happen.

- *Once you have a strategy, determine your tactics.*

Tactics are concerned with the specific plan for a specific battle. Tactical planning, which is based on the strategy, concentrates on the short term and upon more specific objectives. Here's the relationship. A strategy might be, for example, to become the leading producer of robotics in the world. A tactic related to that strategy might be to introduce a line of industrial robots for the auto industry within the next year.

- *Choose an attack strategy.*

Researchers have identified five attack strategies for businesses to consider. The *frontal assault*—von Clausewitz would have called this "boldness"—consists of directly attacking your opponent's strength (Examples: lower prices, more efficient production). *Flanking,* or *encircling*—both of which von Clausewitz heartily recommends—might consist of identifying a weakness in a competitor's geographic coverage or market segments served and then penetrating at several points (Examples: offering an array of more specialized products, bracketing a competitor's product between a higher-priced premium brand and a lower-priced brand. A *bypass* attack, recommended by von Clausewitz because it can cut an army off from its supply sources, consists of bypassing an enemy and attacking easier markets (Examples: diversifying into unrelated products and/or into new geographical markets). Finally, *guerrilla* warfare consists of making small, intermittent attacks on different aspects of a competitor's business, with the goal being harrassment and demoralization (Examples: selective price cuts, executive raids, intense promotional bursts).

- *Watch out for friction.*
Von Clausewitz makes one thing very clear: there is frequently a gap between the formulation of strategy and its implementation, due to what he calls "friction." We call it "Murphy's Law," the ineluctable truth that resides in most management and leadership situations, "Whatever can go wrong, will go wrong." Best to prepare accordingly. How? By conducting, at least in your mind, "what-if" simulations for every critical project you're involved in. Run through each important step, asking yourself, "what's the worst that could happen here?" All too often, you'll discover that your worst-case scenario is the one that's closest to what actually happens. This should come as no surprise. After all, it's war out there!

## CHAPTER 9

# BREAKING THE RULES: IS THERE LIFE AFTER THE POLICY MANUAL?

*Laws not enforced cease to be laws and rights not defended
may wither away.*
— THOMAS MORIARTY

**KEY POINTS**
- BREAKING RULES
- MERE MANAGERS JUST FOLLOW THE RULES; LEADERS KNOW WHEN AND HOW TO BREAK THEM

Self-appointed management pundits are frequently given to hair-splitting. But when it comes to distinguishing between managers and leaders, they may be on to something. Granted, to anyone putting in fifteen-hour days just trying to make next quarter's numbers, separating managers from leaders may seem as useless as rearranging the Titanic's deck chairs. After all, plenty of mediocre managers occasionally show leadership ability. And corporate icons—the likes of GE's Jack Welch, Chrysler's Lee Iacocca, and the late Sam Walton come to mind—also manage: worrying about budgets, resource allocation, and who gets promoted to third vice-president.

Yet separating leaders and managers may be a useful exercise. An early proponent of distinguishing between managers and leaders is Abraham Zaleznik, psychoanalyst and one-time occupant of the Harvard Business School's prestigious Matsushita Chair in Leadership. Zaleznik claims we live in an over-managed and under-led world, and it's causing no end of trouble. The managerial orientation, Zaleznik writes in *The Managerial Mystique*, with its emphasis on form over substance, structure over people, and power relationships over work, is at the heart of the disability of modern business in the United States.[1]

Strong stuff, but he doesn't stop there. He argues that manager-types are handicapped by being born only once, a condition which causes great personal unpleasantness. "While busily adapting to their environment," Zaleznik says, "managers are narrowly engaged in maintaining their identity and self-esteem through others." Then there are the leaders. These stalwarts, in Zaleznik-ese, are twice born. Such future top-dogs, as a result of having suffered some trauma in a former life, possess the fortitude to challenge the status quo, to ask tough questions. This enables them to transform their organizations—to lead. To Zaleznik, this makes all the difference. "Leaders," he goes on, "have self-confidence growing out of the awareness of who they are and the visions that drive them to achieve." Managers, clearly, need not apply.

Zaleznik is not alone in contrasting the limitations of garden variety managers to the virtues of those who can lead. His Harvard colleague John Kotter, for example, while granting that ordinary managers are frequently capable of dealing with complexity (planning, budgeting, goal-setting, refereeing, and the like), argues that it's what they don't do that is the problem: they don't cope with change. That Herculean task, he says, is the unique job of the leader.[2] And choreographing organizational change demands that the leader set direction, create vision, and establish strategy. To illustrate his argument, Kotter has crafted a neat military analogy. Peacetime armies, he says, can be managed. But start a war and you need leaders. No one yet has figured out how to *manage* people effectively into battle; they must be *led*.

The bottom line on all this is that leaders do whatever is necessary to survive and are able to compete effectively in wildly new environments. They do things that managers don't particularly like. Managers fight chaos and disorder; leaders thrive on it.

Management scholar Craig Hickman might well have been thinking about leader-as-chaos-creator when he wrote *Mind of a Manager, Soul of a Leader*. The word "manager," claims Hickman, tends to signify the more analytical, structured, controlled, deliberate, and orderly end of the continuum while "leader" tends to occupy the more experimental, visionary, flexible, uncontrolled, and creative end.[3] His conclusions? Managers are the kind of people who bring the thoughts of the mind to bear on daily organizational problems. Leaders, however, bring the feelings of the soul to bear on those same problems.

Thinkers? Feelers? Once born? Twice born?

The problem with all this is the mutual exclusivity that these categories suggest. True, everyone is cleverly pigeon-holed—but consider the kind of organizational apartheid that can result: managers here, please; leaders over there. The solution, of course, for organizations that are to deal effectively with dramatic changes like globalization, networked information technology, radical new ways of organizing work, and the emergence of a knowledge-based economy, is synthesis and integration. Simply put, today's organizations critically need the best of both worlds, people who can both manage and lead; organizational polymaths who can fuse the objective, linear, rationality of the manager with the aroused consciousness, circularity, and intuitive sense of the leader. Not an easy task.

And one not overlooked in Melville's *Billy Budd*, as you'll discover when you assume the role of Captain Edward Vere, commanding officer of the British warship HMS *Bellipotent*. You'll see that, although Vere attempts to go by the book, he also wrestles with the temptation to create new rules that circumstances seem to demand. And you'll ride Vere's range of emotions as he—and you—discover that the path to successful leadership, as opposed to mere management, is neither easy nor clear; it is strewn with intellectual, emotional, and ethical complexities as well as the frequent need to improvise.

Nowhere, in fact, is the inherent tension between what managers and leaders do better dramatized than in this highly readable story. There's much more here than a mere tale of life at sea. *Billy Budd* is the riveting account of a sea captain's struggle to manage and to lead well while at the same time deciding the fate of one of his most valuable shipmates. As a manager, Captain Vere is bound to do his duty: to follow procedure, to honor the rules, to act, as we might put it, according to the policy manual. But the leader in him dares him to go beyond the book, to create new rules, to consider the unusual, even unique, mitigating aspects of the event and choose an unprescribed course of action. It is this conflict that makes *Billy Budd* a classic tale and a superb case for students of leadership as well as practicing leaders.

That Herman Melville should produce such a masterpiece is not surprising. Following his early career as a professional sailor, Melville, whose biography we began in chaper 6, came back to his home in Boston in 1844 to try his hand at writing. Thanks to his travel experiences in the South Seas, the Marquesas Islands, Tahiti, and Hawaii, Melville could write marvelous descriptions of these lands, describing the people and scenery in ways that fascinated his American readers.

Yet, for all his literary and storytelling talent, his works met with little commercial success and Melville could hardly eke out a living from his craft. As a result, he was forced to work at a number of non-literary jobs and suffered a nervous breakdown in 1856 due, in part, to financial pressures. He became more and more reclusive, even eccentric, as the years passed. *Billy Budd* was Melville's last book, finished only five months before his death in September 1891.

There are two major characters in Billy Budd: the title role, played by a young man who has gone to sea and suddenly been drafted from a merchant ship to a war ship; and Captain Edward Vere, the master of Billy's new ship. A minor but equally influential character, John Claggart, is the master-at-arms, a shipboard position similar to that of a police officer. It is the relationship between these three men that creates the drama and the conflict in the story.

Billy Budd is a young, good-looking sailor (Melville refers to him as "beautiful"), new to sea life, who has come to Captain Vere's man-of-war, the HMS *Bellipotent*, after being impressed from a merchant ship called the *Rights-of-Man*. Billy is a hardworking boy who follows orders well, toils without complaint, and seems to get along with everyone except his nemesis, John Claggart. The master-at-arms, according to Budd's shipmates, "is down on him." Billy, as we've suggested, is innocent, handsome, and seems to have his whole life ahead of him. Claggart is dark, brooding, and full of hatred for the likes of Billy. In his mid-thirties, Claggart is in charge of the ship's weapons, makeshift brig, and enforcement of the shipboard rules. He is not well-liked by the crew, mainly for his vile disposition, but also because it is his job to enforce order.

Then there is Captain Vere, a career British Navy man in his late forties or early fifties, who adheres to the letter of the law aboard his ship.

He takes his service to the Royal Navy quite seriously and has distinguished himself in battle, proved his courage under fire, and been rewarded with the command of his own ship.

### Lessons in Breaking the Rules

As the novel opens, young Billy is comfortable in his job as a "foretopman" aboard the *Rights-of-Man*. Coming alongside the British battleship HMS *Bellipotent*, her impressment officer, Lieutenant Ratcliffe, orders the ship to give up a man into the Royal Navy. Although he is happy on his present ship, Billy cheerfully agrees to go and makes his way to the *Bellipotent* with his few belongings.

Billy's former captain tells Lt. Ratcliffe that Budd is a pleasant young man, liked by all, and a good crew member. As his old ship leaves, Budd waves goodbye to his friends and starts his new life in the navy without much regret. We get the distinct impression from this exchange that Billy has put to sea for the adventure of it all and he does not seem to care much about which ship he is on, as long as he's on the ocean.

Billy adapts to his new ship quickly and shows a knack for work. Simply put, he is a model employee. Melville gives him several interesting characteristics: he apparently knows nothing of his birth, parents, or early childhood and he exhibits a stammer if he is antagonized or frustrated by people or events.

Once he settles into his new life, Billy realizes there is an air of mutiny aboard the *Bellipotent*. As the ship heads to the Mediterranean Sea to join other British ships in battles with the French, he hears stories of successful and failed mutiny attempts that have occurred on other vessels. The *Bellipotent's* captain, Edward Vere, is well aware of these incidents and orders his officers to be vigilant and strict, almost to the point of paranoia. No one will mutiny on his ship.

Vere, as Melville describes him in various passages, is in many ways two-sided. He has proved himself to be a courageous veteran of several sea battles; he is a forceful commander of his ship and men; and he is a strict disciplinarian—his rules and the rules of the Navy are meant to be followed. Yet, he is also fond of books, introspective thought, and the pleasure of his own company. But overall, while he may be a skilled captain, it appears early on that his utter devotion to duty and rules makes him less than flexible. He seems utterly incapable of bending the rules or seeing "beyond the policy manual" should the situation warrant a less harsh approach. Such inflexibility will have a significant impact on Billy Budd as the story progresses. In fact, it makes the story. After Billy accidentally spills some soup on a newly-washed deck, Claggart gives him a hostile reprimand. It's suddenly clear to Billy that he will have trouble with Claggart before this cruise is over.

Critics and scholars have suggested accurately that *Billy Budd* is a novel of contrasts: contrast between Billy's old ship and his new one; and contrast between his former captain (who was benevolent, likeable, and apparently much less concerned with the yoke of discipline) and Captain Vere, a much harsher taskmaster who takes his comfort in following rules. Vere and Claggart contrast as well; one man seeking control, order, and righteousness at all times and the other man seeking to punish his enemies, feed his hidden agendas, and encourage his own hatreds.

And finally, there is the distinct contrast between the easy-going Budd and the malevolent Claggart. Their personalities, behaviors, outlooks, ages, experiences, innocence, and physical appearances are in complete opposition to each other. Since all good drama is based upon contrasts and conflict, their differences make the story powerful.

As the story develops, Claggart has decided to seal Billy's fate once and for all. He tells a crew member to meet with Billy and inform him that a mutiny plot is afoot. Billy rises up against the crew member and threatens him. Claggart will soon turn this contrived mutinous conversation into a weapon against the young man. The trap has been set. Now Billy's innocence and his inability to see Claggart for what he really is will come back to haunt him.

Following an unsuccessful chase with an enemy ship, Captain Vere is on deck when Claggart approaches to tell him that one of the crew members was less than brave during the encounter with the French and further, that same sailor may be ready to organize a mutiny. When Vere hastily asks Claggart who this man is, he tells him "William Budd."

Claggart has struck Vere at his weak spot. Vere likes Billy, has considered him for a promotion, and is shocked at this assertion of cowardice and mutinous behavior. To get to the bottom of it all, Vere orders Claggart and Budd to meet in his cabin for a private conference. At the meeting, Vere orders Claggart to repeat his charges in front of Billy. Billy, speechless with shock, disbelief, and growing rage suddenly reaches out with his fist and strikes Claggart squarely across the forehead. The master-at-arms falls to the floor, dead from the blow to his skull. Vere tries to tend to his fallen officer but it is too late. He gathers his emotions, sends Billy to wait in another room, and calls for the ship's doctor who, after examining Claggart's body, agrees that he is dead.

All this hugely transforms Captain Vere. As Melville puts it,

> ...Captain Vere with one hand covering his face stood to all appearance as impassive as the object at his feet. Was he absorbed in taking in all the bearings of the event and what was best not only now at once to be done, but also in the sequel? Slowly he uncovered his face; and the effect was as if the moon emerging from eclipse should reappear with quite another aspect than which had gone into hiding. The father in him, manifested toward Billy thus far in the scene, was replaced by the military disciplinarian.[4]

Vere tells the doctor he will order his officers into an immediate shipboard court martial to deal with Billy's actions rather than wait to rejoin the British fleet and send the boy to a more formal hearing. The doctor, not wanting to disobey Vere, silently agrees. But along with his fellow officers, he feels they should wait for a formal trial.

For his part, Captain Vere feels trapped. He doesn't really want to prosecute Billy, but the fear of mutiny is constantly in his mind. He worries that if he allows Billy to remain free, or even mitigates the penalty, the crew will think less of him, his rules of order, and his leadership abilities in particular. Forgiveness now, he fears, may cause a mutiny.

At a hastily arranged court martial session, Billy is formally charged with the murder of Claggart. Since Captain Vere was the only witness, he tells the board what happened. Then the first lieutenant asks Billy if the Captain is correct in his description of the facts. Billy tells the court officers that his captain is right, but that Claggart is a liar. He is in fact a loyal servant to the British Navy and the King. He is sorry that Claggart is dead, and he is even sorrier that he killed him, but since he could not speak and his anger got the best of him, he had no choice but to lash out at the man.

When another officer asks Billy whether he was involved in a mutiny plot, he does not tell the court of his encounter with the sailor who tried to implicate him. Instead, he looks to Captain Vere for help; but Vere, not wanting to stray from the case at hand, gives him no help or support and orders the court to focus strictly on Billy's murderous actions. He tells his court that Billy's action requires a sentence of death. The officers soon concur.

There was, in fact, legal precedent for Vere's hoped-for rapid verdict in Article XXII of the 1749 *Principles and Practices of Naval and Military Courts Martial*:

> *If any officer, mariner, soldier, or other person in the fleet, shall strike any of his superior officers, or draw or offer to draw, or lift any weapon against him, being in the execution of his office, on any pretence [sic] whatsoever, every such person being convicted of such offence [sic], by the sentence of a court martial, shall suffer death.*

Vere, in other words, has every legal right to call for Billy's death. This law, obviously enacted as yet another way to dispel any thoughts of mutiny, does not even require such an event like Claggart's murder to end in the suspect's death. Even the mere threat of violence against a superior officer can call for capital punishment after a formal military hearing.

There is also the matter of the enemy nearby. There was, as Vere put it to his officers, no time for hesitation:

> *But while, put to it by those anxieties in you which I cannot but respect, I only repeat myself—while thus strangely we prolong proceedings that should be summary—the enemy may be sighted and an engagement result. We must do; and one of two things we must do—condemn or let go.*

In the meantime, Billy is housed under guard and Claggart's body is buried at sea with full honors. Prior to the burial ceremony, Vere calls his crew on deck and relates the incidents that have happened to Claggart and Billy. He tells them Billy will be hung in the morning. When the crew starts to discuss these events quietly among themselves, the boatswain orders them back to work with his whistle and they disperse.

Billy meets with the ship's chaplain, but understands little about what the cleric is telling him of God, death, and spiritual redemption. He has, in fact, already made his peace with the world, with Captain Vere, and with his present circumstances. He is ready to accept his fate.

Early next morning, Billy is brought by the chaplain to one of the masts of the ship and prepared for his hanging. At the last moment, just before he dies, Billy Budd cries out, "God bless Captain Vere!" After Billy is pronounced dead, some of the crew helps to prepare his body for a burial at sea and the remaining men go back to work.

Later, Vere and the men of the *Bellipotent* fight with a French battleship. While trying to board the enemy ship, Vere is mortally wounded. His lieutenant takes over the fight, captures the French ship, and tows it back to port. As Captain Vere and other wounded sailors are being taken to shore, Vere's last words before dying are, "Billy Budd, Billy Budd."

## Good versus Evil

Billy Budd is a very rich leadership classic, and it is no wonder. The story has many sides. It is at once a novella that tells a tale of good versus evil, using shipboard life as its setting. It also speaks of one man's inability (Vere's) to judge the actions of another (Budd's) under any other context besides what is "purely" right or wrong. From a legal standpoint, it shows how laws can control people rather than people controlling the laws. One of the first things many people ask after reading the story of Billy Budd and Captain Vere is, "Who was right?" And indeed, that's the focal point of the story: Was Vere correct in his handling of Budd's trial? Was there even a need for the trial itself? Did Vere overreact based upon his need to maintain order and be seen as a tough taskmaster, a strict disciplinarian, and a man of the rules?

While there are no easy answers to the Budd case, we can easily form certain conclusions about Captain Vere's leadership style. For him, Budd's case was cut and dried and fell neatly into one of his managerial pigeonholes: "Break the rules, decide on the punishment, mete it out." Rarely did he take counsel from his junior officers. While he lacks the maniacal personality of a leader like Captain Ahab, the approach has some interesting similiarities: "The buck stops here. All decisions end with me. I am the final, and in most cases the only, word."

This "my way" decision-making style becomes quite apparent during Budd's hastily arranged trial. Interestingly, the members of the board find themselves in the same position as Vere in that they are faced with playing two roles as well. They want to get to the bottom of the Budd case and decide it fairly, yet they are faced with making a decision that could be unpopular with their boss. So, faced with the choice between deciding for Budd and against Vere, or siding with him, however tacitly, they must agree with his judgment, verdict, and subsequent death sentence.

Further, the culture of their organization plays a large part in how they must make their decision with Billy. In the male-dominated environment that is the *Bellipotent*, there is no room for weakness or, worse yet, the appearance of weakness. Men are men and ships are ships and Captain Vere and his officers have chosen to live and work in this fear-based, punishment-oriented environment. We can almost guess how Vere will respond. Why? Because he has already revealed himself to be a mere manager, a slave to the rule book, instead of a leader.

While he may mean well, his decisions are clouded by two criteria: what the rule book says and how his decision will look to his men and his officer colleagues. He is what he is, a by-the-book manager who can't find a way to compromise or look at Budd's case in nonjudgmental, unbiased, or even compassionate terms because none of those three abstractions can be found in the table of contents or index of his rule book. Good leaders, however, know from experience and intuition that you can't always go by the rule book. Every situation is different, every person involved with that situation is different and, more importantly, has his or her own side of the story to tell.

As a leader faced with a difficult decision or a personnel problem to solve, you need to put your own feelings aside, no matter how difficult it may be, for just enough time to collect all the facts, listen to all sides, and then, if time and the situation warrants, collect opinions from interested participants, knowledgeable third parties, or even from someone who is not associated with the problem or the people at hand. No one can fault you if you spend some extra time gathering information, soliciting opinions, or asking for advice. Frankly, if the decision is important enough, you'll want to do this to protect yourself from future problems.

Vere's problem was that he failed to take any of these information-collection steps. The officers on Billy Budd's court martial board certainly had their opinions as to what might have happened between Budd and Claggart; about Claggart as a man and an officer; why Budd responded with an attack on Claggart; what questions they might have wanted to ask of Billy; and even what they thought should be done to adjudicate Budd's case. Vere missed all of this because he wanted to show everyone he was a take-charge leader and because the group felt too threatened to respond with anything other than a rubber-stamp approval of Vere's wishes.

## Chameleon Qualities: Changing to Match the Situation

We've suggested before, in chapter 4, that leaders often act like chameleons, changing roles, management styles, or decision-making approaches to fit the situation at hand. If all this sounds familiar, it should. Vere's self-induced transformation from soulful father figure to military taskmaster simply dramatizes that which is indispensable in any successful executive: the capacity to assume roles, to be, at various times, both leader and manager, moving fluently from one behavior to the other depending on the situation. There's nothing hypocritical here, nothing deceitful. Vere's facile gearshifting, in fact, has a long and hallowed tradition in the military. Sandhurst's John Keegan, who investigates the nature of heroic military leadership in *The Mask of Command*, claims that successful leaders, like entrepreneurs and athletes, must possess a strong theatrical impulse.[5] The leader of men in warfare, he writes, can show himself to his followers only through a mask, a mask that he must make for himself, but a mask made in such a form as will mark him to men of his time and place as the leader they want and need.

Lest you think wearing the mask of either the leader or manager works only in the military, consider this: such chameleon-like ability has been celebrated for years in business organizations too, most notably in a now classic *Harvard Business Review* article entitled "How to Choose a Leadership Pattern."[6] The idea is straightforward. Executives need, exhort the authors, a repertoire of leadership and management styles: various habits of behavior which they favor during the process of directing and influencing co-workers. Like Vere, you can pick anything from boss-centered leadership to subordinate-centered leadership. It's a simple matter of selecting from seven leadership styles along a continuum.

To almost no one's suprise, Ken Blanchard, who reduced excellence in management to a half-hour read in his 1983 bestseller *The One Minute Manager*, has recently made all this even more elementary.[7] Positing just four leadership situations, he tidily matches each with a corresponding role for the leader to play. If, for example, you're saddled with unwilling and unable subordinates, argues Blanchard, simply assume the role of petty tyrant and nasty manager: tell them what to do. Willing but unable subordinates get only slightly better managerial treatment. Transforming yourself into company pitchman, you sell them your ideas. Unwilling but able subordinates get brought into the fold by a modicum of leadership which allows them to participate in your grand plans and strategies. But if you're lucky and unusual enough to be blessed with subordinates who are both willing and able to carry out your every wish, lead away. For this situation, Blanchard breezily recommends a kind of leadership that might be characterized as benevolent neglect: kick back and delegate.

The lesson is that you, too, may have to switch roles. Like Vere, you may at times need to be, as Melville hauntingly puts it, like that "...moon emerging from eclipse which reappears with quite another aspect than which had gone into hiding."

But it requires a modicum of flexibility. Vere's inability to see more than one side, usually his own and no one else's, leads to his downfall. And while it's hard to say Captain Vere's "by the rule book" approach led to his own death during the battle that closes the book, it certainly leads to the immediate, and quite unfortunate, death of Billy Budd.

What this boils down to is that good leaders know the answer is not always found in the rule book. They recognize the obvious need for the rule book, better known as the employee manual or their firm's policies and procedures manual. They know that without it, there would be anarchy. We need rules at work just as we need rules at home, in the streets, and in society. We couldn't function in an atmosphere without them, yet we need to be flexible in our interpretation of them. Some might respond: "It's not right to allow people to interpret the rules as they see fit. This means that if someone thought the rule against stealing jewelry from a store didn't apply specifically to him, he could walk right in and take as many diamonds out as he could carry."

We're not denying the need for uniformity in the application of rules; we're only suggesting that in some cases, it's necessary to look harder at the facts and see if the punishment fits the offense. Leaders know when and how to bend the rules, not just to meet their own personal goals but for the good of their people or the good of the organization as well. It's this same argument—enforcing the "letter" of the law" as opposed to enforcing the "spirit" of the law—that confuses the Budd/Vere dilemma.

Vere supporters might say, "It's in the sailors and soldiers' procedures manual. You can't threaten or hit a superior officer. If you do, it's a capital offense." And Budd backers would counter with, "That's certainly true. The rule does require that punishment, in its purest application. But the rule book fails to take in the context, the circumstances, and the situation surrounding its use." They make an important point. It is the context and it is the circumstances that drive good leaders to act with the best interests of the group in mind.

A criminal defense attorney who practices law in a small East Texas county seat puts it this way, "Many of the people who typically sit on my criminal case juries already have their minds made up as to my client's guilt or innocence before my side of the trial even starts. They say, 'Well, the sheriff arrested that man and he's a law officer, so he must know what's right. He wouldn't have arrested him if he didn't think he was the guilty party. And if we have any questions about what to do, we'll just look and see what the law book says.' It's my job to convince them that it's not always 'what's in the law book' that decides guilt or innocence." As a leader faced with a problem that requires "the rule book," you first need to decide if this is in fact a situation that has more than one side; is it one that has room for thoughtful interpretation? Careers can be ruined by a "Rules be damned. I'm going to do things my way, every day" approach to management.

The concept of situational leadership sums up the balance needed between these two extremes. In its essence, situational leadership is exactly what it says—you make your leadership decisions based on the situation. This is not to say you have to be wishy-washy and make everyone happy, but rather that you weigh each problem or opportunity on its merits, flaws, or impact on the organization or people, and then make your decision accordingly.

The benefit of this approach is that it offers you a built-in way to be flexible, unlike Captain Vere, in your thought processes and decision-making. You can find an acceptable resolution without causing a major rift in the management principles that are important to you or tied to your value systems. When the situation calls for you to be tough, you can take that approach; when the problem calls for a cool head and more thought before you act, you can gather your facts, ponder them, and then decide; and if the situation calls for an immediate decision, you can trust your experience and intuition to help you make the right choice.

### The Leader as Seller
If you'll recall from our study of Prince Hal in chapter 2, we pointed out that he had a certain charisma and the ability to communicate with different types of people on their own levels. Walking through the camp of

his soldiers dressed in disguise, Henry was able to listen to their thoughts and feelings and fears. He talked "to" them, rather than "at" them, a quality Captain Vere sorely lacked.

For his part, Vere tended to be aloof, distant, and preoccupied with his thoughts. When one of his men came to him with a problem, he gave the impression that he was bothered by the interruption. Further, he lacked that quality of charismatic communication we saw in Melville's other sea hero, Captain Ahab (chapter 6). For all his faults, Ahab knew how to motivate his sailors and get them to buy into his grand scheme. But in the case of Captain Vere, recall that on two occasions the crew voiced their misgivings about what had happened to Billy. The first came during Vere's announcement of his crime and punishment, and the second followed Billy's hanging. Clearly, we see an unhappy, confused, and apprehensive crew.

Unlike Vere, good leaders know how to sell their actions. Melville made this clear when he compared the kind of leadership Admiral Horatio Nelson was capable of to Vere's more "bookish" style:

> In the same year with this story, Nelson, then Rear Admiral Sir Horatio, being with the fleet off the Spanish coast, was directed by the admiral in command to shift his pennant from the Captain to the Theseus; and for this reason: that the latter ship having newly arrived on the station from home, where it had taken part in the Great Mutiny, danger was apprehended from the temper of the men; and it was thought that an officer like Nelson was the one, not indeed to terrorize the crew into base subjection, but to win them, by force of his mere presence and heroic personality, back to an allegiance if not as enthusiastic as his own yet as true.

Like the famous Nelson, leaders must sell their ideas or their decisions to their constituents, just as a successful salesperson sells his or her products or services to customers.

### Floating Trial Balloons: Selling It to the Crew

People want to feel as if they are not isolated, not "out of the loop." Yet Vere could not and did not sell his treatment of Billy Budd to his crew. And interestingly, he did not even bother to sell his approach to Billy's court martial board, but because of his use of coercive power ("I am in charge, I am the captain of this ship") he influenced the outcome of their decision anyway.

But while the trial board may have been swayed by his rank and position as their leader-of-last-resort, Vere's crew was not. The first they heard of the Budd incident was after Vere had already made his decision—not a good tactic for any leader. Worse, they had no time to react to the death of Claggart, Billy's involvement in it, nor the trial and sentence.

Imagine how you might feel if your company president called your entire organization into an auditorium, went up to the lectern and said, "We've sold the firm to a company in Taiwan. If you want to transfer there, you can, otherwise, you're all out of a job." Needless to say, after the president dropped this pair of bombshells, howls of protest and astonishment and angry questions would surely spring from the audience.

This was precisely Vere's failing. To be an effective leader, you must take the time to sell new ideas to your people or run the risk of their not supporting you when you need it. This is not to say you always have to get complete buy-in from everyone, only that you have to give people the chance to digest the information and respond to it in their own way. This is especially true of critical information, career-affecting news, or other events that can influence people in very specific ways. You've got to pre-sell it, sell it, and then follow up on what you've sold. Political candidates and their campaign managers call this "floating a trial balloon." They do it all the time.

The "trial balloon" technique calls for you to foreshadow an idea that may already be in the works. By putting it out to the people, you can gauge early responses, interests, and criticisms. What you hear from them may influence what you do next. If you get overwhelming support, your choice is clear. If you get middling support, with equal amounts of positive and negative remarks, you may have more information-providing to do. And if your trial balloon gets "shot down," then you know you should either tread very lightly or abandon that course of action all together.

In Captain Vere's case, the use of trial balloons to provide information to his crew could have been invaluable: "There has been a dreadful accident. During a meeting between myself, Mr. Claggart, and Billy Budd, the two men got into a fight and Mr. Claggart died of his injuries." Response to this statement would no doubt have been quick and emotional. After letting the crew vent their feelings, Vere could have said, "I will be conducting a full investigation into this matter. It is my intent to get to the bottom of this and I will need your help. If anyone has any information about this incident that might be useful, please talk to one of our senior officers and ask him to report back to me." Notice here that Vere has not asked his crew to line up outside his cabin door in order to pass information to him; he can use his chain of command to accomplish the same thing. In the military-ruled, male-dominated, honor-oriented environment that is the *Bellipotent*, this would allow his men to save face and still tell the truth about Claggart.

Vere's next trial balloon should come right after this information-gathering, feedback process. "Now that we have collected all the facts in the case, we will convene a court martial trial board to take testimony, review the events, and come to a decision. We will call on several of the crew to help us with this process." Again, this provides the crew with more information and the last part takes the onus off them for having to appear on their own. Anyone who testifies can tell his peers he was called to do it.

Vere's final trial balloon might be stated like this, "We have come to our conclusions with the trial board and its inquiry. Based on the evidence and the testimony from the participants and knowledgable crew members, it has been decided by the board and myself that Billy Budd is guilty of the crime of murdering a superior officer. As you know from the manual, there is no choice but that Billy Budd be hanged for his crime."

While this process would certainly take most of the drama and conflict out of Melville's story, it does illustrate an effective use of the trial balloon as a way to sell hard, distasteful, or difficult news to your people.

### Confrontational Meetings

Thomas Paine observed in *Common Sense* that "... the harder the conflict, the more glorious the triumph." About war, that may be true. But it is seldom true in management, as anyone who has tried to settle disagreements between two quarrelsome co-workers knows. (It is estimated that managers spend about 40 percent of their time refereeing conflict.) In a conflict situation, a superior typically arranges to get the disputants together. Assuming the role of dispassionate arbitrator, he or she encourages them to state their respective views directly to each other, calmly and rationally. "With skilled leadership and willingness to accept the associated stress by all sides," read the management texts, "a rational solution can almost always be worked out." Such an event is called a "confrontational meeting."

But confrontations can also fail. When Captain Vere summoned Billy Budd to his cabin to face Claggart, the confrontation triggered not reason, but disaster. Melville describes Vere's fateful decision to bring the two antagonists together:

> At first, indeed, he was naturally for summoning that substantiation of his allegations which Claggart said was at hand. But such a proceeding would result in the matter at once getting abroad, which in the present stage of it, he thought, might undesirably affect the ship's company. If Claggart was a false witness—that closed the affair. And therefore, before trying the accusation, he would first practically test the accuser; and he thought that could be done in a quiet, undemonstrative way.
>
> Having determined upon his measures, Captain Vere forthwith took action.
>
> Whereupon, "Mr. Wilkes!" summoning his nearest midshipman. "Tell Albert to come to me." Albert was the captain's hammock-boy, a sort of sea valet in whose discretion and fidelity his master had much confidence. The lad appeared.
>
> "You know Budd, the foretopman?"
>
> "I do, sir."
>
> "Go find him."

It spelled catastrophe. The problem, of course, is that confrontational meetings are highly overrated. Captain Vere expected Budd to defend himself. Instead, he was mute. Vere presumed Budd would behave rationally. Yet he acted anything but rationally when he struck the blow that would kill Claggart.

What should Vere have done? Seeing to it that everyone aboard the ship was riveted to his organization's own overarching purpose—beating the enemy—rather than mired in their own petty squabbles, as were Claggart and Budd, might have helped.

A bit of common sense and even restraint is important here. Good leaders know there is a balance between totally avoiding conflict or meddling in every single personnel or relationship problem that appears.

Sometimes you have to let people work things out for themselves and other times you have to step in with a firm word and offer solutions, directives, or enforceable decisions.

Whether the conflict is based around some type of power struggle between people, teams, departments, or divisions, or simply between two people, one of the best ways to handle these potentially difficult and distracting events is to use what psychologists call the techniques of venting and validation. Your skillful use of each offers people an effective way to talk out their frustrations, explain their side or point of view, and then hear words of support that encourage both sides to work together to find an acceptable solution.

Here's an example of how venting works: let's say one of your salespeople comes storming into your office upset that someone in the marketing department failed to send promised product catalogs, price lists, brochures, and other sales literature to an important customer. Before you take up the argument, help this salesperson vent his frustrations. Allow him to rant and rave about the inglorious marketing department and its occupants until he is finished. (This could take five minutes or fifty, but in either case, you'll probably recognize the signs. He'll either stop to catch his breath or slump back into his chair and say, "There, I've said it. Now I feel better.")

And it's true. At this point, once the salesperson has released his pent-up feelings and had the chance to talk it out, you can start the process of validation. Some sample validation phrases might include: "I know how you must feel. This kind of mistake can really make you feel frustrated. I understand exactly what you're feeling. It's perfectly understandable that you might respond to their mistake in this way."

Here's an important key: it's not whether or not you agree with the salesperson that the marketing department erred; that can be decided at a later time. What's important about venting and validation is that it's an anger management process. It allows people to use you as a sounding board for their frustrations. Venting helps them release their emotions and validation shows that you have empathy toward their problems.

It's your job to allow the process to continue. Don't go overboard and join in with statements like, "You're right! Let's go over to marketing and give those jerks a piece of our mind!" It's up to you to allow your employees to vent in the safe confines of your office. Most people, once they've had the chance to blow off some steam, will feel better as a result and, more importantly, will be able to look at the situation in a more generous light. Unless they're the type who harbor grudges, keep silent agendas, and seek revenge in other destructive ways, one venting session is usually enough to get them away from their thoughts of anger and more focused on problem solving.

And the second step, validation, is just as important as the first. You don't need to coddle your employee or otherwise go overboard in your support. Your approach to effective validation is to make the person feel as though you understand their feelings, can identify with what they are thinking, feeling, and saying and, most importantly, that these feelings are perfectly normal.

You may recognize these techniques as ones used by psychologists to counsel victims of trauma, violence, injury, or the death of someone close. What they say to these patients is, "You have every right to feel sad, afraid, or angry. These kinds of emotions are common with your experience. Let's talk more about what you're feeling right now."

The upside of venting and validation is that it can really go a long way toward clearing the air. Sometimes a fiesty blowout can help your people know their voices can be heard. Just remember not to lose your objectivity, try to stay in control, and keep personal, racial, gender, ethnic, ageist, or other spiteful attacks out of the process.

## How to Run Task Forces (and Not Let Them Run You)

The trial board in Billy Budd plays a role not unlike the chorus in many Greek plays. Sophocles used the chorus in *Antigone* as a device to help Creon make his decisions. Among its many literary uses, the chorus can serve as the conscience, the fortune-teller, or the announcer of news. In Melville's *Billy Budd*, the officers of the court martial board are not allowed to develop into their full chorus-like potential. It's clear from the start that Captain Vere is running the show, pulling the strings (for it was he who picked the trial board members, including a marine officer who, not being a sailor, knew nothing of the rules of law and order aboard ship), and making the final decisions.

It was a sham. The members weren't allowed to voice their real opinions, and everyone in the room from Billy on down was too fearful of Captain Vere to say, "Let's investigate this further," or "Can't we take more time to talk about the people and the issues involved in this case?"

The trial board in Billy Budd was like many other task forces we've seen in many organizations. Their usual definition is a "temporary committee created to handle specific company problems or focus on new opportunities." But what appears in print often differs from what goes on behind closed doors. Too often, task forces, ad hoc committees, and other so-called temporary groups take on a life of their own. Ending an existing committee or group can be like killing Frankenstein's monster— you either may need lots of help or a very sharp axe.

Task force groups can take on the form of strategic planning groups, committees designed to handle specific projects (new product development, a large real estate or building plan, relocation efforts, selling the firm or some of its subsidiaries or divisions, etc.) or even crisis teams, created to deal with some internal corporate disaster or outside event.

But if all these groups were formed from the beginning under the impression that membership in the group and the life of the group was going to be a finite event, stick to that plan. When it's time for them to disband, close them up for good and move on to other areas. If it's necessary to re-establish the group at a later time (to deal with new problems or new opportunities), you can restaff it then, mixing predominantly new members with a handful of veterans to bring fresh ideas to the decision-making processes. All too often, it's the members of the committee rather than the circumstances or the need for the group's existence who make the decision to stay in force in the first place. This is usually counterproductive and a big waste of everyone's time.

Committee membership shouldn't be designed to resemble a country club perk. If people on the "outside," that is, not on board the committee or group, don't get the same perks and privileges as those on the "inside," it can cause hurt feelings, resentment, and that same idea of factionism we described above.

And even in the rare event that a committee or an ad hoc group needs to take on permanent status, at least have enough sense to restock the group with fresh faces at intervals. If the committee's work affects the health and welfare of the company, then everyone should have a chance to have their say. Ask for volunteers after a suitable amount of time and allow new people to speak their mind. As one executive puts it, "Committees are like sharks. They either move along or they die."

The *Bellipotent*'s tribunal failed to move, and Billy died. No wonder Melville's *Billy Budd* is one of those stories about which readers often say, "I wish it had turned out differently." The story offers an example of unbalanced leadership, of a near fanatical dependence on the rule book, and the inability by one leader to see the difference between doing things right and doing the right thing.

It has been said that manager do things *right*, and leaders do the *right thing*. Surely Melville's great story of Billy Budd forces us to consider whether or not Captain Vere did the right thing. These are the kinds of decisions every leader is faced with time and time again. Next time you find yourself struggling with a classic case of ethical decision making, keep the following points in mind.

- *When you delegate,* delegate.
  Captain Vere's handling of his drumhead court, his task force, was destructive. His increasing domination of the group killed creativity—the natural impulse to forge alternative solutions. Delegation became direction; monologue replaced dialogue. Yet, like many traditional managers, Vere looked at decisions through by-the-book, binary lenses. In this case his on-off, yes-no approach led him to consider only two options: Budd dies, Budd goes free. Neither alternative, really, was acceptable. Simply put, Vere's two-dimensional (and very simplistic) view created a classic "lose/lose" situation. Really empowering his task force and then responding favorably to its recommendation could have resulted in a much more acceptable course of action.
- *Ethical decision making is deeply affected by context.*
  Simply put, your organization's culture will drive your decision making. In Vere's case, there is irony here. In turbulent, chaotic times (read war), leaders make far better decisions if they are adaptive, malleable, open, diverse, and flexible. Yet military organizations, today's and the 19th-century British Navy, encourage anything but such suppleness. Instead, they are highly centralized, mechanistic, bureaucratic, tending to promote uniformity, loyalty to the system, and strict adherence to rules, regulations and procedures. It's a world, perhaps necessarily, in which policy manuals drive decisions; as in Vere's, the result is, of course, that individuals in such organizations have little leeway in choosing alternatives. Not surprisingly, they find themselves frequently

imprisoned in in little two-dimensional boxes. At its worst, this is the world not of leadership, but of mere management.

- *Leaders wear "masks."*

Vere's self-induced transformation from soulful father figure to military taskmaster clearly dramatizes that which is indispensable in any successful leader: the capacity to assume roles, to be, at various times, both dictator and benevolent friend, moving fluently from one behavior to the other depending on the situation. There's nothing hypocritical here; nothing deceitful. Vere's facile gearshifting, in fact, has a long and hallowed tradition in the military and elsewhere. Sandhurst's John Keegan, who investigates the nature of leadership in *The Mask of Command*, claims that successful leaders, like entrepreneurs and athletes, must possess a strong theatrical impulse. The lesson is that leaders, unlike managers, frequently have to switch roles, to put on a "mask."

- *Timing is everything.*

In *Billy Budd*, Captain Vere grapples with something equally as important as assuming the mask of command. It is timing. Like many leaders, Vere attempts to master time, to invoke a sense of urgency in order to force action. His actions suggest how time can be used as an instrument of power and influence. Research has confirmed that the ability to manage temporal forces is a critical leadership skill. In leadership, as in most endeavors, it is axiomatic that it is as important to determine *when* to do something as it is to determine *what* to do. Well-timed actions frequently succeed; contretemps almost always fall victim to their own inauspiciousness. And in the emerging conventional wisdom about leadership, the need for adroit timing has become formulaic: Quickness is critical to leadership success.

- *Press for alternatives.*

Vere considered only two options, hang or exonerate. Sadly, he did not recognize that he had more than two degrees of freedom. He had room to lead. He could, as his shipmates, and precedent, suggested, have simply delayed, referring the matter of Billy Budd to the admiralty when the *Bellipotent* next reached port. He might have had Budd convicted and then mitigated the penalty. He could have exonerated Billy and then shared his reasoning with the crew. Or he might even, as a mover and shaker among investment bankers at one of our recent seminars suggested, have told a *medicinal lie* (after all, only he and Budd witnessed the fatal blow). All these possibilites, of course, Vere did not consider.

- *Informal groups can be as important as formal groups.*
Organizations are made up of both formal and informal groups. The former consist of traditional organizational units—departments, committees, task forces, and so forth. On board the *Bellipotent*, for example, the foretopmen, such as Billy Budd, are a formal shipboard group. Informal groups, on the other hand, emerge as a result of individuals' needs and common interests. Such ragtag cliques can exert a huge impact on the organization. This is precisely what happened when one of Claggart's flunkies distorted his description of Billy Budd's behavior to him, making it sound as though Billy disliked and did not respect him. The point is that in order to be an effective leader, you've got to be as aware of the strengths and aims of informal groups as you are of formal ones.

- *Break, or at least bend, a rule now and then.*
Lest this seem like a form of corporate anarchy, a recent lesson from that phoenix-about-to-rise-from-the-ashes, IBM, might help. Western Union's consumer services division recently was about to purchase personal computers for its 14,000 agents throughout the United States. Yet there were many obstacles to the deal, and Western Union was close to closing a deal with one of IBM's competitors. As the IBM marketing rep put it, "the customer handed us a set of requirements we hadn't seen before. To meet them, we needed help from four other IBM organizations. We got it by throwing away the rule book. The point? Out went the rule book, in came the business. Think what it can do for you. Consider what it might have done for the hapless Captain Vere.

## CHAPTER 10

# How to Be the Ultimate Turnaround Manager: Churchill and the Allied Victory in World War II

*The nation had the lion's heart. I had the luck to give the roar.*
—WINSTON CHURCHILL

## KEY POINTS
- PERSUASIVE COMMUNICATION
- THE EFFECTIVE USE OF RHETORIC AND NETWORKING

If you've been saddled with the task of turning your failing organization around, consider this story of Britain's triumph over Nazi Germany in World War II. With Winston Churchill as your guide, you'll discover how the power of words can help a leader mobilize and motivate followers.

In this chapter, you'll read excerpts from three of Churchill's wartime speeches to see how vital the ability to communicate can be. You'll learn how the ability to motivate and inspire, coupled with never-ending perseverance, can enable any organization to triumph over its opponent.

And you'll come to see that in leadership it's not the possession of information that counts, but the use you make of that information that often spells the difference between victory and defeat.

## Winston Churchill: The Great Communicator

One of the more famous photo portraits of Winston Churchill, known as Britain's "great lion," shows him seated and looking out at us with a slightly stern face, his brows knitted and his chin firm. Dressed in a suit and leaning a bit forward, the photo fairly screams "Leadership!"

There's no doubt that Churchill had the "command presence" of a leader, that quality of inner self-assurance and confidence that makes other people take notice. Clearly, however, it was more than just command presence that made Churchill an effective leader. After all, most of his followers, who heard his speeches only over the radio, certainly couldn't see him. But what they heard were the words of an effective communicator—a leader whose speeches decisively and unequivocally conveyed to the British during World War II a need for action, a plan for action, and the expected results of that action.

Although Churchill took an active role in determining many of the strategic decisions of the war, that was not his greatest contribution as a wartime leader. Rather, it was his ability to motivate and inspire his people to prepare to fight Germany after the collapse of France in 1940. And his toughness and his reassuring presence as the ad hoc leader of free Europe gave hope to many other countries as well.

For such a task he was well prepared. Winston Churchill was fascinated by soldiers and the military from the time he was a boy. Born at Blenheim Palace in 1874 to parents who were members of Britain's landed gentry, Churchill enjoyed a comfortable and secure childhood. His grandfather was the Duke of Marlborough, a highly respected and valiant military commander, so it's no surprise that Churchill's early interest in the military was encouraged and rewarded.

He attended Royal Military College at Sandhurst, where he learned the skills and tactics of military leadership. Graduating in 1894 as a commissioned officer, Churchill fought in campaigns in Cuba, India, Egypt, and the Sudan in Africa, countries where Britain had a political or geographic stake. Upon returning home, he wrote his first book, *The River War,* which detailed his experiences in the historic battle at Omdurman, a city in the northeast of Sudan.

After running unsuccessfully for his first political office, he began work as a newspaper reporter. Sent to South Africa to report on the fighting there, he was arrested and jailed by the Boers. After three weeks he managed to escape. His dramatic escapade was well-reported in the

British newspapers and, riding the wave of positive publicity as a valiant hero, Churchill was elected to Parliament in 1900 as a member of the Conservative Party.

He soon clashed, however, with the members of his party over their desire to create a large British army and in 1904 joined the Liberal Party instead. The following year, as undersecretary of state for the colonies, he urged the adoption of a policy granting limited self-rule to South Africa as a way to end the fighting there. When the Liberal Party came to power in 1906, he ran for re-election and was selected as president of the Board of Trade. In 1910 he became Home Secretary, and when miners in South Wales went on strike, Churchill sent the militia to quell the unrest. He followed the same policy during a national rail strike. Appointed First Lord of the Admiralty in 1911, he oversaw the modernization of the British Navy, turning it into a professional fighting force in time for his nation's entry into World War I in 1914.

But the fortunes of war were not on Churchill's side. When the Germans moved through Belgium and put Antwerp under siege, Churchill was sent with a navy division to help Belgium. Instead they were badly defeated when the Belgiums surrendered to Germany.

Later, in 1915, his decision to use the navy to attempt to break through the Dardanelles near Turkey proved to be poor military strategy. Of the approximately 500,000 men sent to the area, over 40,000 were killed or missing in action, and another 200,000 injured. When the Conservative Party regained the majority in parliament the next year, Churchill, with few allies in the face of his military mistakes, was forced to resign from office.

Returning to active military service, Churchill became a strong anti-communist, attacking communist ideology and providing military support for anti-communist factions fighting in the Soviet Union. In a general election in 1922 he lost his seat in parliament, but two years later, as a member of the Conservative Party again, he was returned to Parliament. He was named Chancellor of the Exchequer (the U.S. equivalent to our Secretary of the Treasury), but Britain's fragile economy did as little for his career as World War I; at his recommendation, the nation returned to the gold standard, which further weakened its foundering economy. Labor unrest added to his problems, and he spent much of his time embroiled in labor matters, handling strikes, dealing with unions, and condemning strikers in the newspapers.

After losing yet another election in 1929, Churchill spent the next ten years out of office, but certainly not out of touch. He continued to meet with political leaders from other countries and work on the sidelines of British politics. Alarmed by Germany's move to re-arm (in violation of treaties signed at the end of World War I), he warned Britain of the dangers of appeasement and urged that the country's air force be built up.

When Britain entered World War II in 1939, Churchill found himself once more in the position of First Lord of the Admiralty for the Royal Navy. And once more, his forces were badly defeated by the Germans, this time in the battle for Norway. Yet it was Prime Minister Neville Chamberlain who resigned as a result of the defeat. Churchill, as a member of a new coalitional government, became his nation's prime minister.

He became deeply involved in planning and directing the war effort, which at first did not go well—the collapse of the French line necessitated the evacuation by sea of British troops which had been fighting in France. Later, however, the British air force later succeeded in driving back the German air attack on England in what was known as the Battle of Britain.

Although Churchill remained a strict anti-communist, the onset of the war had forced him to consider forming an alliance with Russia. Because Russia was an opposing force to Hitler's Germany, he put aside his personal beliefs in the interest of harmony among the nations allied with his own. He also formed strong ties with the United States, who came to England's aid with troops, war materials, and ships.

But while he may have had to side with Stalin (as evidenced by the historic meeting at Yalta between Stalin, Churchill, and Franklin Roosevelt), Churchill never changed his mind about communism. He was willing to work with the Communists to defeat Hitler, but he could not embrace their ideology. In 1945, it was he who created the term "the Iron Curtain" to describe the physical and psychological boundary between western and eastern Europe.

Churchill's "finest hour," and that of his nation, came together in the closing years of World War II. With his nation on the brink of defeat several times, Churchill went on the radio as the prime minister of Britain to give several moving, motivating, and invigorating speeches that rallied British troops and civilians alike.

The end of World War II in 1945 also brought an end to Churchill's position as prime minister. But he continued to live the life of the elder statesman. Serving as leader of the opposition Conservative party from 1945–1951, he again took the position of prime minister from 1951–1955. In 1955 he retired from public service, and spent the last ten years of his life working on a four-volume *History of the English Speaking Peoples*.

On January 20, 1965, at the age of ninety, Britain's great lion died. Yet his speeches live on, their rhetoric still as powerful and moving as it was fifty years ago. Rightly so, Churchill has gone down in history as the most significant English leader of the last one hundred years.

### Churchill's Speeches: Lessons in Communication, Motivation, and Persuasion

To truly understand the value and power of Churchill's speeches, it's important to understand the events that led up to them. Quite simply, Britain was at war with a seemingly invincible foe: Adolph Hitler.

From his early rise to power following Germany's humiliating defeat in World War I, Hitler had a plan to put every European country under his domination. In the years before the actual start of World War II, one nation after another fell to Hitler's soldiers. When Chamberlain's attempts to appease Hitler and stop his aggression (by ceding part of Czechoslovakia to him) failed, France and England declared war on Germany. But Hitler's army was on a non-stop march across Europe, conquering every nation in its path. And with the fall of France to the Third Reich, Hitler set his sights on Great Britain.

As such, Churchill's overall mission was singular and crystal clear: defeat the advancing German forces. For that reason, in speeches before parliament and to the British public, he attempted to rally the nation to not only fight, but defeat, Germany.

While the world remembers Churchill as a great orator, he was not always one, due in part to a congenital speech impediment. His skill as a polished and accomplished speaker came about only as the result of very hard work throughout his young adult life. Just as the great Greek and Roman orators practiced speaking near a roaring ocean to increase the strength of their voices, or spoke with pebbles in their mouths to improve the clarity of their diction, Churchill practiced his spoken words over and over. He memorized the speeches of well-known British politicians, an exercise that not only influenced his style of delivery but taught him the skills of rhetoric, the art of persuasive communication that he used so effectively in his wartime speeches. Churchill's speeches were not full of off-the-cuff or impromptu remarks; they were well-written, well-rehearsed, and well-planned events. They included stage directions, precise language, and colorful images designed to motivate his audience or sway them to his point of view.

Yet early in his career as a military leader and political decision-maker, Churchill's speeches, while certainly grandiose, were often ill-timed, or to use today's parlance, "politically incorrect." His style of communication—his extensive use of rhetoric—offended some rivals, confused his audiences, and often failed to help his cause with the people in his party. And as he switched party alliances back and forth, his speeches often seemed to contradict each other, making his listeners distrust what he said.

Further, because he was fully committed to the beliefs and ideals he espoused, he had what to others was the irritating habit of saying, "If you don't take my advice, your plans will fail." He seemed no team player, and this arrogance made him few friends in or around parliament.

But while these aspects of his character were liabilities for Churchill before the outbreak of World War II, they became assets once the war began. With German bombers in the air over England, the nation needed a leader capable of great rhetoric and even greater reason, of unshakable grit and dogged determination. They found these qualities in Churchill.

It was the first of these talents that propelled Churchill onto the world stage. As Britain's prime minister and leader of his nation's war efforts, his unparalleled speeches during World War II served three main purposes:

1. They informed Churchill's fellow politicians as to what was happening with the events of the war, particularly as they related to the health and safety of England.
2. Specific speeches were designed and written to provide both comfort and motivation to a highly disturbed British civilian and military population.
3. Many served as announcements to the Allied forces—the U.S. in particular—that England was committed to victory and would fight, with their allies and alone, until Hitler had been conquered.[1]

And these three purposes, looked at in the context of a world at war, help us to see why Churchill had such a dramatic impact upon his nation. He had become a charismatic and persuasive speaker whose speeches illustrate the leader as communicator, the communicator as motivator, and the motivator as mobilizer of his people.

To illustrate Churchill's use of the spoken word to accomplish his goals, we have selected three of his best known speeches.

His "Blood, Toil, Tears, and Sweat" speech was given by Churchill to the House of Commons on May 13, 1940. He had just been appointed the new prime minister following the resignation of Neville Chamberlain, who had taken the blame for Britain's defeat by the Germans in Norway. But as you may recall from the biographical information about Churchill, he was the First Lord of the Admiralty during that battle and bore some responsibility for the loss. Nevertheless, it was Churchill who took over for Chamberlain, and at a time when the country was beginning to reel from the effects of the war. In this speech, Churchill asks his fellow politicians to support his formation of a new government.

The "Arm Yourselves and Be Ye Men of Valor" speech was broadcast to the entire country on May 19, 1940, only six days after the previous speech. Hitler had already captured the Netherlands, Belgium, and Luxembourg, and was on his way to defeat the French. Here, Churchill tells his citizens and the world, in no uncertain terms, that Britain will fight Hitler with everything it has.

"Their Finest Hour," perhaps Churchill's most famous speech, was given to the House of Commons on June 18, 1940, and then broadcast on radio to the entire country four hours later. At this point, France had already fallen to Hitler and the German force was preparing to take on Britain. Churchill spoke about girding the nation for Hitler's impending invasion and gearing up for the Battle of Britain, a fight that would become the first and biggest air battle of the war.

### A Clear and Consistent Message

Churchill's speeches, as we've pointed out earlier, were never impromptu, but rather written and rewritten until they conveyed exactly the meaning he wanted. In his wartime speeches, his message and his aims were not only well-thought out but consistent. In different ways, he repeated the same themes over and over. There was no confusion about what was happening, about what the country needed to do, or why it needed to do it.

Leaders understand the value in giving that kind of consistent message to their people. Some people need to hear something more than once before they believe it, and some probably weren't paying attention the first time or two anyway. But more than that, consistent repetition of your message enables people to believe in you and in what you're saying. The manager who repeatedly jumps from position to position on an issue, or daily changes his mind about what the goals of the department are, loses credibility fast. Why should anyone believe what is said this week, or work toward implementing it, when it's only going to change next week anyway?

Churchill makes his position very clear in his opening statement to his fellow politicians in his "Blood, Toil, Tears, and Sweat" speech:

> *I beg to move that this House welcomes the formation of a Government representing the united and inflexible resolve of the nation to prosecute the war with Germany to a victorious conclusion.*

This statement is brief but powerful. In it, Churchill accomplishes a number of things: he makes it clear that he plans to fight the Germans with a complete and unbending effort; he puts his bipartisan colleagues on the spot by asking them to join his fight (a position they can hardly say no to); and he announces to all his resolve that Britain will defeat Germany. He goes on to tell the assembly that he has staffed the various critical War Cabinet positions in one day, "on account of the extreme urgency and rigor of events." It is clear that Churchill is not taking a let's-wait-and-see attitude. He knows trouble is coming and wants to convey a sense of immediacy to the House.

Then Churchill asks for the support of his colleagues, while again conveying the need to act quickly. It is here that he also makes the point that leads to the title of his speech:

> *In this crisis I hope I may be pardoned if I do not address the House at any length today. I hope that any of my friends and colleagues, or former colleagues, who are affected by the political reconstruction, will make allowance, all allowance, for any lack of ceremony with which it has been necessary to act. I would say to the House, as I said to those who have joined this Government: 'I have nothing to offer but blood, toil, tears, and sweat.'*

Could there be any greater sacrifice from a leader? And will anyone dare to argue with the authority he has presumed when it's clear there's no time to waste in wrangling, and when he has also made it clear he's not doing it for his own glory? As with the opening, Churchill has skillfully put his colleagues on notice: he is already moving out smartly to save England and would hope that they follow his example in their work.

As he closes this speech, Churchill makes it clear that what lies ahead will be difficult, will require many sacrifices and losses, and will challenge the will of the British people to succeed. But the will to win will not falter, he says. Britain's aim is victory at all costs:

> We have before us an ordeal of the most grievous kind. We have before us many, many long months of struggle and of suffering. You ask, what is our policy? I can say: It is to wage war, by sea, land and air, with all our might and with all the strength that God can give us; to wage war against a monstrous tyranny, never surpassed in the dark, lamentable catalog of human crime. That is our policy. You ask, what is our aim? I can answer in one word: It is victory, victory at all costs, victory in spite of terror, victory however long the road and hard the road may be; for without victory, there is no survival. Let that be realized; no survival for the British Empire, no survival for all that the British Empire has stood for, no survival for the urge and impulses for the ages, that mankind will move forward towards its goal. But I take up my task with buoyancy and hope. I feel sure that our cause will not be suffered to fail among men. At this time I feel entitled to claim the aid of all, and I say, 'Come then, let us go forward together with our united strength.'

In his conclusion, Churchill asks and answers the important questions on every British subject's mind. What's our policy? What's our goal? Simply and unequivocally, to wage war against the invading Germans, fight them using every possible means, and win no matter what it takes.

It's clear from this dramatic oration that Churchill's speech was designed to, in theatrical terms, "bring down the house." His opening is reasoned and thoughtful, he explains what he's done and why, he conveys the urgency of the situation and asks for the support of his colleagues. But then, as the speech draws to a conclusion, Churchill's words become more impassioned and emotional as he appeals to national resolve, national pride, and national unity.

In each of his wartime speeches, Churchill also raises the bone-chilling specter of the end of the "British" way of life if Germany is victorious. In effect, he says, "Folks, if we lose, our country is done for. We will no longer be 'England,' as we have been 'England' for so many centuries." Can there be any worse consequences of defeat—not just the loss of life and property, but the destruction of the very foundation of all that's British?

Churchill's final statement: "... let us go forward together with our united strength" reiterates a theme common to all his speeches: the need for unity of purpose and unity of effort. He knows he cannot prepare for war, or fight the war, alone. Throughout the speech he has made clear the need for political solidarity. He asks his political supporters and opponents to focus on what's good for Britain and not let petty partisanship, bickering, or jealousies get in the way of the real issue: victory over Hitler or the end of Britain as we all know it.

Yet Churchill doesn't leave his listeners with this dire predication as the last thought. He ends on a positive and upbeat note: "But I take up my task with buoyancy and hope ... let us go forward together with our united strength." This is his call to action, action not motivated by fear but because their cause is just and right, and will succeed.

When Churchill gives the next speech, "Arm Yourselves and Be Ye Men of Valor," only six days have passed since he spoke to the House. But the situation has worsened. Hitler's invaders have taken Holland, the French army is weakening and in some places has already been overrun. Churchill uses this speech to emphasize again, to the entire country, some of his previous themes: the need for unity and for unshakable resolve.

This speech is his first public address to the people of England since he took over as Prime Minister and, as before, his opening paragraph grabs the listener's attention:

> I speak to you for the first time as Prime Minister in a solemn hour for the life of our country, of our Empire, of our Allies, and, above all, of the cause of Freedom.

With that kind of powerful opening, it's a sure bet no listener tuned out or turned off the radio!

Churchill then defines the problem: the German forces have broken through French defenses; bombers, tanks, and other armored vehicles are making headway toward England; and behind the machines marches Hitler's infantry. So while he commends the French for their bravery and the Royal Air Force for its bombing work, the need for continued vigilance continues. "It would be foolish to disguise the gravity of the hour," says Churchill.

It's time, he suggests, for British troops to take the battle to the Germans instead of waiting for them to attack. It's time to meet the enemy on *Britain's* terms:

> The Armies must cast away the idea of resisting behind concrete lines or natural obstacles, and must realize that mastery can only be regained by furious and unrelenting assault. And this spirit must not only animate the High Command, but must inspire every fighting man.

Here's a clarion call to take an offensive rather than defensive posture, and at the same time it's a vote of confidence in the British forces. "We will not be intimidated," is Churchill's message.

What an important lesson for leaders who want to inspire their people to do more than they thought possible: let them know you believe in them, their abilities and their commitment to the cause and that you expect nothing less than success as the result.

Still, Churchill doesn't attempt to downplay the seriousness of the situation. He makes it clear that in spite of the accomplishments of Britain's defenses, in the air, at sea, and on the ground, further confrontation with German forces is inevitable:

> We must expect that as soon as stability is reached on the Western Front, the bulk of that hideous apparatus of aggression which gashed Holland into ruin and slavery in a few days will be turned upon us. I am sure I speak for all when I say we are ready to face it; to ensure it; and to retaliate against it.

There's some powerful imagery here, as well as emotion and passion, that grabs the attention of Churchill's listeners and reminds them of the grave danger the nation is about to face. Here Churchill's not simply stating facts, he's using words as a tool to inspire and motivate his listeners to take action.

He continues in this vein by repeating a theme from his previous speech: The very existence of all that is British, and all that Britain holds dear, is at stake.

> *Our task is not only to win the battle—but to win the war. After this battle in France abates its force, there will come the battle for our Island—for all that Britain is, and all that Britain means. That will be the struggle. In that supreme emergency we shall not hesitate to take every step, even the most drastic, to call forth from our people the last ounce and the last inch of effort of which they are capable.*

Again the message is clear: our very future as a nation is up for grabs. And having said that, Churchill tells the people what they must do to help preserve England. It's an unquestioned call for action, something leaders know is necessary if they want people to move forward and embrace their cause.

His conclusion to this speech is similar to the end of his speech before the House of Commons: a rousing call to arms, and a reminder that England is fighting for that which is just and right.

> *Centuries ago words were written to be a call and a spur to the faithful servants of Truth and Justice: 'Arm yourselves, and be ye men of valor, and be in readiness for the conflict; for it is better for us to perish in battle than to look upon the outrage of our nation and our altar. As the Will of God is in Heaven, so let it be.'*

Churchill has also introduced the value of honor in this passage: It's better to die fighting for our country and what we believe is right than to surrender, survive, and live for even one day under Hitler's rule. That may seem like an extreme statement, but these were extreme times. Churchill's avowed willingness to die protecting England is an emphatic reminder to his people that his belief in their cause is unwavering. He knows that as their leader he must appear sure and unshakable in his resolve if he is to gain their aid and support.

Finally, we come to Churchill's "Finest Hour" speech, made to the House of Commons on June 18, 1940, and broadcast to the nation four hours later. France has fallen to Germany, and Churchill gives this long and detailed speech to explain why he doesn't think the same thing will happen to Britain.

Churchill begins the speech with a solemn and detailed history of the recent military events involving his nation's forces. He reflects on recent French losses and why, due to mismanagement, miscommunication, and a general lack of readiness, more British divisions were not in a position to help France defend herself. He presents this status report in a matter-of-fact fashion, noting that while the results are unfortunate, it's necessary now to stay focused on the fight ahead:

> *I am not reciting these facts for the purpose of recrimination. That I judge to be utterly futile and even harmful. We cannot afford it. I recite them in order to explain why it was we did not have, as we could have had, between twelve and fourteen British divisions fighting in the line in this great [French] battle instead of only three. Now I put all this aside. I put it on the shelf, from which the historians, when they have time, will select their documents to tell their stories. We have to think of the future and not the past .... Of this I am quite sure, that if we open a quarrel between past and present, we shall find that we have lost the future.*

Churchill then injects a note of confidence about the outcome of this upcoming battle between Britain and Germany. He notes that even though he told the House two weeks earlier that it was possible the French line would crumble, he remains optimistic:

> *... I made it perfectly clear that whatever happened in France would make no difference to the resolve of Britain and the British Empire to fight on, 'if necessary for years, if necessary alone.'*

Churchill again tells all who are listening that Britain's determination to fight remains strong. He then offers reassurances to his own people by noting the number of allied countries who have committed to help them, along with a host of British civil defense forces ready to defend the villages and the countrysides.

Churchill leaves no doubt in the minds of his listeners that the German forces are a tough lot. It will take all England can do to beat them:

> ... the enemy is crafty and cunning and full of novel treacheries and stratagems. The House may be assured that the utmost ingenuity is being displayed and imagination is being evoked from large numbers of competent offices, well-trained in tactics and thoroughly up to date, to measure and counterwork novel possibilities. Untiring vigilance and untiring searching of the mind is being, and must be, devoted to the subject, because, remember, the enemy is crafty and there is no dirty trick he will not do.

Churchill wants people to understand the seriousness of the situation they are facing. But he also wants them to know that, as their leader, he is on top of the situation. So he follows his warning with reassurances that plans are being made to defeat the foe.

For the balance of the speech, Churchill offers additional assurances of England's preparedness to bolster his argument that Britain will not go the way of France. He talks about the men and arms his country has at its disposal and how they be used to defend the nation. He reminds the nation that they have every reason to believe they will triumph over Germany, again inserting a message of hope into his assessment of the battle they are about to face:

> I have thought it right upon this occasion to give the House and the country some indication of the solid, practical grounds upon which we base our inflexible resolve to continue the war.... I can assure them that our professional advisors of the three Services unitedly advise that we should carry on the war, and that there are good and reasonable hopes of final victory.

And then he emphasizes that message again when he says:

> Therefore, in casting up this dread balance-sheet and contemplating our dangers with a disillusioned eye, I see great reason for intense vigilance and exertions, but none whatever for panic and despair.

In the final words of this most courageous, moving, and powerful speech, Churchill says the words that are most often quoted of him. (To capture its true strength, try reading it aloud).

> ... the Battle of France is over. I expect the Battle of Britain is about to begin. Upon this battle depends the survival of Christian civilization. Upon it depends our own British life, and the long continuity of our institutions and our Empire. The whole fury and might of the enemy must very soon be turned on us. Hitler knows that he will have to break us in this Island or lose the war. If we can stand up to him, all Europe may be free and the life of the world may move forward into broad, sunlit uplands. But if we fail, then the whole world, including the United States, including all that we have known and cared for, will sink into the abyss of a new dark Age made more sinister, and perhaps more protracted, by the lights of perverted science. Let us therefore brace ourselves to our duties, and so bear ourselves that, if the British Empire and its Commonwealth last for a thousand years, men will still say, 'This was their finest hour.'

The final message of this speech reiterates the themes Churchill has stressed over and over: the need for unity, the strength of Britain's resolve, the threat not only to freedom but to all that is British, and the reminder that their cause is just and right. And the rest is history. Final outcome: England and the Allies victorious, and the German forces defeated. Like all great leaders, Churchill knew that strong words, followed by strong actions, are an effective way to unite and motivate others to do what needs to be done.

Churchill's speeches are, without question, a testimony of how a leader can use the power of communication to unite and influence individuals to work toward a common goal. Fortunately, your task as a leader does not require motivating a nation to take up arms against another nation. But it may require motivating people in your organization to meet some other problem head-on. Today's business leaders often face daunting situations where a real turnaround in attitude and morale and belief in the organization can make all the difference. Churchill's speeches offer leaders a wealth of lessons on how to motivate people and get them to join forces to solve a problem, whatever it is.

**Persuasive Communication: Using Rhetoric**

Leaders understand the power of using one single message to unite and get their people moving. For President Bush it was, "Free Kuwait!" For President Kennedy it was, "We will put a man on the moon before the end of this decade." For Captain Ahab it was, "Find and kill Moby Dick!" For Martin Luther King it was, "Now is the time to bring about racial equality for everyone in America." And for Winston Churchill, his message was equally as compelling: "We will fight the enemy whenever, wherever, and forever, and we will win."

Consider the following excerpt from his June 4, 1940, speech:

> *We shall not flag nor fail. We shall go on to the end.... We shall fight on the seas and oceans, we shall fight with growing confidence and growing strength in the air; we shall defend our island whatever the cost may be. We shall fight on the beaches, we shall fight on the landing grounds, we shall fight in the streets, we shall fight in the hills; we shall never surrender.* [2]

There is absolutely no question about what Churchill is saying here. The strength of his rhetoric is his repetition of a single message: we shall..., we shall..., we shall. Not we might, but we shall. There can be no misunderstanding, no confusion, in the minds of his listeners about what the goal is.

Churchill also understood the value of invoking an emotional response from his audience. He didn't want them sitting there passively listening, he wanted their hearts and minds and feelings engaged, he wanted their blood stirred, their passions aroused. Love of homeland, concern for loved ones already fighting the war, indignation that Hitler would be so bold as to attack England—these are just some of his listener's emotions to which Churchill appealed in his speeches.

And it's no secret that Churchill used fear as a motivator. Fear is a powerful emotion, one that can force or enable us to do things we might not otherwise do. We've all heard stories of great courage or bravery: about the woman who rushes back into a burning house to save her child, the soldier who storms a machine gunner's lair to save his platoon, the man who finds the superhuman strength to lift a beam off his buddy and drag him to safety as the building collapses around them. When you hear or read news accounts of people who have done such courageous acts, their explanation of their actions often is similar: "I don't know what came over me." "I didn't think, I just reacted to the situation and did it."

Getting people to react to the situation is precisely the point of Churchill's speeches. And because fear is a powerful motivator, he uses it to help drive home his message: if we do not fight hard today, there will be no tomorrow; if we don't join together to fight a common enemy, then our lives will change forever.

For all of our sacrifices in the U.S. during the war years, we never faced the greatest threat: that of invasion. We didn't have Hitler's army poised to cross our borders, we didn't hear the sound of his plane's droning overhead. England did, and the fear people felt was very present and very real. Churchill knew that, and he boldly used that fear to help bring people together and convince them to take action against that fear.

But don't forget. Churchill's use of fear as a motivator was balanced by invoking two other emotions as well: pride and hope.

> *My confidence in our ability to fight it out to the finish ... has been strengthened....*

> *I do not at all underrate the severity of the ordeal which lies before us; but I believe our countryman will show themselves capable of standing up to it....*

His speeches, grave, filled with examples of real dangers, nonetheless included a message of faith and inspiration that said, in effect, I know we will succeed, no matter the odds.

There's a reminder for leaders here: words have the power to inspire, encourage, motivate, and bring about change within an organization. If your business is facing troubled times, you can bet your people know it, and you can bet they're afraid. Rather than ignore or dismiss those fears, acknowledge them and use them as motivators to get people working together to turn the situation around. And along the way, don't forget to convey to them your belief in their ability to make things happen.

If people need to be sold on an idea, persuaded to take a course of action that you know will work, don't make them guess what it is. Grab them by their emotions and tell them. A plan for change, backed by enthusiasm, can be the catalyst you need to get people to help you fight your big battles or change the things that need changing.

## Charismatic Communication

Churchill had intense personal charisma, a physical bearing and presence that commanded people's attention. His speeches also were charismatic; the strength of their rhetoric and the power of his words caught people's attention and sparked their imagination. Churchill's speeches were emotional—not table-pounding, shoe-banging emotional affairs like Nikita Khrushchev's United Nations speech, but rousingly and grippingly emotional nonetheless. Both his choice of words and his style of delivery contributed to a sense of leashed emotions and energy just waiting to burst forth. People felt that energy, they heard in his voice the urgency to act, and they responded.

As Churchill's skillful use of rhetoric teaches us, persuasion is not about who has the loudest voice but about who expresses their ideas the most clearly and compellingly, who captures the enthusiasm, and the emotions, of their listeners. There is room in any organization for emotions—it's not all just hard data and facts. An enthusiastic, energized workforce is a powerful tool. A discouraged and disheartened workforce is a powerful liability.

Many businesses understand the importance of harnessing emotions to make things happen. It's hard to imagine a company sponsoring a big convention for its people or its industry without bringing in a well-known motivational speaker to inspire the troops. These events can take on an almost carnival-like atmosphere that make it hard not to get caught up in the moment. Often, even the most cynical employees will later admit that they were captured by it all, at least for a short time.

And that's part of what communication is all about—capturing the attention of others in order to lead them in the direction they need to go. Great leaders are great communicators. They can write and speak well in ways that get their ideas across powerfully and successfully. They use visual imagery that people can see and respond to with action. They know how to use their body language in an effective, positive, and motivating way. They don't enter a room with their shoulders slumped or their eyes locked to the floor; when they come in, people take notice because their posture, eye contact, and body positioning all say, "Sit up and take notice."

Churchill was a master at getting his listeners' attention. He knew that his effectiveness as a leader depended first on getting people to listen. And there's more than one way to get your audience to sit up and pay attention, as the following story illustrates:

A man was scheduled to give a Toastmasters speech on the subject of getting and holding an audience's attention. The Toastmasters organization has been in business for decades and has trained many good speakers in making a powerful, compelling, take-charge speech. (If there's a local chapter in your area, you might enjoy attending a meeting just for the speaking tips you can pick up.)

When it was time for his speech, the man strode to the lectern, thanked his audience and began. The longer he spoke, the more animated he became, gesturing wildly and raising his voice as he made each point. And as he reached the end of his speech, he exclaimed, "And you really have to believe in your message! You have to make people think you'll do anything to keep their attention!" With that, he quickly removed his suit jacket and tore his shirt completely off his body in one swift motion!

His audience was aghast for a brief moment and then of course gave him loud applause as he held the torn shirt above his head. He told them later that he had bought an inexpensive dress shirt and ripped out some of the seams to make it easier to remove in a flash. How's that for creativity, ingenuity, and grabbing attention?

We're not suggesting that you go to the lengths this speaker did, but the point to remember is this: Never ignore the importance of getting your audience's attention. No matter how critical your message is, it won't make a difference if no one is listening.

Grabbing the attention of the people in your organization is something you as a leader may need to do on a regular basis. And it's not always a clear and immediate threat to your organization that may demand that you get people's attention—sometimes it can simply be that people have become too complacent and comfortable in their jobs.

If you see this happening, if people are becoming apathetic and work is moving along sluggishly, when there is a great deal of time-wasting and game-playing going on, it might be necessary for you to stage a "Locker Room Pep Talk." Movie-based "Locker Room Scenes" such as this have the coach or manager breaking bats, throwing helmets, or otherwise making a mess of the place. Obviously you don't need to resort to similar tactics, but on those rare occasions when your people are due for this kind of treatment, don't hold back your voice or your body language. Let them have it, making it clear what practices and situations you want changed and that you expect them to change immediately.

## Overcoming Communication Barriers

Churchill relied on words to create visual images for his radio audiences, to make them "see" what was happening, and to make the situation real enough to them that they were willing to act. Not having visual support was not all bad, because it forced him to focus people's minds on selected images he felt were important. His words didn't have to compete with multiple images that might distract listeners and make them miss the point of the message.

Distractions are just one of the barriers to communication a leader must overcome in order to become an effective communicator. Other barriers can result from your method of communication, how well you express yourself, and how well the other party listens. Clearly, some methods of communication work better than others in gaining people's attention; consider the list below, in ranking order of best to worst.

*First Best: Face-to-Face.*

Face-to-face communication is the most powerful because your listener can see and hear you, read your body language as well as listen to your words. If you're excited about something, the other party will feel your passion. If you have doubts, those will be visible as well.

Further, unlike using the telephone or communicating on paper, it's much tougher to lie, hide the truth, or mask your feelings when you're working one-on-one. Perhaps this is why some managers who fear conflict, or dislike making "difficult scenes," will fire people over the telephone or send bad news by letter; it's easier to deal with unpleasant emotions if you don't have to do it face-to-face.

*Second Best: By Telephone.*

As the telephone companies like to remind us, the phone is the "next best thing to being there." If you can't arrange face-to-face communication with someone, the immediacy and convenience of the telephone is certainly valuable.

However, it's important to keep in mind that not being able to see the person with whom you're interacting does set up a communcation barrier. Unlike face-to-face communication, the telephone listener can't observe your facial expressions and gestures to help them interpret your message. As in Churchill's broadcast speeches, the tone of voice you use, the words you use and the ones you emphasize will be extremely important in assuring effective communication takes place over the phone.

*Third Best: By Memo, Letter, or Fax.*
There is a lot to be said for the power of the pen. Sometimes putting something in writing is better than a phone call. You can make sure all your important points get covered. There's less chance for misunderstanding about exactly what was said. Written communications can be carried around by the recipient to be read and studied at his or her leisure. And they provide a permanent record of the communication.

Of course, none of the above really matter if your communications are not written effectively. Somewhere during your career you've probably worked for someone whose memos left you scratching your head in puzzlement over what they said. Obviously, that's not effective communication.

So if you can't write well, get help: effective leadership requires effective communication. Take a course at night, buy a good book on the subject of business writing, and start making a conscious effort to improve your writing skills. People do judge you (and your business or organization or association) by the words you use. Write well and you will command a certain respect from people; express your ideas clearly and capture people's attention, and you're on the say to getting them to act.

A drawback to written communication is that you receive no immediate response from the other party, there's no opportunity for the give and take of a face-to-face or phone conversation.

*Fourth Best: E-mail, Voice Mail, or Other Machine-Managed Communications.*
There are few executives or managers today who don't have at least some familiarity with E-mail, voice mail, or one of the dozens of new on-line computer systems that are springing up across America. While this technology can make our business and personal lives easier, there are some people who use this technology as electronic "gatekeepers," putting up a new barrier to communication.

Case in point: Have you ever called people and never, ever reached them by phone? It's always, "I'm away from my desk, so leave a message on my voice mail and I'll get right back to you." Some people use their voice mail systems like a shield. No matter what time of the day or night you call them, you can never speak with a live person.

Communicating via E-mail has basically the same advantages and disadvantages as other written communications. There's one additional advantage however—you may very well get an almost immediate response on your computer screen. The flow of communication back and forth via computer becomes a written conversation. And it won't be long before we'll all be communicating via interactive terminals, bringing us full circle to face-to-face communications, even when the other party is 3,000 miles away.

### Your Core Values: What Makes Your Company Tick?

In his speeches, Churchill referred often to values that were important not only to him but to the citizens of England: liberty, justice and freedom as the foundation of the "British" way of life. These are the values that we're fighting for, Churchill reminded his listeners, along with peace and a sense of safety and security in our way of life.

Churchill knew that references to values can be an effective part of persuasive communication. Whether they are organizational or personal values, understanding the values your people hold dear is important in helping you communicate with them in a way that is meaningful and motivating.

What are the company's values? What is most important to your organization? If you don't know, you can start by asking these questions:

What are my organization's basic core values?

What is the reason we are in business?

What are the things we hold important here?

What does our mission statement say, to our executives, our managers, our employees, our competitors, and our customers?

Answering these questions in detail could take weeks, and if you don't know the answers, chances are good that you're not alone. The process of working to find the answers can be a valuable exercise for all involved, so don't give up.

As you examine this idea of core values and core beliefs, consider the following list of "jump starts" to get you thinking in the right direction:

We will...

We agree to...

It is our goal to...

We want our company to reflect...

We want our customers to feel we are responsive to their needs and we will work hard to exceed their expectations.

We want our employees to feel like this is a safe place to work and grow.

Our service strategy is...

Our corporate culture is based on...

These are the ethical values, principles, and ideals we hold important...

We seek to foster a nourishing work environment by...

Sometimes it's difficult to get into the kind of reflective, thoughtful mood you'll need to answer these starter statements correctly. But don't let the size and scope of the exercise daunt you. This is not something that has to be done by next week. Instead, work with the statements, alone or with others, as you have time. Because in the end, the more you learn about your organization's values, the better able you'll be to motivate and lead the people who are part of that organization.

## Bearing the Yoke

Churchill bore much of the responsibility for helping his nation prepare to fight Germany. A critical part of that responsibility was motivating a frightened populace to unite against an advancing army. He motivated them in two ways—by offering an unending stream of encouragement and by serving as the point man for the nation's never-give-in position.

As difficult as it may be, as a leader you may sometimes find yourself bearing the weight of the world on your shoulders when times are tough. Your people will be looking to you, as England's citizens looked to Churchill, for leadership in difficult times. In short, part of being a leader is being ready and willing to carry the burden of fear for your people and to outwardly project a calm and confident attitude that says to your people, we will succeed.

That doesn't mean you should present a false front, pretend that everything's great when it's not. Churchill certainly didn't hold back the seriousness of the coming conflict from the public. But he also, over and over, said to England: "Together we can do it. Together we can succeed."

There are many CEOs who have sailed with their firms directly into the shoals of bankruptcy, court-ordered reorganization, and near total financial failure. As true leaders, they stuck with their people, led the charge, and never gave up. Their confidence and belief in the organization and their people never wavered. The final result? Together, they were successful in the end. As one observer has put it, "tough times never last, tough people do!"

Learn from Churchill—help your people understand the problems your organization is facing and, equally important, show them what's being done to solve the problem and how they can help. Then ask for that help, expressing at the same time your confidence that with their help, success is assured.

Some Churchillian lessons to keep in mind:

- *Practice, practice, practice.*
  We once asked a college president friend of ours, a real spellbinder, to tell us how he became such a successful speaker. His answer? "Lots of practice." Apparently the old saw about how to get to Carnegie Hall is accurate. This was as true for Churchill as it is for you. His oratorical skills were developed only as a result of much hard work. He had a speech impediment. His speeches were not spontaneous but very carefully prepared. They were worked and reworked to make them perfect. He even used stage directions.

- *Learn the "language of leadership "*
  There's a special language of leadership. It is based, according to leadership scholar Jay Conger, on the leader's ability to address four categories of followers' beliefs. First, you've got to convince followers that your organizational mission is important because it furthers their values (you can do this by describing the current situation as impeding those values and develop a vision of how this situation could be changed). Another approach is to convince your followers that what you want them to do is a necessary precondition to acting according to their values. A third way of crafting commitments through belief is by identifying an antagonist, then convincing your followers that they must unite against this "enemy." Fourth, you must address the feasibility of your mission. If those eager followers don't believe it's doable, they'll soon lose their enthusiasm.

- *Don't forget style.*

  Be sure that your language is adjusted to your audience. Realize that your presentation to the board must sound, look, and feel vastly different from your harangue at the factory. Why? Different constituencies respond to different communication styles. Effective leaders know this and employ a variety of linguistic approaches. Learn to employ a variety of repetition, rhythm, balance, and alliteration. Perhaps most important, don't use what has become so typical in business communications, i.e., hedging phrases and a questioning tone at the end of every sentence.

- *Beware of becoming a "Chamberlain."*

  The contrast between Churchill and Neville Chamberlain is dramatic. Chamberlain, as case writers Michael Green and Donald Birn point out, "describes his meeting with Hitler in a factual and descriptive way. He never expresses his feelings nor does he attempt to use an emotional appeal to build belief in his audience. He tries to downplay the need for war, given that war is a nightmare and a fearful thing. Yet he doesn't drive the point home with any vivid imagery. He ends on the note that it is not clear to him that there are great issues at stake worth plunging into a war for. He leaves the listener with the impression that he is indecisive, has no clear direction nor conception of the problem. He does not inspire confidence in himself or in his course of action." Maybe that explains one of history's most cruel double entendres: the word "chamberlain" also means bedroom attendant.

- *Break down the barriers to communication.*

  Realize that we all assign different meanings to the same word; we see things differently. Remember that Chamberlain perceived Hitler's signed declaration of friendship toward Britain as a guarantee of "peace for our time." Yet Hitler perceived this as a strategic delay while he built up his forces. Churchill, on the other hand, perceived all this as "the complete surrender of the Western Democracies." One way to prevent this kind of confusion is to be certain that, as sender, you make certain your message has been received and is understood.

- *Match your "intelligence system" to the situation.*

  Churchill clearly mastered the art of intelligence gathering.

You'll need to do the same, particularly if the environment your organization finds itself in is unstable and unpredictable. Without it, you won't be able to cope with the changing environment. Simply put, uncertainty in the environment is what drives organizational intelligence. Best to face the fact: it's time for data banks of information, extensive networks of communication, and the ability to process that avalanche of data.

## CHAPTER 11

# YOU'VE GOT TO LEARN
# HOW TO FOLLOW
# BEFORE YOU CAN
# BEGIN TO LEAD

*I must follow the people. Am I not their leader?*
—BENJAMIN DISRAELI

## KEY POINTS

- LETTING YOUR PEOPLE LEAD YOU; PASSING THE BATON

There's a popular book on the market today called *The Handbook of Leadership*.[1] In this scholarly standard-issue manual, you'll find thousands of leadership theories, nearly everything you always wanted to know about the subject and maybe more.

Strangely, however, there's no companion volume called *The Handbook of Followership*. And that's too bad, because followers, not leaders, account for more than 80 percent of the success of any project. For this reason, we thought it important to plumb the considerable wisdom of a little-known Renaissance tome on the art of "bringing up the rear" called *The Book of the Courtier*. In it, the author, a 16th-century bon vivant named Baldessare Castiglione, recounts a series of conversations held at the court of the Duke of Urbino in 1507. Discussing everything from flattery to fornication, the participants' rambling discussions provide a veritable textbook on the art of being a good follower. Such pithy advice sold well. *The Book of the Courtier* was the most widely read handbook on princely behavior in the 16th and early 17th centuries.

## Who Was Castiglione?

If you lived in 15th-century Italy, one of the better jobs was that of a "courtier" to a prince. In those times, a courtier served as the right-hand man (there were no women allowed to take this post) to the prince, acting as his closest advisor, confidant, major domo, aide in matters of the palace, and his lieutenant on the field of battle.

It's a bit hard to find an exact modern-day equivalent to the courtier, but it will help if you think of the prince as CEO and the courtier as his closest assistant and alter ego. Senior vice-presidents, directors, staff assistants and so forth come to mind.

This was not an uncommon job in Renaissance Italy. Every prince was expected to have a whole gaggle of courtiers. Men in these aide-de-camp posts were not like butlers or "yes-men," but rather more like the prince's step-brother, not related by birth or royalty, but still on familiar terms. They served as counselors, listeners, advice-givers, and as their "seconds" during battles.

Of all the courtiers living and working for princes in 15th-century Italy, Baldessare Castiglione was probably the best, the "courtier's courtier." No doubt for this reason, *The Book of the Courtier*[2] was immensely popular. There was also a bit of the voyeur in it, offering as it did a glimpse into a lifestyle most people could only dream about. It gave access and entry into the lives of royal people, their homes, thoughts, loves, ambitions, desires and, more importantly for our sake, their ideas about leading and following.

*The Book of the Courtier* served as a kind of policies and procedures manual for courtiers-in-training. And it was history's first unabashed "how-to" book, providing lessons in everything from dealing with a tyrant boss to how to give advice, be a good listener, give feedback safely, follow orders, enforce rules, harness the sins of pride and arrogance (in both yourself and your leader), and how to keep the peace.

Its author was born near Mantua, Italy, in 1478. He studied in Milan, where he learned to read Greek. He entered his first princely court in Milan and worked there for a time before returning home to Mantua. He later joined the court of Guidobaldo da Montefeltro, better known as the Duke of Urbino. His time at Urbino was critical to his development as a courtier and it was there that he met the real-life characters who appear in *The Book of the Courtier*.

Castiglione later served as the Duke of Urbino's ambassador to Pope Leo X, who had met Castiglione at the Urbino castle. After the death of the Pope, Castiglione was appointed the papal representative in Spain for the court of Charles V. When Castiglione died in 1529, he had served his whole life as a courtier in one form or another. He had worked for a variety of different ruling men, from princes to Popes, and this gave him enormous insight into the traits of leadership.

## Castiglione: Lessons in Followership

In *The Book of the Courtier*, which is written in dialogue form, the author traces four conversations which occurred at Urbino in 1507. These talks were part of a kind of verbal entertainment between the Duchess of Urbino, some of her aides, and a somewhat raucous group of noblemen and military officers who stayed at or visited the palace at Urbino. The aim of this panel was to determine the characteristics, skills, and traits necessary to be the "perfect" courtier. It was an experienced lot. As one of Castiglione's characters put it:

> ... it would perhaps be hard to find an equal number of cavaliers as outstanding and as excellent in different things, quite beyond their principal profession of chivalry, as are found here: wherefore, if there are anywhere men who deserve to be called good courtiers and who can judge of what belongs to the perfection of Courtiership, we must rightfully think that they are present.

Each of the men who contributed their advice and counsel to this discussion had been courtiers and/or soldiers. In short, they had gained the wisdom that comes from a life filled with observation, discussion, and action.

Although Castiglione was not present for the discussions, he later collected remembrances about the conversations from various participants. From these recollections he wrote *The Book of the Courtier*. In it, the participants banter back and forth in the manner of good friends attending a convivial dinner party as they grope for a definition of the ideal courtier.

The first night's conversation covers the background, breeding, education, and experience necessary to become a good courtier. On the second night, the group discusses the best way to work with and for a prince, especially if he is autocratic or, worse, tyrannical. On the third night, the talk turns to affairs of the heart and how a good courtier can best serve himself in physical love relationships (sorry, but that's for another book). And on the fourth and final night, the group discusses the moral values necessary to be a worthy courtier.

By all accounts, the hostess of this affair, the Duchess of Urbino, was a beautiful and fair-minded woman respected by the courtiers who enjoyed her friendship. Castiglione calls her house "the very abode of joyfulness" to suggest that people were allowed to express themselves freely, without fear of ridicule or punishment. This made the house of Urbino a perfect setting for this kind of idea-generating discussion. All of those present were on comfortable terms with each other and felt free to speak of their ideas and ideals of courtiership, as well as ask probing questions of the others.

The first characteristic of a good courtier is nobility, says one of the participants, Ludovico da Canossa. He argues that "... it almost always happens that ... those who are most distinguished are men of noble birth...."

There's a reason for that, he claims. Men who are not of noble birth don't have a family tradition of achievement to uphold, so they don't have the "force and quality" to do virtuous things.

> For noble birth is like a bright lamp.... And since this luster of nobility does not shine forth in the deeds of the lowly born, they lack that spur, as well as that fear of dishonor, nor do they things themselves obliged to go beyond what was done by their forebears; whereas to the wellborn it seems a reproach not to attain at least to the mark set them by their ancestors.

Da Canossa seems to be saying that leaders and others who rise to positions of responsibility are born, not made, a stand that would certainly be debated today. And it was then, too. Gasparo Pallavicino, another participant, interrupts to contradict the idea that being of noble birth is what makes a good courtier. It's what people make of themselves and their opportunities, he argues.

*... I would adduce many instances of persons born of the noblest blood who have been ridden by vices; and, on the contrary, many persons of humble birth who, through their virtue, have made their posterity illustrious.*

It's not always who someone *is* that matters, he suggests, but what someone *does*. There are many other causes, other than one's station at birth, that affect "the differences and the various degrees of elevation and lowliness among us," he concludes.

Da Canossa, who maintains his position that only those of noble birth can become good courtiers, mentions what he believes is another characteristic of a courtier. He puts it this way:

*... that certain grace which we call an 'air,' which shall make him at first sight pleasing and lovable to all who see him; and let this be an adornment informing and attending all his actions, giving the promise outwardly that such a one is worthy of the company and the favor of every great lord.*

In other words, it's important to develop an outward bearing and presence that says to others, "I'm qualified, experienced, and ready to handle whatever comes my way with skill and aplomb."

Da Canossa then concludes that above all, the courtier must be a man of arms, and known among men as "bold, energetic and faithful to whomever he serves." Of the need for this skill, he says:

*... the more our Courtier excels in this art, the more will he merit praise ... we shall be satisfied, as we have said, if he have complete loyalty and an undaunted spirit, and be always seen to have them. For oftentimes men are known for their courage in small things rather than in great....*

The real test, however, is whether a man is *always* courageous, or only when it will impress others:

*But those men who, even when they think they will not be observed or seen or recognized by anyone, show courage and are not careless of anything, however slight, for which they could be blamed, such have the quality of the spirit we are seeking in our Courtier.*

A courtier—or a leader—shows courage even when there is no one around to see it or to praise him. And just as important, he doesn't "make a show of being so fierce that he is forever swaggering in his speech," says da Canossa. The good courtier knows when to appear tough and when to be gentle, he balances fierceness and compassion, and is moderate in his words and actions.

> *... let the men we are seeking be exceedingly fierce, harsh and always among the first, wherever the enemy is; and in every other place, humane, modest, reserved, avoiding ostentation above all things as well as that impudent praise of himself by which a man always arouses hatred and disgust in all who hear him.*

Here Pallavicino chimes in again, saying he has known few men "excellent in anything whatsoever who did not praise themselves." But that seems reasonable, he adds, because a man's deeds should be made known so that he receives "the honor that is the true reward of all virtuous toil."

But there's a difference between having pride and being prideful, counters da Canossa. A man can and should take pride in referring to his accomplishments, without becoming obnoxious and boastful about his actions:

> *If you took notice, I blamed impudent and indiscriminate praise of one's self: and truly, as you say, one must not conceive a bad opinion of a worthy man who praises himself modestly....*

It's perfectly acceptable for a man to take pride in his work, his skills, and talents. What irks the group is people who have no talents and yet can't stop talking about how good they are. "To be sure," notes Pallavicino, "those persons who are of no merit, and yet praise themselves, are insufferable...."

The discussion continues for some time as the speakers debate the importance of various traits in a perfect courtier. When they reconvene on the second night, the Duke of Urbino asks for a review of the previous evening's discussion. The conclusion is that a courtier must develop many facets of his personality and must exhibit many qualities and skills without calling undo attention to himself. Federico Fregoso, who is leading this second discussion, then adds the following rejoinder:

> ... I say that to win praise deservedly, and a good opinion on the part of all, and favor from the princes whom he services, I deem it necessary for [the courtier] to know how to order his whole life and how to make the most of his own good qualities....

In other words, argues Fregoso, a courtier must make sure that all aspects of his life are in balance with each other. He explains:

> ... let him take care not only that his separate parts and qualities be excellent, but that the tenor of his life be such that the whole may correspond to these parts, and may be seen to be, always and in everything, such as never to be discordant in itself, but form a single whole of all these good qualities....

It's a balance of opposing characteristics and qualities—fierceness versus gentleness, for example—that is the ideal, because each enhances the other. Thus:

> ... gentleness is most striking in a man who is valiant and impetuous; and as his boldness seems greater when accompanied with modesty, so his modesty is enhanced and made more evident by his boldness. Hence, to talk little and to do much, and not to praise oneself for deeds that are praiseworthy, but tactfully to dissimulate them, serves to enhance both the one virtue and the other in anyone who knows how to employ this method discreetly; and so it is with all other good qualities.

As he concludes his analysis of how a perfect courtier should conduct himself, he says there are certain general rules he should follow. The most important is to avoid affectation. Other things he should "consider well" include:

*... what he does or says, the place where he does it, in whose*
*presence, its timeliness, the reason for doing it, his age, his profes-*
*sion, the end at which he aims, and the means by which he can*
*reach it....*

In short, a courtier should always make sure his actions are appropriate to the situation. Yet all the qualities mentioned so far "will not suffice to win him universal favor ... unless he have also a gentle and pleasing manner in his daily conversation," concedes the group. The perfect courtier knows when to speak and when to hold a civil tongue, and he alters his style and method of conversation to suit the situation and the person with whom he is conversing. Just as King Henry V (whom we profiled in chapter 2) learned how to talk with common folk as well as members of the court, so should a courtier.

Fergoso adds another quality to the list that the group is compiling:

*... I would have the Courtier devote all his thought and*
*strength and spirit ... his every desire and habit and manner to*
*pleasing [the prince].*

Another participant, da Napoli, takes exception to that statement: "... it strikes me that you have ... sketched us a noble flatterer," he says.

Not so, replies Fergoso. Flatterers love neither their prince nor their friends, which a courtier should do above all else. There's a difference between self-serving flattery and sincere compliments from an aide to his or her leader. And a wise leader will recognize the difference, relying less and less on the advisor who seeks to flatter with insincere compliments or by always agreeing with everything the leader says.

By saying a courtier should devote himself to pleasing the prince, Fregoso means a courtier should always seek "to obey and further the wishes" of the one he serves. This will come about:

*... if he has the good judgment to perceive what the prince*
*likes, and the wit and prudence to bend himself to do this, and the*
*considered resolve to like what by nature he may possibly dislike....*

This description certainly is not dissimilar to how one would describe a good administrative assistant or junior executive. The modern version of Fergoso's statement might be, "Make the boss look good," by anticipating her needs, understanding his style of leadership, and working to help assure the boss' goals are met.

But Signor Ludovico Pio, another participant, has a question: Is a gentleman who serves a prince bound to obey him in all that he commands, even if it is something dishonorable and disgraceful?

The others respond quickly, with a variety of viewpoints. Fregoso claims they're not bound to obey if the request is dishonorable. Da Canossa says it's not that simple: What if the prince he serves treats him well and has confidence that he will do all that he can for him, and this prince orders him to kill a man. Is he to refuse to do it?

Fregoso replies:

> *You ought to obey your lord in all things profitable and honorable to him, not in those that will bring him harm and shame.... It is true that many things that are evil appear at first sight to be good, and many appear evil and yet are good. Hence, when serving one's masters it is sometimes permitted to kill not just one man but ten thousand men, and do many other things that might seem evil to a man who did not look upon them as one ought, and yet are not evil.*

But how can one distinguish what is really good from what appears to be good? asks Pallavicino.

Fregoso, choosing not to discuss the issue because "there would be too much to say," adds "... let the whole question be left to your discretion."

Should one depart from his lord's commands if by doing more or less he could improve the outcome of the task? questions Pallavicino. Again it is Fregoso who replies:

> *... no doubt, it is a quite dangerous thing to depart from our superiors' commands, trusting more in our own judgment than in theirs ... because if our design should happen to fail, and the affair should turn out badly, we incur the error of disobedience, and ruin what we have to do, without having any means of excusing ourselves or any hope of pardon .... Moreover, in this way we begin the practice of making light of our lords' commands....*

Still, he concedes, there may be times when it is clear to the courtier that the gain, if he were to disregard somewhat the letter of his orders, is likely to be greater than the damage in case of failure. In such cases, he "may set about doing what his reason and good judgment dictate," but only *after* taking into consideration the character of the prince he serves, cautions Fregoso,

> *... for if the prince's character happens to be severe, as is true of many, I would never advise him, if he were a friend of mine, to change by the least bit the order given.*

On the final night of conversation about the qualities of a perfect courtier, Ottaviano Fregoso, older brother of Federico, is chosen to lead the discussion. He asks the group to consider that the merits of certain qualities depend on the use to which those qualities are put.

> *For indeed if by being of noble birth, graceful, charming, and expert in so many exercises, the Courtier were to bring forth no other fruit than to be what he is, I should not judge it right for a man to devote so much study and labor to acquiring this perfection....*

Fregoso is saying there should be a greater purpose for the qualities a courtier is expected to exhibit, and he asks the group to consider that it is this:

> *... to win for himself ... the favor and mind of the prince whom he serves that he may be able to tell him, and always will tell him, the truth about everything he needs to know, without fear or risk of displeasing him....*

Thus if the courtier sees that the prince is "inclined to a wrong action," he will be able, because of his goodness, wit, charm, prudence, and knowledge of many things, to show the prince the harm that will result from this wrong action. At the same time, he will be able to show the prince how much "honor and profit" will come to him if he pursues the just and virtuous action. So while all the other accomplishments a courtier can claim are, "as it were, the flower," says Fregoso, the "true fruit of courtiership" is

*... to bring or help one's prince toward what is right and to frighten him away from what is wrong....*

The problem, continues Fregoso, is that the princes often don't have what they need the most—someone to tell them the truth. Their enemies aren't going to, and among their friends there are few who have real access to them, and those friends who do are wary of angering the princes so they say nothing either; they become flatters who will say or do anything the princes want.

> *From this it results that, besides never hearing the truth about anything at all [including themselves], princes are made drunk by the great license that rule gives; and by a profusion of delights are submerged in pleasures, and deceive themselves so and have their minds so corrupted ... that from this ignorance they pass to an extreme self-conceit, so that then they become intolerant of any advice or opinion from others.*

Here Pallavicino enters the conversation, and says he doesn't think the goodness of mind and other virtues Fregoso says the courtiers should teach their princes can be learned, "... but I think that to those who have them they have been given by nature and by God."

Fregoso disagrees. "Moral virtues are not in us entirely by nature," he says. If virtues were natural to mankind, he argues, we should never become accustomed to vice. He continues:

> *... the laws do assume that virtues can be learned, which is very true; for we are born capable of receiving them and of receiving the vices too, and hence through practice we acquire the habit of both, so that first we practice virtue and vice and then we are virtuous or vicious.*

How should one instruct a prince on what is virtuous? the Dutchess asks Fregoso. He responds:

> *... I should teach him ... among other things that he should choose from among his subjects a number of the noblest and wisest gentlemen, with whom to consult on everything, and that he*

*should give them authority and free leave to speak their mind to him about all things without hesitation; and that he should act toward them in such a way as to show them all that he wished to know the truth in everything and that he detested all falsehood.*

As the discussion moves forward, with much debate about important qualities and virtues of a courtier, Ottaviano makes what turns out to be the final observation:

*Hence, if it were for me to educate [the prince], I would have him take care to govern not only in the ways mentioned, but in much lesser matters, and understand as far as possible all the particular things that pertain to his people, nor ever believe or trust any one of his ministers to such an extent as to give him a long bridle and control of all his rule. For there is no man who is entirely apt in all things....*

Near the end of Castiglione's *The Book of the Courtier*, one of the men effectively summarizes the ways of the skilled courtier. His soliloquy on courtiership tells us what it's like to both be a leader and to serve one as well:

*Therefore, I think that the aim of the perfect Courtier ... is so to win for himself, by means of the accomplishments ascribed to him by these gentlemen, the favor and mind of the prince whom he serves that he may be able to tell the truth about everything he needs to know, without fear or risk of displeasing him; and that when he sees the mind of his prince inclined to a wrong action, he may dare to oppose him and in a gentle manner avail himself of the favor required by his good accomplishments, so as to dissuade him of every evil intent and bring him to the path of virtue. And thus, having in himself the goodness which these gentlemen attributed to him, together with the readiness of wit, charm, prudence, knowledge of letters and of many other things—the Courtier will in every instance be able adroitly to show the prince how much honor and profit will come to him and to his from justice, liberality, magnanimity, gentleness, and the other virtues that befit a good prince;*

*and, on the other hand, how much infamy and harm may result from the vices opposed to these virtues.*

This is good advice to any leader's aide and to any leader wishing to choose one. Hire the person who has read Castiglione!

## Leadership Traits

The traits of courtiership that were so important to Castiglione and his associates in the 16th century are equally important traits for today's leaders and the people who help them run their organizations. And as the discussion about courtiers so aptly illustrates, leaders need others to assist and advise them and oftentimes an individual, working behind the scenes, can do as much for an organization as the more visible CEO. Effective leaders understand this, and look for aides and managers who will fulfill the same role the courtiers did for their princes. It's seldom that these modern-day "courtiers" receive public recognition for their efforts, anymore than they did in Castiglione's time. But good leaders know who did the advance work and make sure their followers understand the value of the aide and counsel.

One way to understand Castiglione's book is to put yourself into the role of one of his princes. These men controlled their respective lands, power, and wealth with the help of their courtiers. Those princes who were wise knew that they couldn't possibly do everything themselves. They needed the help of reliable courtiers to run their houses, oversee their lands, assist them in battles, and guide them to make decisions based on wise counsel rather than haste, greed, or impetuousness. And so it goes in business today.

Effective leaders know they can't run their organization by themselves, no matter how hard they work. They must delegate responsibility to others, as the princes did to their courtiers, and they must have people whose advice and assistance they can depend on if their organizations are to run smoothly and their goals are to be met.

Yet it's hard for some leaders to hand over responsibility for areas in the organization they once controlled. As one chief executive's described it: "I built this operation from the ground up. This is my baby. And now you're asking me to let my baby go?"

His point is clear: It can be very difficult for some leaders to relinquish any form of control to others in their organization. But if they don't, their leadership becomes less effective and their organization begins to crumble. And in the process, they'll lose the good followers— the good courtiers—who would have helped to make the organization stronger had they been given the opportunity.

As one observer wrote about delegation and empowerment:

> *To many executives, this is a discomforting topic. It means a surrender of power and an acknowledgment that the people who make the widgets, sweep the floors, and run the daily computer reports are as essential to the success of the company as those with offices in the executive suite.*[3]

Empowering your front line, supervisory, and middle management people and allowing them to take on certain areas of responsibility so that you can concentrate on areas that need your energy and efforts, is not something that will happen overnight. You need to create an environment where followers are encouraged and enabled to become managers and seconds-in-command, fulfilling much the same roles 16th-century courtiers did.

Both the leader and the follower-manager play an important role in an organization, as the discussion of courtiership shows, and each is dependent on the other if they are to be most effective in their tasks.

It is the role of the leader to keep moving forward, seek out new paths, and create new plans. It is the role of the follower-manager to attend to the myriad of details at hand that make it possible for the leader to take on this "new frontiers" role. Leaders need to be aware of what's "out there," they need to focus on the broad picture, on their visions for their organizations, and creatively move their organizations forward. Yet at the same time, someone has to focus on more immediate, day-to-day tasks, responsibilities, and duties, and help implement the leader's goals. That becomes the role of the follower-manager.

The skilled courtier, according to Castiglione—or today's skilled follower-manager—relishes his behind-the-scenes role because he knows it comes with its own powers and its own brand of leadership. And the effective leaders recognize the value of having such individuals helping them lead.

## The Leader as Follower: The Beauty of "Down-Up" Relationships

We think Castiglione would be delighted to learn that his 16th-century ideas are alive and well in our century. Research has borne out his argument that the ideal courtier possesses the capacity to "...dissuade [the prince] of every evil intent and bring him to the path of virtue." Followers, be they courtiers or colleagues, can exert tremendous influence on their leaders. The "ability to manage upward"—or upward influence—can make as important a contribution to organizational effectiveness today as it did in the Italian Renaissance.

It may seem an unusual notion to suggest that a subordinate or follower can influence the direction his or her superior and/or the organization will take. Yet a fascinating study done by J. J. Gabarro and J. P. Kotter at the Harvard Business School revealed that these kind of "down-up" relationships are critical to the effectiveness of an organization.[4] They describe the process as one in which the follower, like the perfect courtier, consciously works with his or her superior to obtain the best possible results for the superior and the organization.

If this doesn't sound like you, don't feel left out. Such "down-up" leadership is not practiced very often. The more common approach, of course, is for followers to take a passive or reactive stance toward their boss, only doing what they're told to do and waiting to be told before they do it. No wonder most people describe the communications channels in their organizations as undeniably "top-down."

Why? Usually, it stems from ignorance. Most people, it seems, don't understand the boss very well. She wants mutual dependence. They think more in terms of *in*dependence. The result is something akin to two ships passing in the night: the folks she relies on simply don't realize how much she depends on them.

The key, obviously, is to let the members of your team know how much you value their help. Understand, and be sure that your subordinates understand, that you and they are often in situations of mutual dependence. Such symbiosis requires a good deal of savvy about the other person—their strengths, weaknesses, working style, needs—and (need we add?) of yourself. It also requires the ability to use that knowledge to build a good working relationship. That means seeking out information about the boss' goals and problems and pressures, just as Castiglione's courtiers did, so you can prepare to help move in the direction of those goals.

The key to helping other people around you take more responsibility for helping you lead effectively starts with your understanding where you are, personally and professionally, in the organization. Your answers to the following questions can help you determine that.

Are you happy with your present job?

Do you see yourself in the same job and at the same company in one year? Five years? If not, do you see yourself doing different work in the same company or different or the same work at another company?

Do you feel your present duties offer you new challenges and opportunities to prove your worth, succeed on a regular basis, and give you a chance for significant advancement?

Would you describe your present relationship with your immediate boss as a good one? What is your gut feeling about his or her leadership skills overall?

How would you rate the people who work for you? Average? Acceptable? Excellent? A combination of each?

Is there one or more employee who currently exhibits the qualities of a good "courtier"?

Do you feel comfortable allowing one or more of these people to take a stronger leadership role, either within your work group or division, or for the organization in general?

Do you feel comfortable taking on a mentor role for one or more of these people?

Do you see opportunities for leadership coupled with "followership" in your organization?

Your answers to these questions can be telling, both about your personal and professional goals and about what you perceive the climate and culture in your company to be for developing follower-managers who can help you and others lead most effectively.

In the worst case, you may not see many chances for you to develop this follower-leader linkage. The time or the personnel may not be right.

In the best case, you may see a number of the opportunities as well as the right people and the right nurturing climate within your organization to allow people to take on new roles of leadership-followership.

If you're in a position to make changes for the better, if you have some strong "courtier" candidates in mind, and if you're willing to help them help you, the following 10-step process can guide you as you seek to change mere managers from followers into leaders.

*Watch.*

In Castiglione's time, a prince didn't just hire the first courtier that appeared at his doorstep. The selection process was long and involved and based upon a number of factors including life and work experience, abilities, the proper character traits, and the desire to serve. You can look for similar qualities in the people around you and the best way to do that is to get out from behind your desk and watch them work. What professional qualities do they exhibit as they work with their co-workers, customers, supervisors, peers, and the people who may work for them? What qualities of leadership do they exhibit under the pressure of deadlines, errors, or during other times when things don't go as planned? Finally, what qualities do they exhibit that are most similar to your own leadership style? Or, how do they differ from your style? Can you find a good fit between the two?

*Choose.*

If and when you feel you've identified the right candidate or candidates for the role of corporate courtier, bring them into your office and discuss your thoughts and plans to see if they align with theirs. Some people are perfectly happy in solid, comfort zone-type jobs and roles and are not looking to change or move up. Other people are more open to change and may be chomping at the bit as you explain what you have in mind. Your selection process should be an informal event that says, "I've watched you work and think you have a number of strengths that indicate you have the qualities of a good leader. I'd like to help you and, in turn, you can help me."

*Teach.*

The learning process should begin immediately. You know from your work the areas where you need help, how you can provide the best examples of leadership, and where you feel your candidate needs the most work and assistance in developing needed skills.

This teaching process can be as formal or informal, as detailed or general, or as lengthy or short as you deem necessary. Remember, you're not running a race just to get to the leadership finish line but rather going on a journey where you gather people and support along the way. And just as this is true for you, it is also true for your corporate "courtier."

*Empower.*

There is only so much teaching can do. Sometimes you have to give people their freedom and let them proceed alone. If they have questions (and if they're sharp), they'll come back to you. Give good people real responsibilities, new challenges, and the hint of danger and difficulty in a new problem, and you'll be surprised at what kind of solutions they will come up with.

And the key to this sense of leadership empowerment comes when they look back and find they didn't need your help to find the solution.

*Step back and watch some more.*

Success is not guaranteed on the first empowerment assignment you give your corporate courtier. You can't make a snap decision and say, "Oh well, this person failed on the first big project. It's back to the drawing board." Learning from mistakes, by trial and error, are valuable teachers. What's most important is whether a person learns from these lessons. That means the best observations you can make as a leader and as an evaluator develop over time, and you can determine how someone reacts not only to success but learns from failure.

As with any new product or service, give people enough time to adjust themselves, find their positions, and do their work. Practice patience in your role as mentor.

*Make adjustments.*

And when you're through watching, you can intervene with suggestions, adjustments, advice, constructive criticism, counseling, and other similar course-correcting help. If people are to learn and develop new skills, they need feedback; they need to know what they are doing right and not so right.

Now is the time to be sensitive, humane, and tactful as you guide your courtiers-in-training in new directions or help them correct problems they have encountered.

*Allow for errors, setbacks, and missteps.*

Stuff happens. As the need for pencil erasers and bandages proves, people make mistakes; some of them can be catastrophic and others minuscule. Your job is to create policies to handle mistakes, to handle your employees, and let everyone get back to work.

New products fail, new services go unused by customers, and new policies and procedures can trip up the best-intentioned employee. Keep your eye on the big picture, focus on the final outcome and on the long-term gains the person is achieving. And again, practice patience. People need to know they will not be dinged for every mistake, and they will want to prove themselves to you again if they make a mistake. Give them this chance.

*Provide never-ending support.*

Good leaders are also good back-slappers. They can prop up people even when it seems as if nothing is going right; they can be walking, talking proof that leadership success is possible. Lots of mere managers can cheer when times are good, sales are high, and the world outside the company doors is looking rosy. A leader knows how to coach, preach, teach, and praise even when the going is rough and it appears nothing more could go wrong.

Make judicious use of hearty praise, positive support, and offer the occasional shoulder to cry on. People need to know they can turn to you for advice and support when things aren't going well, and when things are.

*Empower the followers to become full-fledged leaders and then help them choose their own followers.*

This is an opportunity for the cycle to start repeating itself, for new corporate courtiers to be identified.

*Repeat the process.*

Make sure you do all you can to assure that the cycle does repeat itself. There is always room for good people in every organization.

## Attributes of "Followership"

Perhaps the ancient philosopher-scholar Lao-tzu summed up this concept of "followership" the best:

*A leader is best when people barely know that he exists, not good when people follow him and acclaim him, worse when they obey and despise him. Fail to honor people, they fail to honor you. But of a good leader, who talks little, when his work is done, his aim fulfilled, they will all say, "We did this ourselves."*

It's followership skills—not just leadership skills—that make a leader. Unless you were born into royalty or you're the CEO's favorite nephew or niece, you'll have to start as a follower before you can be a leader. And as Castiglione's courtiers demonstrate, not only is there no shame in followership, in being "in the rear with the gear," there is opportunity—opportunity to serve and make a difference, and become a follower-manager on whom effective leaders depend.

And, just as leaders have their "styles," so to do followers. Robert Kelley, who pondered the little-appreciated role of followers in his compelling book, *The Power of Followership*, discovered five different followership styles, which he described as follows[5]:

1. *Alienated followers.* Skeptical mavericks and devil's advocates whom leaders view as troublesome and adversarial. They think independently and critically, but do not fully carry out their roles. They began as exemplary followers but then withdrew due to lack of trust or unmet expectations.
2. *Conformist followers.* Nonthreatening team players who accept assignments gladly but lack their own ideas, are averse to conflict, and are unwilling to take unpopular positions. Generate few ideas, fear conflict, and need structure.
3. *Pragmatist followers.* Attuned to the organization's political realities, able to work the system and maintain a middle line; play by rules and regulations. Bureaucrats.
4. *Passive followers.* Rely on leader's judgment, taking action only when the leader gives instruction; follow the crowd.
5. *Exemplary followers.* Add value, make positive difference in helping the organization achieve its goals. Focus on goals, take initiative.

Castiglione, clearly, was describing "ideal" or exemplary courtiers or followers. But the important question for you to consider is: how would your boss describe your followership style? Where, on this grid, would he or she place you?

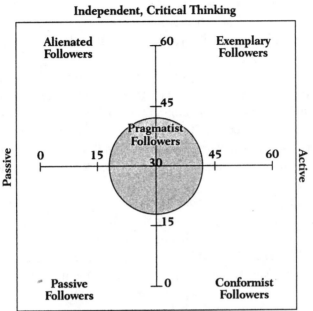

**Back to the Basics: Knowing Your World**

There's an old saying in the U.S. Navy, "We know who does the real work around here; it's the Chief Petty Officers." It's a statement that echoes what the 16th-century courtiers understood about their positions. High-ranking officers could not accomplish their goals without the help of their assistants, aides, and the guy on the line. Generals Eisenhower, Patton, MacArthur, Lee, Grant, Powell and Schwarzkopf may have directed the big battles, but without the work of all those under their command, they wouldn't have won them.

As King Henry V illustrated for us in chapter 2, it pays to remember that. An effective leader knows his or her workers, knows what kind of work they do in the trenches, how they handle problems, how they discover opportunities, what motivates them, what scares them, and why it is they do what they do. And knowing that, an effective leader uses that knowledge to help motivate his or her followers to achieve the aims of the organization.

It's important for you to stop what you're doing occasionally and take a figurative helicopter ride around your organization. You need to observe and understand what's going on in the day-to-day operation of your organization, especially if it has been a while since you left your office to take a look.

Start with your own people or work unit, and work outwards. You don't have to break out a magnifying glass and a fine-toothed comb, just be open to the work going on around you, the atmosphere you sense and the morale of your workers. Keep an open mind in searching for who are serving as real leaders, mere managers, and followers able and anxious to become "corporate courtiers." What you observe may shock, distress, or impress you.

You may find some service-oriented, goal-oriented people, or you may find a bunch of sluggish non-workers. You may see people who don't know the difference between flattery and sincere compliments. You may find people who build added value agreements within the organization and those who can't negotiate without fighting. You may find people who can handle any problem without the need for supervision or those who can't take a step without the need for constant approval.

In any case, your scan of the people around you should reveal who appears to lead, who really leads, who follows in order to lead, who only follows, and who merely manages in the hope that problems and opportunities will leave them alone if they ignore them long enough. With that knowledge, you can begin to identify those individuals who are ready to move into the role of "corporate courtiers."

Castiglione meant *The Book of the Courtier* to be a manual of instruction for any of us who seek to lead, or to follow. For us, his ideas offer insight into leadership development as well as what we will call "followership development." Clearly, Castiglione's book is full of the same kind of problems and challenges that confront today's organizations and the people in them. When you consider the fact that leadership, often, is also a process of following others, you begin to understand why *The Book of the Courtier* is so instructive. Consider these lessons:

- *We are all courtiers.*

  Is there anyone who does not report to someone else? Unless you're one of the fortunate few, we all spend a lot of our time *following*. It is a noble task, we believe. After all, who better can exert *real* influence over the boss? It's called "upward influence." And this ability to manage upward is an important contribution to organizational effectiveness. Your task is simple: to work with your superior to obtain the best possible results for yourself, your boss, and your organization.

- *Be a devil's advocate.*

  You've got to have the courage to disagree at times. Such dissent, when properly dispensed, can improve the quality of decision making. It is also a marvelous curative for that worst of managerial diseases, premature consensus. Castiglione would, however, have recommended that it be reserved for those situations which are fairly complicated and not well structured. Also, when playing this very important leadership role, avoid identifying strongly with one particular position. Focus instead on the process of the debate itself lest you become known as a "carping critic."

- *It's as important to know how to follow as it is to know how to lead.*

  Sure, you want to study leadership. That's why you purchased this book. But it's equally important that you become a student of followership as well. For it's becoming more and more difficult to distinguish the one from the other. In the future, leaders and followers will be more and more interchangeable. Why? Because leadership is a relationship—people interacting with other people. Here's the point. Increasingly, you will find yourself, as a leader, involved in a large number of leadership situations at one time. Since you can't possible run everything (at least we hope you're not that indispensable!), you will often play the role of follower as well.

- *Realize how much they need you.*

  Think about it. How much do you rely on the members of your team? Although you may not recognize it, your boss feels exactly the same way about you. You are, in other words, his or her courtier—the person depended on to understand the organization's lofty mission and to ensure that its goals are achieved. A major part of your success in doing this well depends upon your ability to support your boss. We're not suggesting that you have the word "courtier" printed on your business card and emblazoned on your office door, but be clear about this: Castiglione was right. Educating the boss is a very big part of your job.

CHAPTER 12

# DOING THE RIGHT THING: GANDHI ON THE RULES OF BUSINESS AND LIFE

*I think it would be a good idea.*
—MAHATMA GANDHI,
when asked what he thought of Western civilization

**KEY POINTS**
- RULES FOR LIFE AND WORK
- MERE MANAGERS TRY TO DO THINGS RIGHT; LEADERS DO THE RIGHT THINGS

As the ant once told the elephant, "It's not always size that indicates real strength." It's hard to find a more unimposing figure, physically, than India's late spiritual and political leader, Mahatma Gandhi. But what he lacked in size, he more than made up for in his gigantic leadership—in charisma, speaking skills, and an unflagging desire to lead his people and his country through a period of tremendous civil change.

Gandhi came from average beginnings and rose to become one of the most influential leaders of the 20th century. His message was not just for India, it was for the world: peace for all people, change through nonviolence, and respect for human beings, no matter their political or religious beliefs.

In this chapter, you'll see how this man served as the inspiration for many world leaders to follow, including Martin Luther King, who—as we discovered in chapter 7—took Gandhi's principles of change through civil disobedience and used them to reshape the racial fabric of American society.

Safe to say, Gandhi serves as the "father of the civil rights movement," not just for his country, but for the world. His teachings, "preachings," and writings have elevated him far beyond the role of Indian politician; he was, and still is, a world leader. Using a mixture of deep-seated religious beliefs, his ability to speak to vast numbers of people gathered together, and his understanding of how to give people hope by removing oppression from their lives, Gandhi serves as a model leader.

No wonder it's quite common to see pictures of Gandhi in the homes and offices of Indian people all over the world. An attorney we know has a large photo of Gandhi on his desk. He tells us that he looks at the picture whenever he feels depressed and when he is certain that the world we live in is full of despair. Just looking at the picture, he says, lifts his spirits.

Leaders can do that. And leaders like Gandhi can have a tremendous impact upon our lives. Part of it is identification. Gandhi looked like the people he led, spoke as they did, ate the same foods, and wore the same clothing. His physical presence at the center of a large crowd was cause for great excitement as people clamored to be near him. His speeches could move the masses, in ways we have rarely seen since. And his actions—fasting for causes he believed in, marching across the country, confronting British leaders in his attempt to create free rule for India and for Indians—motivated people to follow him as if he were invincible.

If you believe this kind of impact is the sole province of transcendent luminaries like Gandhi, think again. Consider, for example, Pat Haggerty, former chairman and CEO of Texas Instruments, Inc., whose life, and its impact on followers, has recently been chronicled by a former employee. Haggerty, it turns out, was a leader who eschewed status symbols. They'd only come, he said, between the high poohbahs and the people who did the real work. With this thought in mind, Haggerty insisted that employees "just call him Pat." Somehow he changed people's lives; maybe because he realized that when everyone focuses on common purposes, common people can do uncommon things. Then, too, he admitted his fallibilities—and the fact that for twenty-five years he'd been saying the same daily prayer: "God, grant me the grace to fulfill with wisdom, justice, respect, humility, and humanity my duties to all for whom and to whom I am responsible."

The bottom line on all this is that Haggerty, like his much more famous counterpart, Gandhi, clearly and dramatically enhanced the lives of those he led. You can too.

## Gandhi: Born to Lead

Gandhi was born in Porbandar, India, on October 2, 1869. His father was a chief minister for the maharaja (prince or leader) of Porbandar and his family came from a long line of grocers and moneylenders (the name "Gandhi" means "grocer").

His mother believed in Jainism, a religion that places much importance on the concepts of both nonviolence and vegetarianism, an eating habit prevalent today. Hindu Indians believe all life forms to be sacred and will not eat the flesh of any animal.

Gandhi was influenced by the ideals of his mother, whose life he called "an endless chain of fasts and vows." As a youngster, however, he lived a double life. At home, he behaved in one manner, with strict adherence to his mother's ways; with his friends, however, he secretly smoked, ate meat, told lies, and wore non-Indian-style clothing. Understandably, he felt tremendous pangs of guilt while engaging in these behaviors, especially since they countered everything his mother believed. As he grew to young adulthood, these feelings forced him to make significant changes in his moral behavior that would guide him for the rest of his life. And he adopted his mother's beliefs as his own.

Gandhi married in his early teens and went through standard British-Indian schooling. After finishing school, he traveled to England to study law. In his era, the phrase "the sun never sets on a province of the British Empire" represented the political order of the day. England ruled many countries, including India.

Gandhi passed the bar in 1891 and began practicing law in Bombay, where he found little immediate success. He was asked to go to South Africa to handle legal cases for Indian citizens living there, and from 1893 to 1914 he made his home in that country. During these years Gandhi witnessed many instances of overt racial discrimination against the Indian people in South Africa. As minorities in a foreign land, they did not have much of a voice in their treatment or welfare. Gandhi soon rose to the challenge and became one of the leaders in the movement to challenge British rule, first in South Africa, and later, in his home country.

When he went back to India from South Africa in January 1915, Gandhi became involved in the country's fledgling labor movement. But it was an event in April 1919, known as the "Massacre of Amritsar," which thrust him into action, and later, into national prominence.

At Amritsar, British troops led by a British Indian Army general were protesting an emergency powers act that gave the British unlimited political, military, and civil power. In the melee, 379 unarmed Indian people were killed and over 1,200 were wounded. The result of this barbarism transformed Gandhi from an interested spectator to a dedicated activist. He would leave his comfort zone forever.

Within a year he became the leader of the Indian National Congress, during which time he established a policy of "noncooperation" with the British from 1920–22. He later organized a number of successful protest marches against unpopular British measures, such as the Salt Tax of 1930, and many boycotts of British goods. One of his more famous boycotts involved clothing. He urged his people to wear only "homespun" clothes made from Indian-handmade weaves. He staged several clothes-burning ceremonies at which people threw their British-made clothing onto huge bonfires. He led a number of protest campaigns and, over time, developed his philosophy of nonviolent resistance known as *satyagraha* (or literally, "steadfastness in truth").

As you might imagine, Gandhi was extremely popular with his people and widely despised by British leaders. His unflagging determination and his ability to stick the collective thumb of India into the eye of the British lion caused British pols to stop calling him "that disturbing little man in the robes," and to start taking his demands seriously.

Like Martin Luther King, Gandhi spent some time in British jails and often used personal hunger strikes as part of his civil disobedience techniques. The publicity surrounding these hunger strikes, which often went on for life-threatening weeks, helped rally support among Indian people for his causes and helped put enormous pressure on his British captors. His final term of imprisonment came in 1942–44, when he called for the total withdrawal of the British (the "Quit India" movement) during World War II.

Unlike other Indian political rulers or business leaders who still believed in or followed the strict caste or class system, Gandhi fought to improve the social status of the lowest classes of Indian society, including the casteless "untouchables," whom he called *harijans* (or "children of God"). While these people were referred to as "unclean" by the majority of the Indian population, Gandhi believed that all people were good in the eyes of God and that devout Hindus should accept each other for what they were. While this was not a popular sentiment, Gandhi was quick to point to this inter-class racism; that is, Indians discriminating against Indians, as something that made them no better than the British.

In his later years, Gandhi worked hard to build a better relationship between the Hindu Indian people (who made up the majority of the population) and the many minority groups in India, in particular, the Muslim Indians. The division between these two groups, which still exists in often fierce and violent ways today, caused Muhammad Ali Jinnah, the leader of the Indian Muslims, to help create a separate state, which is now Pakistan. When India finally achieved independence from Britain in 1947, Mahatma Gandhi was so opposed to the India-Pakistan subdivision that he organized a huge protest movement against the plan.

Like his student-to-be, Martin Luther King, Gandhi was assassinated. It happened in Delhi on January 30, 1948, when a Hindu fanatic who mistakenly believed that Gandhi's involvement in the creation of the Pakistani state meant that he supported Muslims over Hindus. He is said to have murmured quietly in Indian as he died, "Oh, God."

Throughout his life, Gandhi exhibited great energy and at the same time, even greater patience. He faced racism, bigotry, and religious and political fanaticism from all sides. Yet he managed to persevere, achieving giant gains after suffering small setbacks. To this end, he demonstrated perhaps the most important trait of the leader: to keep on keeping on.

Gandhi used the ideals of his religion to guide his life. It was his belief that the path to "enlightenment" (the goal of many eastern religions) consisted of a long journey rather than a short ride. As such, he counseled that since we're all on the same path together, we might as well help each other as we make the trip.

Since Gandhi spent much of his time facilitating meetings with disparate groups—the British and the Indians, Hindu Indians and Muslim Indians, etc.—he became an accomplished negotiator. He had excellent conflict resolution skills and possessed that rare ability to see ways for each side to succeed or, barring that, at least to "save face."

Gandhi knew in his heart and in his head that guns and bullets, fists and feet, and words of hate or fury were not the answer to India's problems. Yet his political ideas sent shockwaves throughout his country. Through his protest of the British Salt Tax, manifested by a march across the country to the oceanside sea salt factories; his unconventional boycott of British-made clothes over Indian-made homespun clothing (imagine having to weave your own necktie); and his ability to help the oppressed (Indians) see that they vastly outnumbered their oppressors (the British) delivered a clear message to his opponents: he would be heard.

And he would move others out of their comfort zones. He had the very unusual, and very leaderly, ability to convince his people to give up their collective apathy and to embrace collective action (such as protests, marches, boycotts, publicity campaigns, etc.).

It changed political geography. Today, India rules herself. For his efforts in political, spiritual, religious, and philosophical leadership, Mahatma Gandhi remains India's most famous citizen and one of the world's most beloved leaders.

### Gandhi: Lessons on Humility in Leadership
On September 11, 1906, attorney Mohandas Gandhi convened a meeting of some 3,000 Indian citizens in the South African city of Johannesburg. The purpose of this gathering was to debate the appropriate response to a new ordinance under consideration by the white South African government. Under the proposal, all Indian men, women, and children over age eight would have to register themselves with the police, get fingerprinted, and then carry a personal ID card at all times. Indians who did not carry this card with them both night and day could be fined, imprisoned, or deported. It also allowed South African police to stop an Indian woman on the street or enter her home to ask to see the card. In the Indian community, this new law was akin to slavery, especially since no other minority group in South Africa was required to follow the rule. The mood in the meeting hall, to say the least, was ugly.

Gandhi had helped draft his community's response to this ordinance—absolute and unwavering resistance. One of the leaders on the platform with him urged the angry crowd to approve their resistance plan "with God as their witness." For his part, Gandhi spoke out against the new segregationist law and said that he would indeed make his pledge before God not to obey it. He suggested that "... the government has taken leave of all sense of decency" and that everyone in the room must stand together, even if it meant hunger and suffering, beatings and imprisonment, pain and deportation, or any other wicked injustices. In effect, he said, "I'm ready for it. What about you?"

> But I can boldly declare and with certainty, that as long as there is even a handful of men true to their pledge, there can be only one end to the struggle—and that is victory. There is only one course open to me, [that is] to die but not to submit to the law.[1]

En masse, everyone in the meeting hall rose and swore to God that they would not follow such an egregious law if it passed.

As an attorney, Gandhi knew the power of negotiating from strength and he also appreciated the value of taking a fight to the opponent's home turf. With that in mind and the Indian resistance movement primed for their initial acts of civil disobedience, Gandhi sailed to London to meet with the British Secretary of State of India and the British Secretary for the Colonies.

After much campaigning and argument, Gandhi felt he had convinced the British diplomats not to support the South Africans' racial ordinance. And in fact, as he sailed home, he received a confirming cable: Britain would not support the Black Act.

Flushed with an apparent victory—his first significant one as a leader—Gandhi returned to South Africa with the hopes that the British-influenced government there would follow the lead of England. But it was a Pyhrric victory. While the British government said on the one hand that it wouldn't support the law, time was on its side. Gandhi's trip to England ended in the latter part of 1906; on January 1, 1907, South Africa would no longer be a British colony and could therefore enact any law it chose. Gandhi had been tricked. It would teach him many valuable lessons.

But true to his word, Gandhi did not register under the new racial law when it took effect on July 31, 1907. As a result, he was arrested on January 11, 1908, and sentenced to two months in jail.

The publicity Gandhi received while in jail helped bring the issue to a boil. Less than three weeks into his sentence, Gandhi was released from the jail and brought to a meeting with the leader of South Africa, General Jan Christian Smuts.

Smuts promised to repeal the Black Act if Gandhi could get the Indians to voluntarily "register" themselves. Unlike his Indian counterparts, Gandhi saw the power and spirit of compromise. While his friends believed that Smuts would not honor his promise, Gandhi, who believed in finding the good in all people, was willing to accept Smuts' counteroffer, largely because it allowed both sides to save face. Indians wouldn't be "forced" to register, and the government could still look as if it had retained its power.

As the months passed, negotiations between the two sides deteriorated into name-calling. During this time, Gandhi read a copy of Henry David Thoreau's *Civil Disobedience*. Gandhi had been arrested, along with many of his associates, for failing to keep and maintain his registration card. Thoreau's work, which documents his own overnight prison stay for failing to pay taxes, presents his theory that it was more important to be right than to follow the law. Like Gandhi, Thoreau believed bad laws were meant to be broken. It was, he concluded, his duty to resist unjust laws. He put it this way:

> *All men recognize the right to revolution, that is, the right to refuse allegiance to, and to resist, the government when its tyranny and efficiency are great and unendurable.*

Gandhi took this message to heart. You could not abide a law that was unjust, nor support the people who created it. He vowed to spend his life fighting oppression and the oppressors.

Gandhi soon returned to his homeland. In 1930, Indian leaders were calling for total independence from British rule. While Gandhi believed that change in terms of people's views and their politics was a gradual process dependent on education and experience, he knew the Indian people wanted independence. With some reluctance, he agreed to head the campaign, knowing that it was his duty as the most recognized Indian leader of his century.

His most famous act of civil disobedience came in March 1930. He wrote a letter to the British Viceroy Lord Halifax, saying, in effect, that a new British tax on Indian salt was illegal and he and his associates would use acts of civil disobedience to disobey it.

It was his plan, Gandhi told his followers a few days later, to stage a "Salt March" from Sabarmati, India, to the seaside town of Dandi, a distance of over two hundred miles. On March 12, armed with only a walking stick for support, the sixty-one-year-old leader set off on foot, with a growing number of followers behind him. He made the trip in twenty-four days because, as he said to all who asked, "We are marching in the name of God."

As he walked, people watered the roads for him or laid flowers and leaves in his path. He walked over twelve miles per day, ignoring a horse-drawn cart. And what began as a small band of Gandhi devotees had become several thousand dedicated, devoted Indians by the time he reached Dandi on the evening of April 5.

In the morning, Gandhi and his thousands of followers marched to the edge of the ocean and the great man gathered some salt that had been created by the waves. Lifting it over his head for all to see, Gandhi literally and symbolically broke the law, which said that no Indian citizen could possess salt not made by the British salt monopoly in India. This one small and elderly man had, in effect, thumbed his country's collective nose at the British rulers. The implications of the Salt March led to swift changes throughout the Indian nation.

In response to Gandhi's salt boycott, British troops began making mass arrests of any of Gandhi's followers caught possessing handmade salt as well as anyone who pledged support of Gandhi.

Mass arrests of the supporters and the subsequent protests surrounding these arrests spread across India within days. Literally thousands of people broke the law and made or possessed their own salt. Estimates of the numbers of protesters arrested ranged from 60,000 to 100,000 people. And then on May 5, less than one month after his march, Gandhi was once again arrested for "crimes against the British government." And as usual, he went to jail peacefully, quietly, and with joy in his heart.

With Gandhi in jail, British leaders hoped the salt controversy would die down. Of course, the exact opposite occurred. Gandhi had written another letter, just before his arrest, stating that his supporters planned to march to the Dharasana Salt Works with the intention of disrupting the operation. Led by Indian poet Sarojini Naidu, the protesters reached the gates of the factory only to be kicked and beaten unmercifully by the British troops. One by one the Indians approached the gates and one by one they were battered and attacked until none were left standing. Several people died and over 320 were badly injured.

In the end, this one act of nonviolent protest and Britain's violent response turned the eyes of the world on the British presence in India. World outrage came swift and loud. By the end of 1930, British leaders in England and India knew they had lost their final battle with Mr. Gandhi and his loyal supporters.

And while it would take many more years until India would be completely free from British rule, the seeds for change had already been sown. Gandhi's ideas for non-violent civil disobedience had come to full fruition.

### Humility in Leadership: It's Not Noise, It's Presence

Gandhi was a believer in manual labor and simple living. He spun the thread and wove the cloth for his own garments and insisted that his followers do so too. He disagreed with those who wanted India to become an industrial country. He urged his country to seek its own way in the world. He strove to show his people that they were capable of self-rule, a fact that most British leaders scoffed at then.

And he was full of energy. Gandhi seemed to be a man who become more valiant and courageous as he grew older. He was never content to sit back and let circumstances dictate the health of his nation; he wanted to be the change agent for his people and for his land. An appropriate motto for him could have said, "Follow my example, take my lead, and never stop moving forward."

We've come to expect executives to fly first-class, be driven about town in stretch limousines, eat at three-star restaurants, and generally get the kind of treatment reserved only for the very rich. But when it comes to business leadership, unostentatiousness and even a modicum of modesty are "in." Take F. Kenneth Iverson, CEO of Nucor Corporation, the steel-producing giant. A reporter describes him as anything but pretentious. "He drives his own car to work. He flies regularly to visit Nucor's twenty-two plants—but not on a corporate jet, because the company doesn't have one. Instead, Iverson sits in coach and carries his own bag. His corporate headquarters is hidden away on half a floor of a four-story building across from a suburban shopping mall in Charlotte, North Carolina. Iverson does have a corner office, but it's cramped and utilitarian by CEO standards. Nor is there an executive dining room. When

Iverson treats his top execs to lunch, they often walk across the highway to Phil's Deli."[2]

Humility, not showiness, seems to be part of Iverson's leadership magic. As he puts it, "Reduce any difference between management and anyone else at the company—destroy corporate hierarchy." It's a style that seems to be working. Nucor hasn't had a losing quarter in twenty-five years!

But if ever a man met the dictionary definition of "humility," it was Gandhi. From his early experiences in South Africa to his work for India's revolution of independence from Britain, to his later years as the nation's political and spiritual leader, he always exhibited a sense of quiet grace, sublime strength, and power.

And his understanding of how groups respond to their leaders teaches us two things: sometimes leaders lead by speaking, with the power of their words; and sometimes leaders lead by doing, with the power of their actions. He knew instinctively that there was a time to talk and a time to leave the speeches for the politicians and simply do what needed to be done. The salt march began as his own idea; that is, he said, "I will march to Dandi," and then along the way, he picked up thousands of supporters. Over the three-week period, Gandhi marched through towns where thousands left their jobs and their their homes just to be with him. Indian people marching with him said it all: "Gandhi is our leader. He is in the front, leading and guiding us."

But he was also what lately has become known as a "servant leader."[3] The key to Gandhi's greatness was that he was seen as a servant first, a leader second. Perhaps the best way to put all this is to understand that there are two types of leaders today: One type says: "I am leader; your job is to follow me." The other says: "Where would you like to go? I'll aid you in getting there."

It's a concept that has a fascinating provenance: an incident in Herman Hesse's story, *Journey to the East*. Professors Julius Jackson and Douglas Gutknecht, who have analyzed Gandhi's servant leadership, write that: "A character, Leo, is a servant doing menial chores for a group on a journey. In a subtle way, Leo is the glue that holds the group together and that makes the group meaningful. However, when he leaves, the group disbands and the journey is ended. Years later, one of the members of the journey finds Leo is a great and noble leader of a religious order. This had never been acknowledged when Leo was doing the chores. Leo was actually the leader all of the time, but he was servant first because that was what he was, deep down inside."[4]

Servant leadership seems to work. Jack Balousek, one-time CEO of ad agency Foote, Cone & Belding's San Francisco office (he's since moved on to become president/chief operating officer of FC&B North America) is a case in point. Talk about loyalty. Even folks Balousek's had to let go call him with new business leads. It seems he's a master at building relationships. And he is a self-proclaimed "servant leader." As he puts it, "The role of management today is really different than it was five or ten years ago. Back then, management was expected to know all the answers and tell everyone what to do. Today the roles are reversed. I work for the people who work for me."[5]

Reversing work roles so dramatically can call for Draconian measures. Gandhi, for example, was willing to be more than a figurehead; he was also willing to go to jail for his beliefs. This was more than just grandstanding, more than a mere symbolic act. Gandhi demanded that he be arrested to demonstrate his willingness to put himself and his freedom at risk for his beliefs. Such sacrifice, of course, was part of a strategy: Whenever Gandhi was arrested, his subsequent incarceration (even if it was only for a brief period) rallied his supporters even more.

The point of all this is that you, like Gandhi, must lead by example. You must go down on the frontlines with your people. It's not enough to say, "You go forward and I'll catch up later." It's more necessary to say, "Come this way with me. We will go together."

### The Power of Sacrifice

As John F. Kennedy said in his inaugural address, "Ask not what your country can do for you, but what you can do for your country." Gandhi embodied this idea. He possessed that rare ability to sacrifice himself for others. Of course, this commitment was helped hugely by his religious beliefs—Hindus believe that there is good in all people.

Upon his arrest for violating the rules of the Black Act, Gandhi was said to have told the judge in effect, "Please give me your maximum punishment. I am the leader of these people and I have encouraged them to break this law. Therefore, I deserve the brunt of your punishment." Faced with this admonition, the judge sentenced Gandhi to jail "without hard labor." Gandhi had helped his jailer save face. The judge could still carry out his sentence as if he were in control of the situation, and for his part, Gandhi received a less harsh sentence when he was fully prepared for a more strenuous one.

As you consider Gandhi's life and work, ask yourself what sacrifices you're prepared to make for your team, your work group, your unit, or your division. What commitment are you willing to make toward the success of your entire organization?

**Bearing the Brunt**
Gandhi's story dramatically demonstrates that assuming the torch of leadership often brings with it the price of pain. Like Churchill, Cleopatra, and King Henry V, Gandhi bore the weight of his nation on his shoulders. He knew that in order to expect hard work from others you must first do hard work yourself. No matter how hard they work, you work harder. And no matter how difficult their burden is, yours is greater.

Shakespeare describes this "yoke of leadership" better than any other writer in *Henry V*:

> *We must bear all. O hard condition,*
> *Twin-born with greatness, subject to the breath*
> *Of every fool whose sense no more can feel*
> *But his own wringing! What infinite heart's ease*
> *Must kings neglect, that private men enjoy!*
> *And what have kings, that privates have not too,*
> *Save ceremony, save general ceremony?*
> *And what art thou, thou idol Ceremony?*
> *What kind of god art thou, that suffer'st more*
> *Of mortal griefs than do thy worshippers?*

It was a sense of "ceremony," no doubt, that impelled Gandhi to tell people that he actually enjoyed his time in jail because it allowed him to pray, fast, and read good books. But there was more. Faced with the option of incarceration or fighting, Gandhi chose the path of least resistance. He knew that going to jail for his beliefs was a critical tactic in his grand plan for the rebirth of a British-free India.

Sacrifice, of course, is more than just "falling on your sword" for the good of the group. This event should have a purpose, a reason behind it. There should be a reason for you to take the heat, even if it's only for the good of the morale of the group. Sometimes you'll need to absorb the blame as a way to protect your people from those who want to do them harm; sometimes you'll have to do it so that others can have someone to blame for their mistakes. Sacrifice without a point, as Gandhi might say, is a waste.

## The Yoke of Greatness

Even the most confident leaders are plagued by self-doubt. Surely Gandhi, too, must have gone through periods of painful soul-searching as he set his revolutionary course of action and asked his people to follow. While these feelings are common, they shouldn't be paralyzing. While Gandhi may have had occasional doubts, he overcame them and kept going. After all, his leadership role didn't allow time for indecision.

Put simply, Gandhi willingly bore the yoke of leadership. Whether it was through his campaign of passive resistance—using his own hunger strikes, the call for people to make their own homespun clothing, peace marches, boycotts, or strikes—Gandhi knew he needed all of his energy to bring self-rule to his country. Once he accepted the initial challenge to go to South Africa as a young lawyer and begin the fight for Indian civil rights, he'd realized his true calling. Like it or not, he would have to be a leader of people and their nation.

Martin Luther King, who learned much from Gandhi, was also not completely comfortable in his role as the leader of the black civil rights movement. As you'll recall from our discussion of King in chapter 7, he thought he was too young and too inexperienced to take on such an important leadership role. Thankfully for his followers and the nation, they did not agree with his self-deprecating evaluation and thrust the yoke of leadership on his shoulders.

And so it may be with you, in your organization. You may not want some important project or critical problem thrown onto your desk with orders from on high to "handle it," and yet these things happen. Part of being a good leader is realizing you will have to leave your comfort zone from time to time and go off and fight the big battles or tackle the big quest.

## Gandhi's Seven Deadly Sins

Every great leader needs guideposts to signal the way. Mahatma Gandhi, we are told, had his. They are summarized in a piece entitled

"The Great Soul." As you make the transition from manager to leader, we think you'll find these proverbs, which immortalize seven deadly leadership sins, invaluable:

1.  *Wealth without work.*
    Gandhi knew from his dealings with the British that a middle-level, desk-riding English bureaucrat made more money in one month than most Indian people made in one year. And it's not that Gandhi particularly despised people with money; he just thought that the gap between the very rich and the very poor was corrosive. As he put it:

    > *How heavy is the toll of sins and wrongs that wealth, power and prestige extract from man.*

    Gandhi was no stranger to hard work. Even at age seventy-nine, he was a robust figure, actively involved in politics, diplomacy, and—need we say?—leadership.

2.  *Pleasure without conscience.*
    As a Hindu, Gandhi believed in the importance of moral character. He spoke frequently of the need to prevent one-upmanship from ruining the Indian social structure. And as a person who fasted and prayed every day, he knew there was no value in hedonism, or taking only the rewards of life without paying for them with honest labor. Certainly he was unwilling to put personal pleasure before the needs of others. Neither should you.

3.  *Knowledge without character.*
    These two traits must go hand in hand. As Gandhi put it, "If my character made a gentleman of me, so much the better." He knew from his experiences as a diplomat and a leader that there are plenty of people in the world who possess intelligence without honor, smarts without ethics, and pragmatism without humanity. He believed these combinations to be dangerous, in that they coupled rare and powerful weapons with the absence of goodness.

4. *Commerce without morality.*

*... one thing took deep root in me—the conviction that morality is the basis of things and that truth is the substance of all morality.*

Like Rule #3, this proverb exhorts leaders to beware of success without ethics. The wealthy business person who is immoral will trample competitors and then lose everything.

5. *Science without humanity.*
Gandhi was killed only a few hours after a *Life* magazine reporter asked him about the effects of the atomic bomb dropped on Hiroshima two and one-half years earlier. His response:

*The science of war leads one to dictatorship pure and simple. The science of nonviolence alone can lead one to pure democracy. Nonviolence is the only thing the atom bomb cannot destroy.*

As a firm believer in nonviolence and a tireless advocate of its use, for Gandhi, the welfare of all people must be the most important aim of science.

6. *Religion without sacrifice.*

*For me, politics bereft of religion are absolute dirt, even to be shunned. Politics concerns nations and that which concerns the welfare of others must be one of the concerns of a man who is religiously inclined, in other words, a seeker after God and Truth....*

Hindu religion is built on sacrifice, and Gandhi's life offered one example of one personal sacrifice after another: fasting to save food, silent prayer, giving his food to people less fortunate so that they could eat, offering his extra clothing to people who had never had new clothes, and in the end, giving his life with-out regret.

7. *Politics without principle.*
   Politics was Gandhi's life. From the time he left law school in England until his death, he always had his hand in the game of diplomacy and the art and science of government. It had its rewards. As he put it:

   > *It is to me a matter of perennial satisfaction that I retain generally the affection and the trust of those whose principles and policies I oppose....*

   How many political or corporate leaders can make this same claim today?

   Mohandas "Mahatma" Gandhi served as the agent for change for an entire nation. He devoted his life to the service of others and to making a better India for all its citizens. He worked tirelessly, in the face of great odds and even great oppo-sition. By bearing the weight of a nation on his own, he was able to succeed and prove that might does not always make right.

## Leadership as the Right Thing to Do

In this book, we have made numerous comparisons between the mere manager and the leader. The former, we have argued, does only what is expected (or less), takes few risks, makes little effort to serve, train, empower, or lead others, and in the end makes little contribution to the success of the organization or to his or her own personal or professional success.

Conversely, we have defined the budding or developing leader as a careful risk-taker, a diligent and tireless worker, a rule-breaker when necessary, a naysayer when necessary, an empowering force for the peo-ple who work for the leader, a questor, a skilled and charismatic com-municator, and—perhaps most importantly—someone who is not satis-fied with the status quo, someone who will not stay locked into a comfort zone that prohibits new experiences, new challenges, and new ways to take action.

And we have said (paraphrasing leadership scholar Warren Bennis), "Mere managers may do things right, but real leaders do the right things." But there's more. Listen to Gandhi:

> *It's the action, not the fruit of the action, that's important. You have to do the right thing. It may not be in your power, may not be in your time, that there'll be any fruit. But that doesn't mean you stop doing the right thing. You may never know what results come from your action. But if you do nothing, there'll be no result.*

# AFTERWORD

As this book testifies, we think the heroes of literature mirror our own humanity, our strengths and frailties, our ability to lead and manage. And they certainly teach those of us who are willing to get to know them, their struggles, and their victories, to see a bit more deeply into our own lives, both personal and professional. And, as we've discovered in our seminars, managers find—frequently to their great surprise—that the lessons of literature "have legs." Educational experts refer to this as "transference," the ability to use what is learned back at the office. Whatever you call it, it is invaluable, because it means that the learning doesn't stop at the classroom or when the book is closed. It means that at last a modicum of permanent change occurs; change that can be chanelled toward greater productivity, a chance to achieve that reached-for goal, or an opportunity to take a quantum career leap.

At the end of each of our seminars, we go around the table and ask each of the participants to describe briefly the most important thing they've learned that they can take back to work with them. We've compiled the results, one taken from the summary at the back of each chapter in this book.

Herewith, the *Timeless Leader* Success Guide:

1. *Plato—When things get too comfortable around here, it's best to take cover.* It's called complacency, and it is a terminal organizational disease. And it doesn't just happen to the giants like IBM. But wherever it occurs, the stagnation that results is classic. You've no doubt witnessed it. A friend founds a small company that becomes a leader in its industry, commanding respect, high prices, and even higher margins. This seems to be a career made in heaven. Increasingly, however, something all-too-human happens. Your friend becomes overconfident, even arrogant. He or she is in the comfort zone. Feeling invincible, a disdain for customers develops. Then sales begin to stagnate. Profits plummet. A key customer chooses another supplier. A product is recalled. Smaller, more agile—and, we might add—less comfortable companies begin to capture share of market. Employees are laid off. A plant closes. It's a near-mythic journey you must avoid.

2. *Prince Hal—Remember that leadership is about transforming.* Prince Hal consistently focused on England's well-being and on unifying his realm. Perhaps a little less grandly, you need to do the same thing. He also exhorted his men to perform beyond what they think they are capable of. All this is called "transformational leadership." It's the ability to get people to focus on team goals rather than individual ones; to increase the need to achieve at a higher level. The result is that everyone finds new satisfaction by doing more than they ever thought possible.

3. *Antigone—Remember that it's part of the leader's job to disagree.* Unless you spend most of your time on another planet, you'll find that frequently the *right* thing to do is to oppose the status quo, to rouse followers to act against the established way of doing things, to reform your organization. The key, of course, is to be sure that (1) what you're trying to accomplish is good for the organization, not just you, and (2) that you keep your eye on the long-term goal so as to not find yourself mired down in righteous indignation along the way. Also, don't make the incorrect assumption that going to battle with the boss is necessarily bad. Sure, you may feel you're avoiding conflict in the short term.

But—over the long haul—best to get what's nagging you off your chest. It'll help your self-image as well as provide you with the information you need to do your job better.

4. *Willie Stark—Be willing to share the limelight or even take a lesser role.* Sometimes, quiet leadership is more powerful than basking in glory. In these cases, it's not always who's right, but what's right. Taking all of the credit is perfectly acceptable in certain situations, especially if you did all the work or took a project from start to finish. In other cases, it might be best to fall back on a more humble stance and let your employees get the praise. One of the elements of real leadership is your ability to empower other people so that they can feel more of a sense of achievement. Just as you don't always have to win every battle, you don't always have to take the credit.

5. *Cleopatra—Connecting is everything.* The operative word, of course, is *networking.* At this, Cleopatra was without equal. Her formula was simple. She could best meet her leadership needs by connecting with the needs and desires of Caesar and Antony. Such ability to discover, embrace, and enthusiastically support key players' goals and aspirations is as much a part of successful leadership today as it was in Cleopatra's time. Females seem to be better equipped for this sort of thing than males. They disdain traditional organizational structures like the hierarchical ladder. Instead, they place themselves at the center of things and "connect" to all those around them as if by invisible strands or threads.

6. *Captain Ahab—Question. Don't tell.* Too many managers simply announce goals to their employees. Big deal. It's a monologue, a top-down game in which few listen and fewer buy in. But Ahab knew better. He got his men to commit to his goal not by telling but by asking. Sure, the most famous line in the book, as we've said, is its opening three words, "Call me Ishmael." But the real magic starts when Captain Ahab asks, "What do you do when you see a whale, men?" And he doesn't stop there: "What do you do next, men?" he asks. Then, "What tune is it ye pull to, men?" The effect of this barrage of questions was as dramatic as it was immediate: The crew, because they participated actively in the process of setting objectives, quickly made the boss's goal their own.

7. *Martin Luther King—Create a dialogue that focuses on interests.* Frequently neither side knows what the other wants when there's conflict. Get out a pen and a piece of paper and ask each person to make one list of their interests and another list which guesses about the other side's interests. (At the very least, this gets them both working and not shouting at each other. What's more, it clarifies each side's position without your having to act like an interrogator trying to extract information from disgruntled people.) Then have the sides exchange or explain their lists. Often, this step alone is enough to get them to start saying closure statements such as, "You need that? Well, I can do that for you if you do this for me."

8. *Von Clausewitz—Think strategy.* Strategy is to the leader what an income statement and balance sheet are to the accountant. Strategy is a road map that shows you where you are going. It is an overall plan. And strategy in business is similar to strategy in war. It is long-term. It is determined by top management. It provides general goals toward which the organization should strive. And, perhaps most importantly, strategy must match resources and skills found within the organization with the task at hand. Simply put, if you don't have the resources and skills necessary to achieve your goal, you badly need a new strategy.

9. *Billy Budd—Break, or at least bend, a rule now and then.* Lest this seem like a form of corporate anarchy, a recent lesson from that phoenix-about-to-rise-from-the-ashes, IBM, might help. Western Union's consumer services division recently was about to purchase personal computers for its 14,000 agents throughout the United States. Yet there were many obstacles to the deal, and Western Union was close to closing a deal with one of IBM's competitors. As the IBM marketing rep put it, "the customer handed us a set of requirements we hadn't seen before. To meet them, we needed help from four other IBM organizations. We got it by throwing away the rule book. The point? Out went the rule book, in came the business." Think what it can do for you. Consider what it might have done for the hapless Captain Vere.

10. *Winston Churchill—Beware of becoming a "Chamberlain."* The contrast between Churchill and Neville Chamberlain is dramat-

ic. Chamberlain "describes his meeting with Hitler in a factual and descriptive way. He never expresses his feelings nor does he attempt to use an emotional appeal to build belief in his audience. He tries to downplay the need for war, given that war is a nightmare and a fearful thing. Yet he doesn't drive the point home with any vivid imagery. He ends on the note that it is not clear to him that there are great issues at stake worth plunging into a war for. He leaves the listener with the impression that he is indecisive, has no clear direction, nor conception of the problem. He does not inspire confidence in himself or in his course of action." Maybe that explains one of history's most cruel double entendres: the word "chamberlain" also means bedroom attendant.

11. *Castiglione—It's as important to know how to follow as it is to know how to lead.* Sure, you want to study leadership. That's why you purchased this book. But it's equally important that you become a student of followership as well. For it's becoming more and more difficult to distinguish the one from the other. In the future, leaders and followers will be more and more interchangeable. Why? Because leadership is a relationship—people interacting with other people. Here's the point. Increasingly, you will find yourself—as a leader—involved in a large number of leadership situations at one time. Since you can't possibly run everything (at least we hope you're not that indispensable!), you will often play the role of follower as well.

12. *Gandhi—Bear the yoke.* Gandhi's story dramatically demonstrates that assuming the torch of leadership often brings with it the price of pain. Like Churchill, Cleopatra, and King Henry V, Gandhi bore the weight of his nation on his shoulders. He knew that in order to expect hard work from others you must first do hard work yourself. No matter how hard they work, you work harder. And no matter how difficult their burden is, yours is greater.

# NOTES

## Chapter One

Some material in this chapter was adapted from "Plato: *The Republic*," a Hartwick Classic Leadership Case, and accompanying teaching notes written by Gerald McCarthy, managing director of OLV Associates in Worcester, Massachusetts, and Associate Professor of Management Edward Ottensmeyer of the Graduate School of Business at Clark University.

1. Plato, *The Republic*. Richard W. Sterling and William C. Scott, eds. New York: W.W. Norton and Co., 1985. All quotations are from this text.
2. Paul Carroll, *Big Blues: The Unmaking of IBM*. New York: Crown Publishers, Inc.
3. Suzanne Bay, "Tapping Change: Quality Pays Off at Greenfield Industries", *BusinessWest*, September 1, 1994.
4. Oscar Suris, "Retooling Itself, Ford Stresses Speed, Candor," *Wall Street Journal*, October 27, 1994.
5. Peter Vaill, *Managing as a Performing Art*, San Francisco: Jossey-Bass, 1989.

## Chapter Two

Some material in this chapter was adapted from "The Henriad, by William Shakespeare," a Hartwick Classic Leadership Case, and accompanying teaching notes written by Associate Professor of English Richard Burke of Lynchburg College and Professor of Management Douglas F. Mayer of Hartwick College.

1. William Shakespeare, *The Riverside Shakespeare*. G. Blakemore Evans, ed. Boston: Houghton Mifflin Co., 1974. All quotations are from this text.
2. Edwin Crego and Peter Schiffrin, *Customer-Focused Re-Engineering*. Burr Ridge, IL: Irwin Professional Publishing, 1994.

3. Steven E. Prokesch, "Mastering Chaos at the High-Tech Frontier: An Interview With Silicon Graphics' Ed McCracken," *Harvard Business Review*, November–December 1993, p. 135.
4. Ibid.

## Chapter Three

Some material in this chapter was adapted from "Antigone: A Woman Challenges Authority," a Hartwick Classic Leadership Case, and accompanying teaching notes written by Thomas R. Martin, Jeremiah Chair of Classics at the College of the Holy Cross, and Richard B. Larson, Organization/Human Behavior consultant and adjunct professor at Assumption College and the College of the Holy Cross.

1. Dudley Fitts and Robert Fitzgerald, Editors, *The Oedepus Cycle of Sophocles*. New York: Harcourt Brace Jovanovich, 1977. All quotations are from this text.
2. Karl Albrechtl and Steve Albrecht, *Added Value Negoatiating*, Burr Ridge, Illinois: Irwin Professional Publishing, 1993.

## Chapter Four

Some material in this chapter was adapted from Robert Penn Warren's *All the King's Men*, a Hartwick Classic Leadership Case and accompanying teaching notes written by Director of Independent Studies Robert Colley and Professor of Management Dennis Gillan, both of Syracuse University.

1. Robert Penn Warren. *All the King's Men*. Orlando, FL: Harcourt Brace and Company, 1974. All quotations are from this text.
2. "Southwest Airlines' Herb Kelleher: Unorthodoxy at Work." *Management Review*, 1 January 1995.

## Chapter Five

Some material in this chapter was adapted from "Constructing Charisma: Cleopatra of Egypt," a Hartwick Classic Leadership Case and accompanying teaching notes written by Thomas R. Martin, Jeremiah O'Connor Professor of Classics at the College of the Holy Cross; and Richard Larson, Organization/Human Behavior consultant and adjunct professor at Assumption College.

1. Plutarch, *Parallel Lives*. Dr. Thomas Martin, trans. All quotations are from this text.
2. Marjorie Williams, "All About Anna," *Vanity Fair*, September 1994, p. 60.
3. Faye Rice, "How to Make Diversity Pay," *Fortune*, August 8, 1994, p. 32.
4. Ibid.
5. Sally Helgeson, *The Female Advantage: Women's Ways of Leading*. New York: Doubleday, 1990.

## Chapter Six

Some material in this chapter was adapted from "Herman Melville's *Moby Dick*," a Hartwick Classic Leadership Case and accompanying teaching notes written by James A. Bostwick Professor of English Welford Dunaway Taylor and Professor of Management Systems James C. Goodwin, both of the University of Richmond.

1. Herman Melville, *Moby Dick*. Norton Critical Edition. New York: W. W. Norton, 1967. All quotations are from this text.
2. Matthew Shifrin, "Last Legs?" *Forbes*, September 12, 1994.
3. Shawn Tully, "Stretch Targets." *Fortune*, November 14, 1994.

## Chapter Seven

Some material in this chapter was adapted from "Martin Luther King's Jr.'s 'Letter from Birmingham Jail,'" a Hartwick Classic Leadership Case and accompanying teaching notes written by Associate Professor of Economics and Business Margaret Maguire and Associate Professor of History and Black Hispanic Studies Ralph Watkins, both of the State University of New York at Oneonta.

1. Martin Luther King, *Why We Can't Wait*. New York: Joan Daves Agency, 1963. All quotations are from this text.
2. Linley Gwennap, editor, *Microprocessor Report*, quoted in The *Wall Street Journal*, "Apple Finally Gives In..." by Jim Carlton, October 17, 1994.
3. Margaret J. Wheatley, *Leadership and the New Science*. San Francisco: Berrett-Koehler, Publishers, 1992.
4. Judith M. Bardwick, "Danger in the Comfort Zone," *Small Business Reports*, Vol. 17, No. 4, April 1992, pp. 68–71.
5. Karl Albrecht and Steve Albrecht, *Added Value Negotiating*. Homewood, Illinois: Business One Irwin.

## Chapter Eight

Some material in this chapter was adapted from "Carl von Clausewitz *On War*," a Hartwick Classic Leadership Case and accompanying teaching notes written by Professor of German Wendell Frye of Hartwick College and Associate Professor of Philosophy Michael K. Green of the State University of New York at Oneonta.

1. David Howarth, *The Armada: The Spanish Story*. New York: Viking Press, 1981.
2. Carl von Clausewitz, *On War*. J.J. Graham, trans. Hampshire, England: Routledge, 1962. All quotations are from this text.
3. Brian Dumaine, "Corporate Spies Stoop to Conquer." *Fortune*, Nov 7, 1988.
4. Steven Flax, "Know Your Competitors." *Fortune*, May 14, 1984.
5. Michael Gershman, *Getting It Right the Second Time*. Reading, Mass.: Addison-Wesley, 1992.

## Chapter Nine

Some material in this chapter was adapted from "Herman Melville's *Billy Budd*, Sailor," a Hartwick Classic Leadership Case, and accompanying teaching notes written by Professor of English William Brown of Philadelphia College of Textiles and Science and Associate Professor of Management Claudia Harris of North Carolina Central University.

1. Abraham Zaleznik, *The Managerial Mystique*. New York: Harper & Row, 1989.
2. John P. Kotter, *Harvard Business Review*. May/June, 1990, p. 103.
3. Craig R. Hickman, *Mind of a Manager, Soul of a Leader*. New York: John Wiley & Sons, 1990.
4. Herman Melville. *Billy Budd, Sailor*. New York: Bantam Doubleday Dell, 1965. All quotations are from this text.
5. John Keegan. *The Mask of Command*. New York: Viking Penguin Inc., 1987.
6. Robert Tannenbaum and Warren H. Schmidt. "How to Choose a Leadership Pattern," *Harvard Business Review*. 51, no. 3. May–June, 1973: 162–164 ff.
7. Kenneth H. Blanchard, Drea Zigarmi, and Robert B. Nelson. "Situational Leadership After 25 Years: A Retrospective," *The Journal of Leadership Studies*, November 1993.

## Chapter Ten

Some material in this chapter was adapted from "Winston Churchill," a Hartwick Classic Leadership Case and accompanying teaching notes written by Associate Professor of

Philosophy Michael Green of the State University of New York at Oneonta and Professor of History Donald Birn of the State University of New York at Albany.

1. Robert Rhodes James, *Winston Churchill: His Complete Speeches, 1897–1963*. New York: Chelsea House. All quotations are from this text.

2. David Wallechinsky and Irving Wallace, *The People's Almanac #3*. New York: Bantam Books, 1981.


## Chapter Eleven

Some material in this chapter was adapted from "Baldessare Castiglione's *The Book of the Courtier*," a Hartwick Classic Leadership Case and accompanying teaching notes written by Associate Professor of History Peter G. Wallace of Hartwick College.

1. Ralph Stogdill, *The Handbook of Leadership*. New York: Free Press, 1974.

2. Baldessare Castiglione, *The Book of the Courtier*. Edgar Mayhew, ed. New York: Doubleday Dell Publishing Group, 1959. All quotations are from this text.

3. Michael Kinsman, "It's the how of employee ownership that's key," *San Diego Union-Tribune*, October 1, 1993, p. C-1.

4 J. J. Gabarro and J. P. Kotter, "Managing Your Boss," *Harvard Business Review*, Jan-Feb, 1980, 92-100.

5. Robert E. Kelley, *The Power of Followership*. New York: Doubleday, 1992.


## Chapter Twelve

Some material in this chapter was adapted from "Mahatma Gandhi," a Hartwick Classic Leadership Case and accompanying teaching notes written by Assistant Professor of Philosophy and Religious Studies Julius Jackson and Assistant Professor of Sociology Douglas Gutknecht, both of San Bernardino Valley College.

1. Louis Fischer, *The Essential Gandhi*, New York: Random House, 1983. All quotations are from this text.

2. John A. Byrne and William C. Symonds, "The Best Bosses Avoid the Pitfalls of Power," *Business Week*, April 1, 1991, p. 59.

3. Robert Greenleaf, *Servant Leadership: A Journey into the Nature of Legitimate Power and Greatness*. New York, Paulist, 1977.

4. (Teaching Note) "Mahatma Gandhi," Hartwick Classic Leadership Case, Hartwick College, 1994.

5. Shelley Garcia, "Executive of the Year: Jack Balousek," *Adweek*, April 1, 1991, p. 23.

# BIBLIOGRAPHY

Albrecht, Karl and Steve Albrecht. *Added Value Negotiating.* Burr Ridge, IL: Irwin Professional Publishing, 1993.

Byrne, Robert. *1,911 Best Things Anybody Ever Said.* New York: Ballantine, 1988.

Chappell, Tom. *The Soul of a Business.* New York: Bantam, 1993.

Clavell, James. *Sun Tzu and the Art of War.* New York: Dell, 1983.

Clemens, John K. and Douglas F. Mayer. *The Classic Touch.* Burr Ridge, IL: Irwin Professional Publishing, 1987.

Cleary, Thomas. *Mastering the Art of War.* Boston: Shambhala, 1989.

Cohen, William, A. *The Art of the Leader.* Englewood Cliffs, New Jersey: Prentice Hall, 1990.

Deshimaru, Jean Taisen. *The Zen Way to the Martial Arts.* New York: Dutton, 1982.

Fischer, Louis. *The Essential Gandhi.* New York: Random House, 1983.

Garfield, Charles. *Peak Performers.* New York: Avon, 1986.

Garland, Ron. *Making Work Fun.* San Diego, CA: Shamrock Press, 1991.

Griffith, Samuel B. *Mao Tse-Tung on Guerilla Warfare.* New York: Praeger, 1961.

Hyams, Joe. *Zen in the Martial Arts.* New York: Bantam, 1979.

Korda, Michael. *Success!* New York: Ballantine, 1977.

Leonard, George. *Mastery: The Keys to Success and Long-Term Fulfillment.* New York: Dutton, 1991.

Luecke, Richard. *Scuttle Your Ships Before Advancing*. New York: Oxford University Press, 1994.

Melville, Herman. *Moby Dick*. New York: W.W. Norton, 1967.

Merkin, Lisa, and Eric Frankel. *Trivial Contest*. New York: Avon Books, 1984.

Miyamoto, Musashi. *The Book of Five Rings*. New York: Bantam, 1982.

Peter, Laurence J. *Peter's Quotations*. New York: Bantam, 1977.

Roberts, James L. *Cliffs Notes on Moby Dick*. Lincoln, Nebraska: Cliffs Notes, 1961.

Robinson, Peter. *Snapshots from Hell*. New York: Warner Books, 1994.

Rowes, Barbara. *The Book of Quotes*. New York: Ballantine, 1979.

Rubinstein, Jonathan. *City Police*. New York: Ballantine, 1973.

Semler, Ricardo. *Maverick!* London, England: Random House, 1993.

Snodgrass, Mary Ellen. *Cliffs Notes on Billy Budd*. Lincoln, Nebraska: Cliffs Notes, 1991.

Sophocles. *Works of Sophocles*. Trans. by Dudley Fitts and Robert Fitzgerald. New York: Harcourt Brace Jovanovich, 1977.

Vickers, James, E. *Cliffs Notes on Julius Caesar*. Lincoln, Nebraska: Cliffs Notes, 1980.

Warren, Robert Penn. *All the King's Men*. New York: Bantam Books, 1974.

# INDEX